FRENCH CONNECTIONS

Martin James is an internationally published music critic who has contributed to some of the UK's leading music magazines. He was part of the editorial team that produced the legendary dance music magazine *Muzik* and has written for *DJ*, *Mixmag*, *Electronic Sound* and *Urb*. He also regularly contributed articles about jungle, drum & bass, UK hip hop, dub reggae and electronic music to the *Guardian* and the *Independent*.

Martin has written several books about urban and electronic music and culture and is also the author of the definitive biography of The Prodigy. Now in its third edition, *We Eat Rhythm* covers the band's early years and was written in close collaboration with The Prodigy. The second part of the biography *We Live for the Beats* will be published in 2024.

Martin is Professor of Creative and Cultural Industries at Solent University, Southampton, where he lectures on underground music and the music industry.

State of Bass: The Origins of Jungle/Drum & Bass

We Eat Rhythm: The Prodigy Story Part 1

Dave Grohl: All of Him

Moby: Replay – His Life and Times

Funk Soul Brother: Fatboy Slim

Media Narratives in Popular Music (with Chris Anderton)

Understanding the Music Industries
(with Chris Anderton and Andrew Dubber)

FRENCH CONNECTIONS

From Discotheque to Daft Punk –
The Birth of French Touch

MARTIN JAMES

First published in the UK by Sanctuary in 2003
This edition published by Velocity Press 2022

velocitypress.uk

Printed and bound in Great Britain by Clays Ltd, Elcograf S.p.A.

Cover design
Hayden Russell

Typesetting
Paul Baillie-Lane
pblpublishing.co.uk

Photography
Mark Stringer

ISBN: 9781913231163

CONTENTS

To Lisa, Ruby Blue, Felix Drum and Bella Pearl... always.

Also dedicated to my generous brother in beats,
Philippe Zdar (1967–2019). RIP, my friend.

ACKNOWLEDGEMENTS

Why a book about French dance music? Well, it all started by accident, really. I was in Paris early in 1994 interviewing Chris the French Kiss of Yellow Records fame, when a chance discovery of the BPM record shop in Bastille opened my eyes to a new development in French dance music. Sure, I'd long been aware of the rave scene in France (I even went to and wrote about a few free parties and club events in the early 90s). I was already a fan of Laurent Garnier and Eric Morand's FNAC and F Communications, but this was something new. A sound that seemed to draw on the influences of hip hop as much as dance culture. I didn't know it then, but I was witnessing the beginnings of what was to become French Touch.

In the five years that followed this first trip, my visits to Paris became so regular that Eurostar thought of naming a train after me! I was the first UK journalist to interview many people who would become seen as the leading players. I wasn't the only journalist writing about these artists, but only Mixmag Update's Frank Tope could claim to have covered the scene to quite the same level. A fact that led to an accusation in the French media that I was partially responsible for the hype that quickly surrounded these artists. A hype that everyone claimed to hate but used to the fullest advantage. My involvement extended to popularising the term French Touch, although I also stand accused by French media, among others, as being responsible for coining the term. It would be more accurate to say I borrowed it from French cinema and applied it to the music in print. French academics have gone to extraordinary lengths to prove I didn't coin the term in the years since. So I reiterate, I popularised the term French Touch and in so doing liberated it from the close quarters of Paris club culture.

So, through my visits, I discovered a city without a club culture but a country with a well-organised free party scene. I found a scene that was largely run by a rich elite from the posh suburbs of Paris and an underground movement that vibrated the foundations of the urban projects. I discovered a country with a long history in both dance and experimental music, but a mainstream stuck in the pop songs of the 80s. I also experienced the dichotomy of a pro-Techno Parade government at complete odds with a public (and police) that considered dance music to be all about drugs. But above all, I found a love of dance music that reminded me of the golden age of party culture in the UK.

For so long ignored by the rest of the world, France had been able to develop at its own pace. It is often claimed that their relevance was less valid just because they were a few years behind the UK and Germany. But it is this slow start in the face of a hugely oppositional public that turned France into a hotbed of talent.

French Connections: Daft Punk, Air, Super Discount and the birth of French Touch offers an insight into the events, artists, DJs and producers that helped create the contemporary dance music climate in France. There are some omissions, though. Firstly, if everyone who had even been involved in dance music in France got a mention, this book would just read like a telephone book. So I have had to act as a gatekeeper, reserving judgement on who the most important figures were.

Furthermore, I omitted people I considered to have had little bearing on the actual dance culture. For example, Jean Michel Jarre may be world-famous as a synth virtuoso, but my consideration was that his work had little influence on French dance culture. His music was firmly rooted in the rock aesthetic. Although it can be argued that he made synthesisers more popular among young musicians, his input into the sampling and ecstasy culture of the house and techno generation is debatable.

Similarly, Deep Forest; although they enjoyed huge global success with their world music/ambient crossover, their influence on the development of dance culture in France was tiny. They did, however, do a huge amount to promote the world music/dance fusion sound that had some impact on

France. However, this musical development is worthy of a book unto itself and, I feel, not so important in the story I have focussed on.

When I started this project, I was determined that the French Touch sound that became popular at the end of the 90s would not be the book's main focus. However, as I interviewed people, I found it was impossible to avoid it. Everyone uses this development as a reference point. It either denotes the artists' sense of belonging or underlines their sense of otherness. It was therefore impossible to avoid.

A quick note about the structure of the book. It doesn't follow linear narratives. Histories don't follow straight lines but events overlap. To understand the present, it is often necessary to overlay the past. So this book might jump from disco back to *musique concrete*, it might skip between decades, but it's through this that I attempt to make sense of the messy lines of historical retelling.

French Connections: Daft Punk, Air, Super Discount and the birth of French Touch presents a series of vignettes woven into a historicising fabric. As a result, some interviews are replayed in the present tense while others are delivered in the past tense. This provides some detail with added urgency.

It is also important to point out that this story may be drawn from a huge amount of research, but it is tempered by subjectivity. Therefore, it is a version, or a remix, of the events, with my own musical journey at its axis. And, as I have already said, that journey started with the French Touch – purely accidentally.

I'll never forget one of my trips on Eurostar. I was with Jonathan from POP Promotions, journalist Veena Verdi and photographer Mark Stringer. We were on our return journey and we'd all been hitting the red wine a little too heavily. Stringer was then caught by a guard and chastised for smoking. So he dutifully moved to the corridor between carriages and re-lit his cigarette. When he returned to his seat, he jokingly said he'd chucked the butt out of the window. The next morning the news came through that there had been a fire in the tunnel. Ours was the last train to get through. For weeks after, we convinced Stringer that he'd started the blaze. Even though we all knew that you couldn't open the windows on the train. But he was drunk; we all were. So who knows what he might have done.

So my first thanks go out to the people on that trip. Jonathan, a good friend and great PR, Veena, a fine writer with an encyclopaedic knowledge of music and finally, Mark Stringer – a top snapper with whom I've had so many adventures and sunk far too much wine with over the years.

Next, I would like to thank the man who opened my eyes to the great music coming out of France, Chris le Friant aka The French Kiss. And for the same reasons all at BPM and Rough Trade.

For their help throughout this project (whether now or in the past) my heartfelt thanks go out to the following: Laurent Garnier, Eric Morand and all at F Comm, Philippe Zdar and Boombass; The Daft Punk boys, Pedro Winter and Gildas; Etienne de Crecy, Pierre-Michel Levallois, Alex Gopher and all at Solid through the years; Air's Nicolas Godin and Jean Benoit Dunckel; Philippe Ascoli, Marc Teissier du Cros, Alice Retif; Arnaud Boivin from Ya Basta records, Jean Jacques Perrey, DJ Cam, Indy Vidyalankara at Sony UK, Antoine Gouiffes, Olivia Guzzo and Gregor Woitier at Sony Music France, Dimitri from Paris, Laurence Mueller (Virgin France) and Carla Williams (Virgin UK – you are a star), DJ Gilb'R and Didier Cohen from Versatile Records, Kid Loco, Dax Riders, Guillaim Atlan and Isabelle at Lafesse Records, Cerrone, Eric.Vandepoort and Fabrice Dubard at Universal France, Eddie Ruffett and Richard Dawes at Universal Polydor (UK), Sean and Karli at PIAS (UK), Yannick from Pro-Zak Trax, Manu le Malin, Arnaud Frisch and all at Uwe, Tampopo, Talaga, Vitalic, Terence Fixmer, JC from Active Suspension, Philippe from BiP_Hop, Alexander Escolier, Jean Marie Koné at Radio FG, Philippe Grundler from Catalogue records, Eric Ghiglion from Big Wave, Jean from Scandium Records, Epileptik Productions, Alain Zerahian from Pamplemousse Productions, Ben at LaPlage Records, Boris Picq at Black Tambour, Pascal Vitalic, Eric Trosset at Comet, David Duriez at Brique Rouge, Yann-Erik from SoulShake , Anne from Allobrox, C.Bass at N.R.V. Records, Christophe Tastet and Benjamin Diamond, Olivier Champeau from Les Disques Bazoline, Fabrice at Grossomodo Productions, Fakir Music's Patrick Droit and the guys from Grand Tourism, Funkorama etc, Alessandro aka Al Ferox, Pierre-Olivier (aka P.O.) at Missive Music, Pascal at Rotax Disques, Olivier (Teo Moritz) from Superhuit, Eric Ghiglione at Big Wave, Chloe Bartoletti, Steve Lhomme, Christophe Vix-Gras, Patrick Vidal, Didier Lestrade, Mathieu Minelli at Chateau Rouge, Juantrip'… and if I've missed anyone out here, my sincerest apologies. Phew.

I would also like to thank Colin and all at Velocity Press for resurrecting this book, giving me the chance to make tweaks and for providing a cover that finally says what the book is about.

And finally, as ever, my love goes out to the families (the Thomas clan and the Tansey tribe), but most of all, my deepest love to Lisa Jayne, Ruby Blue and Felix Drum – I love you all more than I could say.

Peace,
Martin James

INTRODUCTION

In the final years of the twentieth century, the dance music emerging from France suddenly seemed to be everywhere. Every time you turned on the TV, listened to the radio or even went shopping, the sounds of French house music seemingly filled the air. It was the sound of filtered house. A style that was rejected wholesale by the dance music elite of Paris just as quickly as it had first appeared.

However, it did represent the coming of age of a country that had for so long been considered to be lagging behind the cutting edge of European musical expression. In 2003 French academic Philippe Birgy argued that this period was part of the invention of a tradition, suggesting that French Touch was related to external forces taking hold of domestic creative voices to give themselves 'a local existence'. While his focus on authentic tradition appears to preclude French musical identity from the process of pancultural exchange, the truth is that France had a long history of involvement in the development of electronic music innovation, dance cultures and associated subgenres.

Indeed, France had long been the source of revered dance cuts. Its club history reached back to the discotheques of WWII and its compositional innovation could be found in the tape loop and found sound aesthetic of Musique Concrete. French songwriters, producers and artists dominated the disco days, while France also played a part in developing the post-punk mutant disco era. While these latter developments could be argued to be predominantly Anglo-American forms of cultural expression, the influence of France was ever-present.

In 2001 France was one of the most effective exporters of dance music worldwide. According to the French Music Bureau, a government-funded body set up to actively promote French music, domestic electronic music accounted for 47% of albums and 77% of singles sold abroad (rather than in France) in 2000/2001. Furthermore, the country's biggest exports were Daft Punk's *Discovery* which clocked in at around 1.8 million copies, and Air's *10 000 Hz Legend*, which sold around 500,000 units. Indeed according to The French Music Bureau's figures, at least ten albums sold over 100,000 copies that year. All of them were electronic music based.

This then is the story of French dance music. It's a tale that extends way beyond French Touch and those three tracks that dominated the airwaves at the end of the 90s. In fact, there is so much more to France than 'Music Sounds Better with You', 'Lady' and 'Starlight'.

But first, a question...

IS THERE A FRENCH SOUND?

"When you look at every artist's initiative in France, they all go in a very personal direction. It's not just a pure French thing that's going on. The influences are much bigger."

Thomas Bangalter, Daft Punk, Paris

"I would rather say that there are different French sounds. The French house and its techniques were created by Daft Punk and then used by many other commercially successful musicians. The hardcore techno scene with Manu le Malin as the leader created its own sound too. This scene is very organised with labels, parties, associations, and festivals. There is no real electroclash scene as, contrary to what we think, there is only a handful of musicians composing it."

Vitalic, Dijon

"A French *savoir-faire* did exist some years ago when the Super Discount crew and the Daft boys released their first records. A Disco House mix that turned into the so-called French Touch – a journalist and marketing thing, I believe. And what about today? A French sound? There are plenty of good artists in France but the patterns we are all working on are coming from the USA, the UK and Germany. Very few things were invented here during the last twenty years. It's only a question of recycling things with more or less accuracy and attitude; that's it."

Tampopo, Toulouse

"Yes, mostly two types; one influenced by the sound of Detroit, often with melodies but with a stronger European techno touch; the other influenced by 80s sounds with artists like The Hacker or Kiko."

Jean Christophe, Scandium Records, Nimes

"Is there a French sound? Hype would say so, but to me, that sounds stupid. Music has no frontiers. Fashion does, hype does... If you produce music following a fashion or a hype, then you'll sound from the country where this hype started, period."

Benoit Carles, Pamplemousse, Buc

"I wouldn't say there is a French sound. But among all the electronic music coming from France, I can see a link. All compositions seem to be simple. They are never big productions with lots of different and various sounds. But it's usually the minimum required to make the track good. It's a bit like the 'nouvelle cuisine'. You only get a few, but the few are delicate and tasty."

Steve L'homme, Paris

"I feel French productions have an elegant feeling; the productions are sweet, very musical. We've got a very intense and living world music scene; many fusions emerge from these meetings. But I do not really believe French Touch is a French sound. For me, it's a kind of dancing filtered house with disco inspirations from Bob (Sinclar) to Joey Negro."

Benua Carles, RYTHMiX Records – Paris

"I don't think so. There's not a real French sound because there's a lot of different producers with different musical cultures, and I think it's a good thing. But instead of that, in other countries, there's the image of the French producing this fucking French Touch, and I think it's a bad thing... It's a marketing thing."

Teo Moritz, Superhuit, Lyon

1. LA DISCOTHEQUE

"SHE'S... D: DESIRABLE. I: INCREDIBLE. S: SUPER SEXY. C: SUCH A CUTIE. SHE'S: OH, OH, OH."

D.I.S.C.O. Five letters that evoke extreme feelings – from revulsion to celebration, disgust to devotion. The era when Donna Summer first cooed 'I Feel Love', Parliament first wore silver jumpsuits and the Bee Gees first started 'Jive Talkin'' has continued to fascinate designers, artists and musicians alike. In 2002, as the French Touch effect dominated the airwaves, we lived through the final days of the 70s revival and disco's influence could be felt everywhere. Advertising stole its imagery; fashion mimicked its style. And as for the music, everyone from The Clash to Pulp, Dimitri to Daft Punk had taken a piece of the disco pie.

Film director Paul Thomas Anderson grabbed his 15 seconds of disco delight with the 1998 movie 'Boogie Nights'. Along with a brace of filmmakers, he brought the Hollywood machine to add the final stroke of lip-gloss to the make-up of the retro revolution.

The words disco and France have long walked hand in hand. In Paris, Europe possessed a disco capital to rival New York. It was here that the very first discotheques emerged, some of the most famous disco hits were penned and many of the scene's elitist tendencies were first promoted.

Disco's metronomic beats and swathes of chocolate box strings seduced generations of Parisians into dancing and, in many cases DJing. Techno legend Laurent Garnier cut his twin deck teeth spinning the disco-fied sounds of 80s tech-funk as a youngster. Most French Touch stars were nurtured on a diet of disco and techno-funk, while Daft Punk's Thomas Bangalter was literally brought up in the house of D.I.S.C.O. as his father co-wrote the Ottawan smash of the same name.

Little surprise then that as the world jigged to the filtered beats of the late 90s French Touch revolution, it was disco that once again pumped at the music's heart. In many ways, French dance music and disco are inseparable.

"Above everything, disco has strong and deep roots in France," confirms Catalogue Records founder Philippe Grundler. "It is a genre which is deeply integrated in our culture, which explains the later French Touch generation."

For many, disco culture – soundtracked by one-hit wonders, styled with man-made fabrics and documented by faintly ridiculous films about totally ridiculous dancing – was the ultimate in disposability. Worse still, disco was a style that allegedly came to bleach the soul of black music before destroying the heart of rock'n'roll. It was the sound of evil incarnate, the anti-music, five letters that came to subvert and destroy. For D.I.S.C.O. read D.E.V.I.L.

Then again, disco could easily read 'devil may care'. It represented the ultimate in good-time party positivity. It was sound encapsulated by the fractured reflections in mirrored balls, flamboyant flares, towering platforms, open-necked shirts, medallions and mountains of cocaine. Disco was the sound of a world needing an escape from reality.

In the late 70s, the US was suffering from the Carter-era strikes (and near bankruptcy of the country in 1978) while the UK was reeling from the effects of high unemployment and general strikes. Yet despite its escapist aesthetic, disco also represented a dynamic push for change. A change that came in the least obvious ways. For instance, it was an era when fashion became unisex and the dividing line between macho and camp became increasingly blurred. Whereas 60s hippies had decided it was OK for men to have long hair, the doyens of disco turned suited-and-booted men into hunks in stacks. Clint Eastwood wore purple crimplene, Burt Reynolds and Charles Bronson sported beige flares, and an Italian/American actor with an unfeasibly square chin, sparkling blue eyes and dapper white suit became the ultimate symbol of masculinity. His name, of course, was John Travolta, and he represented the perfect snapshot of the era in *Saturday Night Fever*. *A* movie that said to the men of the world, "It's OK to want to be a dancer" and suddenly hip gyration became a symbol of hypermasculinity.

Equality was not one of disco's watchwords. Sex, on the other hand, was. Indeed, it was such an overtly sexual movement that in 1976 American activist Jesse Jackson was moved to take a stand against what he called 'sex rock'. Through PUSH (People United to Save Humanity), Jackson sought to protect innocent ears from such offensive platters as Donna Summer's 'I Feel Love' (a track which Summer herself would condemn some years later after gaining religion in her life) and KC and the Sunshine Band's '(Shake, Shake, Shake) Shake Your Booty'.

Fortunately, he failed dismally. Not only did America succumb to the driving beats and the sexploitative lyrics, but the rest of the world did too. At the heart of it all was the music. Good-time sounds with bearded men singing in falsetto squeaks. Big-haired women belting it out like banshees on angel dust. And a profoundly subversive union of male stereotypes – construction worker, policeman, GI, biker, cowboy and Native American chieftain: The Village People. Perhaps unsurprisingly, a French concept!

With the onset of the 70s, as the new decade closed its doors on the dark days of the late 60s, a wave of optimism spread across the US as the 'tune in, turn on; and drop out' generation embraced the ideology of 'doing it for themselves'. By 1974, two underground subcultures were brewing in Britain and America. On the surface, punk and disco might have appeared diametrically opposed, but they actually had a great deal in common. Where punk sought to cut through the rock bullshit with a burst of petulant anger, disco flew in the face of punk's aggression and aimed straight at the pelvis. It was sex music. While serious efforts to forward racial and sexual integration generally resulted in the pseudo action of peaceful demonstrations, real change was taking place on New York's dancefloors as straight and gay people "got down with the get down" and did The Hustle.

This wasn't the first time discos had been linked with politics of change. During World War II, the word discotheque – a slang term for Paris jazz haunts of the 30s – became synonymous with the French resistance to the Nazi occupation. A ban on dancing to or performing American sounding music was enforced during that time. The underground discotheques, however, carried on playing their favourite sounds regardless.

The very word discotheque is, of course, derived from the French word for library, bibliotheque. It originally meant, quite literally, a collection of recordings. According to Albert Goldman's 1978 book *Disco*, the very first place to use the term was a bar in Rue Huchette in Paris before the Second World War. Called *La Discothèque*, the bar invited its clientele to request their favourite jazz records when ordering drinks.

During the Nazi occupation, Parisians defied the ban on American music by creating underground bars. Gramophones were set up in cellars on the Left Bank. Here the culture of resistance grew as people continued to indulge in their passion for the music of Black America and to listen to their favourite records. The labels of which had been covered over by less offensive titles and artists in order to hide the music source, should a raid ever occur. In a strange twist of events, these underground discothèques would create a pattern of defiance that would become the life force of dance culture in the late 80s and early 90s. While the act of hiding labels would become commonplace among DJs who wanted to keep information to themselves.

In 1947, with hostilities ended, Paul Pacine opened Whiskey A Go-Go in Paris. With its garish décor, wild atmosphere and elite clientele, this club set the blueprint for the modern discotheque. The soundtrack was culled from Black American Jazz while the drink of choice was scotch whiskey, the fashionable drink of the day. This drink inspired the club's décor of garish tartan and at least one wall was covered with lids of whiskey cases. It was a winning formula. Soon Pacine had a string of similar clubs throughout Europe. In turn, he made the concept of clubs specifically for the playing of records chic.

Competition quickly emerged in Paris with Jean Castle's discotheque *Chez Castle* enjoying similar success. By 1960 Pacine was forced to respond with the opening of his renowned *Chez Regine*. The notorious Regine Zylberberg, who had first started as the toilet attendant at the original Whiskey A Go-Go, managed the club. However, thanks to her vivacious character, she soon became the club's biggest attraction. It should also be noted that it had been argued by Maren Hancock in the book *Media Narratives in Popular Music* that Regine can be recognised as the first DJ through her activities at the club. *Club Regine* was run on the concept of elitism. It was an approach that became the norm for Parisian clubs until the late 90s.

"There has always been a discothèque culture in France – what we call Paris by Night," explained Phillippe Escoli, founder of the highly influential Source Records in Paris and later Managing Director of Virgin UK. "The French created, I think, all of these bad door policies. If there is a Studio 54, it's because of La Palace. All the bad aspects of discotheques started in Paris, but it wasn't club culture. It was for Mick Jagger and so on. The music was there but it didn't have the club culture to back it up."

These bad door policies were embraced by Regine Zylberberg, who wanted to present her new club as the only place to be seen. So for the first few weeks, she deliberately kept people out. Despite an empty club, she would place signs outside the venue door saying the club was full almost as soon as the doors had opened. Word soon got around and when she truly opened her doors to the grateful public Chez Regine was instantly rammed.

According to Sheryl Garratt's fascinating account of club culture "Adventures in Wonderland – A Decade of Club Culture", Zylberberg also had a lucky break that would increase the hype surrounding her club.

"Soon after, the American cast of the musical West Side Story came in and showed her a new dance that didn't need a partner, and that was easy for even the most rhythmically challenged: the twist," wrote Garratt.

Unsurprisingly Regine's quickly became the chosen place for the people of Paris to twist and people dancing solo to records became the hippest thing to do. As a result, Paris by Night offered the blueprint for the club culture of the decade that followed. And yet, despite following the trends and developments in the US, it remained strangely stagnant in the years that followed the disco revolution.

Although it wasn't until 1960 that the US opened its first discotheque, *Le Club*, America did grab the concept and run with it to score a global touchdown. *Le Club* was the brainchild of Olivier Coquelin, who brought the Parisian discothèque model to New York and aimed it directly at the city's elite. The next discotheque in the Paris tradition was opened a year later. *Peppermint Lounge* on Manhattan's West 45th Street might have been a sleazy dive, but a residency by minor twist act Joey Dee & The Starlighters sealed its reputation.

Similar clubs opened in San Francisco and New York, while England saw its first discothèques arrive in 1962 with *La Discotheque* in Wardour Street, London and *The Place* in the less cosmopolitan surroundings of Hanley, near Stoke-on-Trent. In both cases, the clubs were purpose-built, with the ambience being as important as the music. The former featured double beds placed on and around the dancefloor, tuning into the increasing sexual freedom of the era. While the latter featured all-black décor, with red lighting, a gold-painted entrance hall, mock leopard skin wallpaper in the toilets, and a small sitting room that was all white with blue lighting. Called 'The Fridge', it was, as Sheryl Garratt points out in *Adventures in Wonderland*, "the first chill-out room".

By the late 1960s, US clubs like The Sanctuary in Hell's Kitchen and The Electric Circus on St Marks' Place used pyrotechnic lighting, while the strobe light had become a regular feature in the clubs of the US and the UK. However, it was an effect that had been initially pioneered in the discothèques of Paris. Furthermore, the US and the UK saw discotheques adopting top quality soundsystems. In England, this caused much concern for the Musicians Union, who considered that the use of soundsystems that were as loud as bands would be detrimental to live musicians. It was an attitude that kept the concept of dancing to records in an inferior position, constantly undermined by the live band. As a result, discothèques had to work harder at creating the right atmosphere to make people want to spend money on getting in to dance to records.

Ironically perhaps, given the central position that the discothèque has in the birth of club culture, in the US the soundtrack of the 60s version was almost exclusively rock! The black soul music of the time barely had a look in. 1976 saw this rock hegemony finally broken. Following a spate of run-ins with Hell's Angels, rock discos looked like being on the way out. Then promoters Steve Rubell and Ian Schrager moved into the heart of Manhattan, intending to create the perfect environment. Enter *Studio 54*, the blueprint for all discos. It opened in 1976 and, in an act of elitism that mimicked the agendas of Parisian discotheques, they only allowed invited people through their doors. These included celebrities like Mick Jagger, Liza Minnelli, Elton John and Truman Capote. One of the featured house performers was Grace Jones, the so-called 'Dietrich of the new decade' whose androgynous looks gave her instant status as a gay icon.

In Erika Haa's *Boogie Nights – The Disco Age*, August Darnell, vocalist with Kid Creole and the Coconuts, describes the buzz that surrounded Studio 54:

"In England now, they have these rave parties, but when people say there's nothing like a rave, I say I saw all of this in 1976 at Studio 54."

There had been another event that was to have a huge effect on the growth and development of club culture. Studio 54 had opened its doors following the huge changes that occurred in the aftermath of one of the most far-reaching political and cultural events of the decade – the Stonewall Riots of 1969.

"Before the Stonewall Riots," wrote Sheryl Garratt in Adventures in Wonderland, "gay bars in America were seedy, furtive places where a lightbulb flashed over the door if someone unfamiliar came in, warning patrons to separate on the dancefloor. Homosexuality was seen as an aberration, a medical condition, something hidden and shameful. By the 60s gay activism was growing in cities like New York, and the more liberated, open approach to sexuality advocated by hippies had begun to break down barriers. But the love that dared not speak its name didn't begin to shout it in the streets until the summer of 1969."

Throughout the year, police had closed down gay bars. The Tele-Star was gone, so too was the Checkerboard and more recently, police raids had forced the after-hours bars the *Sewer* and the Snake Pit to shut up shop. On the evening of 22 June 1969, just as the gay scene was mourning the death of Judy Garland, the New York Police decided to raid the Stonewall Inn at 53 St Christopher Street.

The bar employees were immediately arrested for selling liquor without a licence and customers were invited to file out onto the street, one by one. Here they grouped together to bemoan yet another act of routine harassment of the gay community. However, as the police vans arrived for the arrested employees, the crowd's sense of despair turned to anger. A riot ensued, and the police were forced to take refuge in the very club they'd just closed down!

In today's more tolerant times, it is hard to imagine the Stonewall Riots' effect on the gay community. Immediately after, people were filled with an empowering sense of pride. A mood of hedonistic defiance appeared in the clubs where the older atmosphere of oppression was replaced by a new optimism. The rush of energy thus saw the birth of the contemporary club experience, as discotheques became places where you could lose yourself in an orgy of sex, drugs, music and dancing.

The scene was subsequently set for the disco revolution and growing in the shadows came the sound as D.I.S.C.O. was born.

DON'T STOP THE MUSIC

The generic term disco would not be coined until September 1973 when Vince Aletti wrote the article "Discotheque Rock Paaaaarty" for *Rolling Stone* magazine. However, its antecedents could be found in the Philadelphia sound, pioneered by Kenneth Gamble and Leon Huff. Typified by its lush string arrangements, the Philly sound ensured mega-success for The Three Degrees, Billy Paul and McFadden & Whitehead. But it was with The O'Jays' 1973 hits 'Love Train' and 'Ship

Ahoy', a disco sound was solidified, even if it wasn't defined as such. Also influential in the Philly sound and subsequent disco explosion was Vincent Montana. A member of MFSB – the band responsible for the genre-defining T.S.O.P. 'The Sound of Philadelphia' – he introduced Latino rhythms which became central to disco.

The repetitive rhythms, melodies and vocal hooks of disco could also be found in the early 70s works of Isaac Hayes, particularly in the 1971 track 'Theme from Shaft'. It was Van McCoy's 1975 cut 'The Hustle' though, with its rolling flute refrain, which really pinned down the disco formula. 'The Hustle' came complete with its own dance, as frivolous as the tune itself. With 'The Hustle', however, all strands of the pre-disco aesthetic came together to create a clearly defined musical genre, which could live up to the reputation and style of the discotheques themselves. Years later, Gamble and Huff would have a huge hit with The Trammps' seminal 11-minute epic 'Disco Inferno' that followed the Gamble and Huff approach and reinforced the notion of disco as a genre. From here grew the branches of all subsequent contemporary dance sounds.

"I think you can find the sounds, not the motions of disco, in today's music everywhere," DJ Laurent Garnier told me in 1997. "When I talk about dance music now, it's still disco-oriented. Take US garage and deep house; it's a total follow on from stuff like Loleatta Holloway or all the Salsoul things, you know? Then move on to Jeff Mills' Purpose Maker and stuff like that. All the samples from Purpose Maker are usually taken from disco tracks. I think that kind of New York disco vocal stuff is still followed by the New York guys, and I would say all the more technical stuff has influenced a lot of technical people today."

With the culture of the discotheque so firmly ensconced in the Paris nightlife, it is little surprise that disco music affected a vice-like grip on Parisian culture throughout the late 70s and early 80s. The music's subversive sophistication soundtracked a period of open-mindedness among the leading celebrities that emerged in the late 70s and continued well into the 80s. Furthermore, the music saw the French music industry actively producing and exporting music to the rest of the world.

"During disco, it was the only other time (apart from the post-acid house era) that we produced music and exported it outside of France," confirms Laurent Garnier.

The initial atmosphere of cultural euphoria encouraged French song-writers to seize the sound emanating from the USA, adding their own flourishes of genius along the way. As a result, France became a hotbed of disco talent with numerous global success stories emanating from the country. Despite often being portrayed as a country always at least two years behind the US and the UK in terms of pop culture, the earliest disco rumblings in France came in the same year as 'The Hustle'. The track in question was Bimbo Jet's 'El Bimbo'. It is not strictly a disco record (as the genre had yet to be fully defined), but it represents one of the foundation stones.

With this single, a French producer could be found embracing the sonic developments of Vincent Montana by adding a deep Spanish Cuban flavour to the Philly sound. His name was Claude Moran – one of France's brightest young producers of the era. 'El Bimbo' came as a result of a meeting between Moran and Laurent Rossi (son of French music legend Tino Rossi). Rossi Jnr. recognised the commercial potential of the song and immediately brought in some studio musicians to record the track. 'El Bimbo' was a huge hit in France that year, shifting over 1.3 million copies. Part of the track's appeal came with the fact that it came complete with its own dance routine like 'The Hustle'. 'El Bimbo' may not have had the same kind of global impact as Van McCoy's addition to the pre-disco pantheon, but it did see French dance music seeping into the charts of other countries. Indeed 'El Bimbo' managed to chart in both the US and the UK.

Further success from French artists came a year later with 'Chinese Kung Fu' by French studio group Banzaii, which charted on the US Billboard Charts. However, the group failed to achieve any further notable success, thus underpinning the growing reputation of France immediately pre-disco as a hotbed of one-hit wonders.

Perhaps the defining moment in the early days of disco came with Parisian producer Cerrone. Definitely no one-hit-wonder he would push the bass drum to the fore, thus creating the rhythmic foundation that all disco and later house tracks would follow. His 1976 debut 'Love in C Minor' (released just before The Trammps genre-defining 'Disco Inferno') remains one of the most influential tracks in the disco catalogue. While Cerrone himself is one of the most important figures in disco.

Among the more interesting figures to emerge during this period was drummer and dancer Claude Francois who found a natural affinity with the disco phenomenon. His hits included a French version of 'Oh What a Night' ('Cette Année Là'), 'Magnolia's for Ever' and finally 'Alexandria, Alexandra'. Francois' love of rhythms and complete immersion in the world of dance resonated throughout his music, with the interplay between texture and beats creating a sense of subliminal rhythm. In many ways a sound that pre-empted many of the tricks employed in early house music.

Perhaps one of the earliest doyens of French disco was a man who actually lived in the USA. His name was Michel Polnareff and in 1976, he recorded the seminal 'Lipstick'. A lithe sexual beast of a single, 'Lipstick' lifted the strings of Philly soul, added a disco beat and threw in melodies and hook lines that were immediately addictive to the burgeoning disco generation. Later that year, Mort Schuman wrote and Claude Pascal produced Sex O'Clock USA's lesser-known hit 'Baby Come Home' on the Prelude Label (home of French DJ Francois Kervorkian), underlining France's growing reputation in the process.

However, any achievements made thus far in the French disco world would pale into insignificance next to the duo who would come to be known as The French Wonderboys – Henri Belolo and Jacques Morali. The team would pen some of the disco era's biggest hits by artists as diverse as the Ritchie Family, Patrick Juvet and their finest invention, The Village People!

The Belolo/Morali sound found Moroccan grooves fused with European melodies and Philly strings in their early days. Their first success came in 1975 with The Ritchie Family, an all-girl vocal group recruited through small ads in US entertainment magazines who took their name from their record producer Richie Rome. A 'T' was added as an ineffective form of subterfuge. The trio initially consisted of Cheryl Mason Jackson, Cassandra Ann Wooten and Gwendolin Oliver. However, by 1978 the lineup was made up of three completely different girls: Jacquiline Smith-Lee, Theodosia "Dodi" Draher and Ednah Holt. Thus underlining the fact that The Ritchie Family was, first and foremost, a vehicle for the songs and productions of Belolo and Morali.

The Ritchie Family's first hit single was a rearrangement of the standard 'Brazil' (a song performed 30 years before by Xavier Cugat). The fusion of South-American rhythms and the emotive ambience of Philly Soul resulted in a massive single, which went to #13 on the Billboard Hot Soul Singles Chart and #11 on the Billboard Pop Chart. A year later, in 1976, the duo repeated the success of 'Brazil' with 'The Best Disco in Town'. Further Ritchie Family singles, 'I Want to Dance With You (Dance With Me)', 'Life is Music', 'Quiet Village', 'Give Me A Break', 'I'll Do My Best (For You Baby)' and 'All Night, All Right' faired less well. However, they did all break into the Top 100.

The next successes for Belolo and Morali came with their work for Swiss-born Frenchman Patrick Juvet. Indeed Juvet is notable for being one of the only French people ever to top the US Charts. Juvet already had a name for himself as a pop performer in the David Cassidy/Donny Osmond mould with hits that included 'Les Mots Bleus' or 'Rappelle toi Minette'. However, in the early 70s, he underwent a complete style make-over, re-emerging as a glam rock performer in the style of Bowie's Ziggy Stardust with the album *Chrysalide*.

Success for Juvet was limited beyond France. As with many French performers, he found that the French language translated badly into international sales and despite notoriety in his home country, he was unknown elsewhere. In 1975, in a bid to change this, he moved to Los Angeles, where he picked up on the early disco sound (not unsurprisingly also being explored by David Bowie). Juvet showed Jean Michel Jarre a song he had penned that featured English lyrics on his return to Paris. However, Jean-Michel took the words and placed them with the French composition 'Où Sont les Femmes'. That the song was an international hit was something of an irony. Despite his aim to find an international sound, Juvet found success beyond France, with a French sound!

Around the time of 'Où Sont les Femmes' Juvet met Henri Belolo and Jacques Morali in a lift in New York before bumping into them again later in the night at the famed Studio 54 club. A collaboration seemed to be written on the stars and they quickly agreed to work together. Juvet presented a selection of songs to Belolo and Morali, from which Morali chose the cliched slow disco groove of 'I Love America'. Casablanca Records immediately saw the potential in the collaboration between the French Wonderboys and the French youngster and signed him for three albums. The second of which spawned the huge hit 'Ladies Night'.

However, Juvet became a victim of the lifestyle that surrounded his success as a disco star. He quickly descended into a life of drink and drug addiction and when his 1982 album *Rêves Immoraux* failed, he returned to Paris and entered into a self-imposed retirement from music. The temporary retirement lasted until 1991 when he recorded *Solitude*, an introspective French-language album. It failed to have any impact and soon went out of print.

"Juvet was one of the only people of that era who was most definitely doing it for the love of the music," says Christophe Monier of The Micronauts. "He felt the music deeply."

In 1977 Belolo and Morali launched a group originally intended as a jokey concept, The Village People. As legend has it, while walking through New York's Greenwich Village in spring 1977, the French Wonderboys were captivated by a guy dressed in full American Indian chief gear. They followed him to the bar he worked in as a Go-Go Boy and chatted to him about his style. He explained that a lot of people in the gay community dressed in different costumes to represent everything from sexual preference to cliques they belonged to. It was a subversive twist on the language of the street gangs of the US. Later that night, they went to a club where this was particularly prevalent and they were immediately struck with the idea of a concept group that focussed on the gay community but was sold to the straight world. The first band member was their American Indian chief friend, Felipe Rose. A Frenchman!

Using the same methods as had been used for putting The Ritchie Family they placed wanted ads in relevant papers to put the rest of the band together. Finally, after weeks of auditioning, the other five members were enlisted into the group: Randy Jones, David 'Scar' Hodo, Glen Hughes, Alexander Briley and lead singer Victor Willis. The whole band lived in Greenwich Village, so their collective name was easy to decide upon, The Village People. Before they'd even performed a single song, The Village People signed a contract with Casablanca.

Despite immediate success in the gay bars of the US in 1977 and the subsequent gold-selling debut album, it wasn't until 1978 that The Village People scored their first crossover hit, 'Macho Man'. The single was taken from their second album, which sold two million copies and helped establish the group as an internationally known phenomenon.

In September 1978, the group released their third album. Rather than soften their gay image to ensure greater acceptance in the straight world, they decided to call the album *Cruisin'*, subsequently eulogising the gay nightlife life in full. It was to contain their first international runaway hit, 'YMCA'. A song that not only transcends any barriers of sexuality but also limitations of time to become a karaoke standard the world over.

In 1979 Morali penned a new song after seeing an advert for the US Navy. 'In the Navy' found The Village People exploring what were in many ways gay clichés for the mass consumption of a straight audience. Once again, The Village People enjoyed global success and performed a song that became a standard. By the end of 1979, the band had taken on a new lead singer, Ray Simpson, brother of Ashford and Simpson's Valerie Simpson, and released the live album *Live and Sleazy*. It fared less well than previous releases and acted as a portent for bad things to come. A year later, the movie *I Can't Stop the Music* proved to be a financial disaster, from which The Village People failed to recover.

Although strictly speaking an American front for French producers and songwriters, The Village People represented the epitome of the

French influence on disco throughout the era. There was, however another act that was entirely French, who also enjoyed huge acclaim throughout the time – The Gibson Brothers.

Called "the black Beatles" by The Sun in 1979, the trio first emerged some years earlier as PhalanstÈre. Featuring white frontman Jean Jacques Goldman, the rock and blues influences quartet had won a song competition back in 1970. Their prize was the chance to record a few songs but the resulting demo failed to spark any interest. In 1975 though, they were chosen to play as the house band for a National TV Show starring French TV legend Guy Lux. Now named Martique-Express they performed on several shows before deciding to re-launch as a three-piece disco outfit named Gibson Brothers – after their love of Gibson guitars. What followed was a series of global hits including 'Non-Stop Dance, 'Cuba', 'Oh, What a Life', 'Latin America', 'Tic Tac' and the huge hit 'Better Do it Salsa'. However, none of these singles compared to the success of 'Que Sera Mi Vida' which shifted 45,000 units a day in the UK alone, soon reaching the six million mark.

Notably, the main production and songwriting force behind The Gibson Brothers was one Daniel Vangarde, whose son Thomas (Bangalter) would gain international fame as one half of Daft Punk in the 90s. Among Vangarde's substantial catalogue of hit singles was Ottowan's infamous 'D.I.S.C.O.', which would become one of the scene's defining tracks despite coming at the tail end of the disco era.

Another French act that held a huge influence over the future French Touch scene was Space. The band was formed in 1977 by Didier Maroani, aka Ecama and consisted of Didier Marouani, arrangers Roland Romanelli and Jannick Top, and singer Madeline Bell. The band's first three albums, *Magic Fly* (1977), *Deliverance* (1977) and *Just Blue* (1978), sold over 12 million units globally despite the fact the band never played live. They did appear on television, however, becoming instantly recognisable by wearing space helmets to hide their faces. It was a performance trope that would pre-empt Daft Punk by some 20 years. The reason for remaining incognito was that Marouani was already a successful solo singer signed to Polydor.

Space's launch single 'Magic Fly' was only written as a one-off theme tune for a 1976 television show about astrology.

Marouani would tell Dreamchimney.com, "The producer and I invited my record company to release "Magic Fly" under my name, but the label decided that the composition was not good enough to do this ... My producer found another company, but I could not "light up" under in my own name since the contract with my company remained in force... The suits appeared also because no one could recognize me in it. I had to come up with a creative pseudonym, and I settled on 'Ecama'."

Space would fall apart after the band's producer Jean-Philippe Iliesco refused to support a planned live show after the release of *Just Blue*. Didier Marouani left the band in 1979. Fellow band member Joe Hammer explored new projects while Romanelli and Jannick Top limped on, releasing the album *Deeper Zone* in 1980 to critical indifference. In 1982 Marouani and Joe Hammer performed and recorded as Didier Marouani & Space before becoming renamed Paris-France-Transit following legal action.

Although they would never reach the same heights as achieved through the trio of early albums, Space's legacy has had a huge impact. Their music was a regular feature of the Blitz Club and helped spawn the new romantic scene hooked on synths and outlandish costumes. As a result, they would go on to inspire a generation of synth artists, with their music eventually echoing in the sounds of Daft Punk's *Discovery*. From 2010 the influence they held over Daft Punk has been heard among the movers and shakers of the synthwave scene who adopted the pop techno tones of the Parisian duo without fully recognising where that sound had originally come from. Indeed, Space may be among French music's biggest unsung heroes.

DEATH BEFORE DISCO

From 1976 onwards, the airwaves of the UK and the US were saturated with the disco beat. Ironically, however, the government-controlled French radio stations still refused to play the music, which resulted in stifling the growth of the sound in France. However, disco's influence seeped into the mainstream with a speed that not even the French government could control.

In 1976 the dinosaurs of rock started to embrace the sound to revitalise careers (some of them on the verge of extinction before the disco touch). The Rolling Stones reacted to disco with 'Hot Stuff' in 1976 and delivered 'Miss You' in a 12-inch disco form two years later (in 2002, French producer Mirwais would release an acid house version of the same tune). Even Rod Stewart chose to ignore the bluesy roots he'd emerged with, instead embracing the tacky side of disco with hits like 'D'Ya Think I'm sexy', while the likes of Dolly Parton and Queen even opted to join the disco party. If such respected artists turning their serious music to a seemingly frivolous commercialised sound was hard to take for many fans, then the reaction to David Bowie's disco persona was a step too far. Many fans of Bowie had found his post-Ziggy sounds of the Philly inspired *Young Americans* hard to take. Indeed in his shows recorded for *David Live*, audience members were seen to leave already half-empty venues in their droves. Furthermore, tapes of the concerts exist which clearly capture booing between songs.

Much was made of the fact that people didn't like the way Bowie was the only performer visible on the huge set. The band was hidden behind backdrops, much to their disgust. However, by the end of this world tour, Bowie had rejected the overblown sets in favour of a stripped-down, white light affair; the band were now fully visible. Also clearly audible was his deep love of disco as he started to introduce new songs, including a disco track called 'Nightclubbing', which would turn up a year later on the Kraftwerk inspired Iggy Pop album *The Idiot*, and 'Fame', co-written with John Lennon.

The final dates in the tour found Bowie unveiling his new *Young Americans* world, which fully embraced Philly soul and disco like a long-lost sister. Fans of old were horrified. This even though he'd experimented with Philly strings as long ago as 1974 with '1984' from *Diamond Dogs*.

Despite any negative reactions from his rock fandom, 'Fame' provided Bowie's first US #1 single. He also became the first white artist to appear on US TV show Soul Train. The reasons he gave for why the US hadn't taken to Ziggy Stardust like the UK but had embraced this new disco Dave were simple: "They don't need me. They've got Sylvester." He said at the time of his sense of redundancy in the face of San Francisco based Sylvester, whose outrageous costumes, hi-camp falsetto and gospel-inspired melodies resulted in huge hits like 'You Make Me Feel (Mighty Real) and 'Dance (Disco Heat)' – two tracks would also have huge importance for post-acid house French dance music.

Just as disco hit its commercial peak, the flipside of critical acclaim wasn't far away. Charles Shaar Murray may have declared Chic's 'Le Freak' his NME Single of the Week in 1977 (drawing comparisons to the Sex Pistols' 'Anarchy in the UK'), but the rest of the rock media seemed intent on destroying this so-called 'non-music'. Punk rock was, by this time, the new rock'n'roll. Disco, quite simply, was the new fluff-pop. The rock world vengefully coined the slogan 'Disco Sucks'.

The 'Disco Sucks' campaign was one of the strangest events in the history of music, and one which underlines the passion that music can evoke in people. Inspired by US rock radio's refusal to play disco, Chicago based DJ Steve Dahl took up the cause with his own twist. He arranged a deal with the local White Sox baseball team, whereby fans were allowed into the game for a fraction of the usual price if they brought a disco record with them. The intention was to have a 'disco demolition' between White Sox games.

On 12 July 1979, between matches with the Detroit Tigers, a pile of 20,000 disco records were collected and blown up with dynamite in an anti-disco, pro-rock ritual. The fans were so moved that they started to riot, tearing up anything that wasn't nailed down while chanting "disco sucks!" The second White Sox game was subsequently cancelled and they forfeited the match to the Detroit Tigers.

As Simon Reynolds points out in his excellent book Energy Flash, the events at the White Sox baseball game did, in fact, recall both the Nazi book burnings and the exhibitions of Degenerate Art. He wrote: "Modern day spectacles of *kulturekampf* like Cominskey were impelled by a similar disgust; the belief that disco was rootless, inauthentic, decadent, a betrayal of the virile principles of the true American *volk* Music, rock'n'roll. Hence T-Shirts like 'Death Before Disco', hence organisations like D.R.E.A.D. (Detroit Rockers Engaged in the Abolition of Disco) and Dahl's own Insane Coho Lips Antidisco Army."

Ever the self-publicist, Dahl released his own disco parody in 1979, 'D'Ya Think I'm Disco'). However, his attempts to douse the creative flames of disco were in vain. The genre's influence continued to grow, even managing to crop up within the nihilistic pose of punk rock. P.I.L.'s 'Death Disco' – wrongly assumed to be an attack on the music rather than the discothèques themselves, by now the haunts of drugged up elite masquerading as beautiful people – was directly inspired by disco's grooves. Meanwhile, Ian Dury and the Blockheads immersed themselves in boogie for tracks like 'Hit Me With Your Rhythm Stick' and Blondie had huge success with their punk/disco fusion 'Heart of Glass'.

Rock's more creative artists quickly understood the possibilities of disco, even if many of the fans weren't! A simplified reading of this would suggest white against black racist motivations in the anti-disco movement. Disco was a derivative of black dance-based music, while rock was considered white music – despite its black heritage. On the face of it, rock's hegemony was attempting to suppress the voice of disco.

However, the anti-disco debate was equally loud among the funk fraternity, revealing another aspect of racism. Disco was considered to be black music stripped of all of its ethnicity. In his book *Funk – The Music, The People and The Rhythm of The One*, African diasporic music historian Rickey Vincent argues that it was an example of funk's black fever sanitised by machines for white consumption.

"Disco is a simplified form of non-ethnic, electronic-sounding dance music... The essence of disco is a repetitive simulation of the rawness of black funk, with music extended by machines and not by grooving improvising musicians," he argued.

Furthermore, Vincent rejects the discotheques which employed disco as their soundtrack as sanitised environments, made safe, he argued, for white people.

"This new sound provided a dance experience with easy-to-learn steps, taught at clean clubs typically managed by gays and white ethnics and set on the high-class boulevards (rather than the dank R&B venues on da hood [sic]), and drew a middle-class white American set into the fold."

The racial aspect of disco is further fuelled by the suggestion that white guys who didn't even like the music wrote disco music. They were allegedly after making a quick buck from disco. Dimitri From Paris, one of the leading DJs to have emerged from the French house scene, has reservations about the validity of his own country's position in the disco story. The musicians, he claims, were only in it for the money.

"Actually, I can not see any artistic links between the French and disco," he says. "A lot of the producers only saw disco as a way to make money. It was simple music for them to make. They were banging acts together that were actually studio musicians. Jacques Morelli started producing and put Village People together, and it was so money-driven. These people didn't actually seem to like disco. They were making jazz and suddenly, they started making disco cuts and making money, which the musician despised actually. I don't think any of those people were doing it for the love of it. Cerrone was definitely a money-loving guy. I find it hard to imagine that he was doing it for love. At the time, watching Cerrone on TV, I just thought, 'who's that corny looking guy with a stupid looking haircut playing this huge drum kit.' I didn't like it at all. To me, disco was all about white producers doing commercial music. But then I used to not like disco until I got into house music. Now I know there was a deeper side to disco. But Cerrone wasn't a part of that. Neither were most of the French producers and songwriters."

However, the suggestion that disco was white dance music created by people who didn't even like the sound is one that Laurent Garnier totally dismisses: "O'Jays, The Trammps, they were doing disco. 'Disco Inferno'... they're fucking black. A lot of people today say that techno is the white version of house, but that's bullshit. Saying disco was a white thing is bullshit too."

Rickey Vincent may be correct in his observations on the discotheques themselves as the playground of a white middle-class elite but his protestations of disco's lack of cultural worth are ultimately rejected by the development in dance music in the years that follow. In a development that Vincent inadvertently acknowledges, the European influence of dance culture came with the addition of machines to make music. The machines represented the single most important disco development in the late-70s – the sequenced synthesizer groove as invented by Georgio Moroder on the classic electronic pulse of 'I Feel Love' featuring Donna Summer. And the Teutonic synth coding of Kraftwerk. Two separate strands of electronic music, which were to have long term influence, shaped the trends that followed.

"In the disco time there were a lot of people who were making electronic music," explains Laurent Garnier. "Take Kraftwerk or Onyx. People like that were very, very synthetic in their music. It was all to do with sequencers, synthesizers and stuff like that, and that was called disco then. I met Kraftwerk and they told me the biggest thing for them was that they were making disco music. Too many people want to put things in boxes today, but at that time, there were lots of different things going under the name disco. At the end of the day, the tempo may change, the machines may change, but it's all dance music. Today, if these people did that music now, it would be called techno. The bottom line is that the music is the same."

One of the most famous tracks of the era to employ the synthesized sounds presented by Gorgio Moroder came in the shape of the classic 'Supernature' by Parisian artist Marc Cerrone. A legend in French dance circles who would inspire many of the so-called French Touch producers of the late 90s.

SPACER

As the disco argument raged throughout the US and UK, it seemed as though France had somehow bypassed the controversy altogether. Popular music was still typified by accordion-fuelled vocal songs by artists like Jonny Halliday and (Belgian) Jacques Brel for the wider French population. Despite its growing popularity, disco was, as Rickey Vincent argues, still a phenomenon that centred on the fashionable clubs of Paris and Cannes.

Among these traditional French vocalists was Parisian artist Anny Chancel. Born in 1946, Anny became better known as Sheila, who would become a hugely successful singer in France thanks to her early-60s recordings like 'L'école est Finie' and 'Des Rois Mage En Galillée'. For her performances, Sheila was always accompanied by a troupe of black dancers called the Devotions.

Despite massive popularity in her home country, a worldwide hit still alluded Sheila until her long-term producer and manager Claude Carrere (who would launch the infamous Carrere Records label in the mid-70s) suggested an image and sound change. In 1977 Sheila was reborn as Sheila B. Devotion. She enjoyed moderate success abroad with the hits 'Love Me Baby' and 'Singing in the Rain'. In 1978 she then released a disco-lite version of 'Light My Fire'. Global success finally came for Sheila B. in 1979 when she released the Chic produced 'Spacer' which was Billboard's Hot Soul Single and peaked at #28, remaining in the US Billboard Top 100 for 13 weeks. It was an achievement that was echoed throughout the world.

Also released in 1979 was a single by a French singer in the more traditional style, which became known throughout the world. Existing at the crossroads of disco and Californian rock, 'Born to be Alive' was the work of one-time English teacher Patrick Hernandez. The song was originally penned in 1976 for his group Paris Palace Hotel for their debut album but it was never released due to record company indifference. Hernandez retired from the music business and started farming rare breed cattle.

Two years later, he was searched out by legendary producer Jan Van Loo. While recording the track 'Making Love' with the producer, Hernandez played him 'Born to be Alive'. Van Loo agreed to produce it, but he insisted on a definitive tempo of 133 BPM with live-sounding drums. While they were recording in the studio ex-Paris Palace Hotel drummer Hervé Tolance played Patrick the guitar riff from a live recording of Spencer Davis Group's 'Give Me Some Lovin'. The same riff was subsequently used on the new version of 'Born to be Alive'.

Again French labels were indifferent to the track, but it was picked up by Italian radio and at 1979's Midem Conference in Cannes, he received a gold disc from Italian sales. He was subsequently snapped up by CBS France and immediately sent him out on a massive promotional tour for the single. His show consisted of just himself and backing dancers. Among the dance troupe was the then-unknown performer Madonna. Over the next two years, over 23 million copies of 'Born to be Alive' would be sold worldwide, winning the songwriter 56 gold singles.

Various other French disco artists achieved some success during the disco era. Among them was Vartan (Johnny Hallyday's ex-wife), who had hits with 'Disco Queen' and 'I Don't Want The Night To End'. Also notable were the Parisian group Belle Epoque whose 'Miss Broadway' reached #26 on the Billboard Hot 100 in 1978.

In 1977, studio musicians Slim Pezin, Marc Chantereau and Pierre-Alain Dahan formed the band Voyage. Their eponymous album offered a journey around the world with disco flavoured by indigenous sounds. It was a work that may have proven unpopular at the time, with most French radio ignoring it completely.

The album was picked up by one of the house DJs at Paris' leading discotheque Elysee-Matigon which was hosted by Regine Zylberberg. When the US born DJ was invited to spin at Regine's New York club, he opted to play the Voyage album in its entirety. As a result, US record labels swooped in to sign the unknown French artists. Despite huge interest from Atlantic, Voyage opted to sign for the specialist disco label Marlin/TK Dance. The album sold two million copies in 1978 and, in an act which would be echoed with French artists over the years, Voyage finally found success in their home country.

The self-titled debut Voyage album would become hugely influential over the years, acting as a precursor to French ambient house artists Deep Forest, who enjoyed worldwide success with their world music collages in the 1990s. The second Voyage album *Fly Away* may have enjoyed greater success – it reached #1 on the US Dance Charts in January 1979 – but it was less interesting on a creative level.

The two albums that followed disappeared from sight almost straight after their release in 1980 and 1982, echoing a plight suffered by many disco artists at the turn of the decade. That didn't stop Paul McCartney from inviting them to support him on the first part of his early-80s tour!

One name that can't be ignored is Serge Gainsbourg. Although considered a more traditional French singer in the St. Germain-des-près school of chanson, he embraced the disco inferno with his huge hit 'Sea, Sex and Sun' – written in fifteen minutes on the corner of a restaurant tablecloth. He had also written the disco-fied 'Manureva' for Alain Chanford.

Gainsbourg was born Lucien Ginsburg in Paris in 1928, into a Jewish family that had survived the Nazi occupation through a combination of false papers and quick wits. As a young musician, Ginsburg made a name for himself as the songwriter of choice for many of the major figures of the famed St. Germain-des-près School of chanson. He changed his name to Serge Gainsbourg in 1958 to release his own self-titled solo album. Despite a lack of commercial success, he was critically acclaimed for his sharp observations on life. He also started to gain the tag of misogynist through some of his more chauvinist lyrics. Bringing early hints at the notoriety that would follow.

Serge Gainsbourg was perhaps best known for his 1969 hit with Jane Birkin' Je T'Aime...Moi Non Plus'. Their archetypal heavy breather was originally to have featured Brigitte Bardot. However, as he explained at the time, "she thought it was too erotic and she was married." The Bardot version of the track subsequently remained in the Phillips Records volts for 17 years. Birkin was less reluctant to get involved in the project and her sexual moans and heavy breathing would bring the record global notoriety. Like Gainsbourg, Birkin was no stranger to controversy. Three years before the release of 'Je T'Aime… Moi Non Plus' she had featured in Michelangelo Antonioni's cult film Blow Up'. Her part in the film may have been pretty small, but she had come to the public's attention thanks to the scenes of nudity she was in. At a time when cinema was still trapped by the conservatism of the 50s, such scenes were extremely shocking in the US and the UK.

'Je T'Aime… Moi Non Plus' was released in 1968 and immediately received condemnation. The record was banned in Sweden, Spain, Brazil, and Britain. The Vatican implored the Italian government to banish it. Philips was forced to delete the track and drop it from their catalogue. In the UK, Philips subsidiary Fontana followed suit. Despite strong sales pushing the track to number two in the UK charts. A small company, Major Minor, immediately bought the rights and saw the song climb to number one. Meanwhile, the track was translated into 81 languages elsewhere in the world, including Japanese. By the end of the year, sales had exceeded two million, ensuring Gainsbourg's position as Europe's leading pop star!

'Je T'Aime… Moi Non Plus' was followed by an album *Jane Birkin and Serge Gainsbourg*, which featured such similarly sexual tracks as '18-39'. A year later, he continued the sexual theme with his *69 Annee Erotique* album. Heavy breathing Birkin style would become something of a cliché in disco music, with Parisian Cerrone carving out a particularly fine line in audio eroticism.

The seventies saw Gainsbourg experiment outside music, releasing a feature film of 'Je T'Aime… Moi Non Plus', starring Joe Dellesandro (from Andy Warhol's *Trash*), Jane Birkin and a young, unknown Gerard Depardieu. Gainsbourg also moved into directing television commercials.

He continued to write songs for others, but his best work was for himself on albums such as *Vu de l'Exterieur*, *Rock Around the Bunker*, *L'Homme à Tête de Chou* and *Aux Armes Etcetera*. With this last album in 1976, he made the greatest musical leap of his career, as he became the first white artist to create a major recording in Kingston, Jamaica. He employed the services of legendary rhythm duo Sly Dunbar and Robbie Shakespeare and Bob Marley's group The Wailers for the sessions. As a result, he became the first French artist to record reggae sounds for release in his native country. If this didn't cause enough controversy in the conservative French climate, the album's eventual release in 1979 included a reggae-fied version of the French National Anthem – ensuring in the process further home-country notoriety.

Its release brought denunciations by generals, priests, and politicians. It also incurred the full wrath of Legion d'Honeur, who considered it a serious insult. War veterans subsequently protested at his concerts and even threatened fans and as a result, Gainsbourg's concerts started getting cancelled. More seriously, a bomb threat and 400 paratroopers vowing vengeance in Strasbourg terrified The Wailers so much that they refused to play. Never one to pander to public opinion, Gainsbourg took the stage alone and sang "La Marseillaise" acapella. The entire audience sang along before quietly exiting the venue.

Aux Armes Etcetera sold over 500,000 copies, winning Gainsbourg his first-ever gold disc for an album. Furthermore, despite the protests, he was awarded "best male performer" and "best album" at that year's music awards in Cannes. Ironically Jimi Hendrix's similar reworking of the US National Anthem was an object of pride for Americans, while in the UK, Brian May's guitar soloing version of 'God Save The Queen' in honour of Queen Elizabeth's 2002 Golden Jubilee was met with little more than cynical mockery. Each case provides an insight into the various national mindsets. While the French reaction to Gainsbourg's 'La Marseillaise' gives a rare insight into the level of nationalistic pride that would mark out many of the country's cultural developments over the years that followed.

In 1984 the album *Love on the Beat* was again met with disapproval from the French moral majority. The album's themes touched on homosexuality and incest. However, this was nothing compared to the reaction he would get in 1985 when he created the notorious 'Lemon Incest'. Its notoriety mainly comes from the video that included bed scenes with his daughter, Charlotte.

He once proclaimed, "For me provocation is oxygen," and true to his word, he continued to provoke people (famously he once even declared "I wanna fuck you," to Whitney Houston on live TV) until his death in 1991. Gainsbourg's legacy stretches far beyond his notoriety. His musical explorations, which brought together the French chanson style with contemporary sounds (disco, reggae, etc.), have influenced France's dance producers. Nowhere is this more apparent than with the work of Air. Indeed even house act Cassius claimed him as an influence. Not least because Cassius' Philippe Cerboneschi, aka Zdar, worked with Gainsbourg in his later years and even produced his daughter's 1997 album.

D.I.S.C.O. R.I.P?

As the 1980s dawned, the disco generation went into a rapid decline. The post-disco sounds of new romantic artists like Spandau Ballet and Visage quickly usurped the originators, while the increased wealth of the so-called Yuppie generation broke down the elitism of the 70s. Discothèques subsequently became the playgrounds of the newly wealthy who demanded a new soundtrack. The buccaneering spirit of disco was almost extinguished. The outrageous clothes had gone and the sound had been watered down to AOR mush. Many of the originators concentrated on money-spinning mega-ballads, while acts like Sister Sledge pursued an ever more poppy route.

However, the greatest impact on the disco era came with the onset of AIDS. If one moment encapsulated the end of the disco it was Sylvester's AIDS-related death in 1988. The scene had become ravaged by the HIV virus in the 80s but the sight of Sylvester at the San Francisco Gay Pride March, wheelchair-bound but joining the 'people with AIDS' procession, brought home the grim reality that the glorious hedonism of the 70s was well and truly over.

A gay icon, Sylvester became a symbol of Gay rights by virtue of the fact that, unlike so many others, he didn't renounce his homosexuality as soon as he found success. An act that once more underlined the radical political force at the heart of disco. But where once Sylvester was the high camp star of disco, now he was barely recognisable, cheekbones protruding and hair thinning. A few months after his death, 'You Make Me Feel (Mighty Real)' had a new meaning. As Barry Walters noted in The Village Voice on 8 November 1988: "Now the party lives on in the picket lines, in benefits, and in rallies to keep those like Sylvester alive."

France, too, had its share of AIDS-related tragedies. On 15 November 1991, Jacques Morali succumbed to the effects of the virus. Although he'd been sick for the best part of the 80s, the French Wonderboys hadn't been entirely quiet through the decade. In 1981 they pioneered the Mediterranean Disco sound with artists like Sandy Marton ('People from Ibiza') and Silver Pozzoli ('Around My Dream'). By 1983 they were involved in the revival of Ertha Kitt's flagging career with the disco-funk track 'Where Is My Man?'. The track had no impact on the mainstream, although it was a huge hit on the gay scene. In many ways underlining the extent to which the gay and straight communities had once again become split apart in the face of the misinformed homophobic response to the AIDS epidemic.

Following Jacques Morali's death, Henri Belolo remained actively involved in dance music with his label Scorpio Music. However, the duo's final Belolo and Morali hit production came with a group that was to define the next major musical development to hit in the post-disco era. The group were Break Machine, a black trio who championed the nascent underground dance style breakdance with their single 'Street Dance'. It was a song that was to have a huge resonance with France's African immigrant communities that were starting to develop their own identity within French culture. The onset of breakdance and the subsequent hip hop scene provided the key and French hip hop was soon to become an international tour de force.

One of the key events in the impact of Break Machine on France was the government act in 1981 that allowed radio stations freedom to control their own output. As a result, a whole generation started to hear US dance music and the post-disco sounds of tech-funk were everywhere. On the poppier end of the spectrum, this was represented by Michael Jackson and Cameo, while the underground was represented by The Peech Boys – a group formed by Larry Levan in the mid-80s. Levan was perhaps better known as the man behind New York's most influential club, the Paradise Garage. The tech-funk soundtrack of which would be echoed throughout Paris' discothèques. The house sound that was later pioneered in the club would have a huge impact on French youth.

Larry Levan had opened the Paradise Garage, a concrete garage in SoHo, Manhattan redesigned as a haven for club hedonists. In many ways, it flew in the face of the elitist Studio 54 style clubs and went some way to introducing a more open-door policy. Ironically, in the shadows of the increasingly sanitised ambience of the discothèques, the Paradise Garage reintroduced a raw dirtiness that had been the original atmosphere that went with the clubbing experience. With its pornographic murals and anything-goes atmosphere, the Paradise Garage quickly became a favourite hangout for players on the city's gay scene. Despite, and in many ways as a result of, the effects of AIDS on the community

US dance producer Moby explains what the attraction was for him: "As a white, straight kid from the suburbs going out to these mostly black, gay clubs, was just how foreign and interesting and wonderful it was. It really was alternative. New York was dirty and dangerous and sexual politics were weird, but at these clubs [Paradise Garage and Red Zone], Latinos, blacks, whites, men and women were celebrating."

Musically, the sound of Paradise Garage is pivotal to the development of house culture and the sound of France's leading French Touch producers. Paradise Garage DJs Larry Levan and David DePino would concentrate on the hard-edged, euphoric sounds of the underground. Disco may have become the commercial soundtrack to the dying days of the 70s through to the mid-80s, but Paradise Garage, just like Chicago's clubs, proved that the scene was developing in ways nobody could have ever predicted. Among the sounds the club pioneered were mutant disco and no wave, New York's answer to post-punk and futurism (a precursor to the new romantics). The mutant disco/no wave sound was an interesting departure from the commercialisation of the once-underground disco sound. Very much in keeping with the experimental ethos of post-punk, with this sound artists such as Liquid Liquid, Was Not Was and Material drew a clear line between Sex Pistols, Brian Eno, George Clinton and Afrobeat legend Fela Anikulapo Kuti.

By the mid-80s, Levan began to incorporate electro-funk into Paradise Garage's musical menu. As a member of the Peech Boys, with vocalists Bernard Fowler (later to be found singing with industrial-funk outfit Tackhead), Levan pioneered the sound which would subsequently become synonymous with New York-based producers such as Arthur Baker and Frenchman Francois Kevorkian, and artists from D:Train to Rockers' Revenge.

Despite the earliest efforts of the French Wonderboys, other French producers, songwriters and musicians failed to take up the gauntlet thrown down by the Paradise Garage championed artists. Whether as a result of the social impact of free radio – which essentially de-centred French artists – or perhaps due to a sudden malaise among the next generation of musicians in France, the country seemed to recoil from its position as dance pioneers for some years. Furthermore, the most successful artists like the Gibson Brothers seemed to stop making music entirely. It was as if, without the panache and flamboyance of disco, French producers suddenly lost their cultural foothold.

For a few years at least, French disco was dead and the soundtrack to Paris by Night was being created by the US and the UK.

CERRONE – THE GODFATHER OF FILTERED DISCO

Malligator Records offices, Paris, December 2002

"Now a lot of people argue about who invented disco. And what I think is, the first person that I think did invent disco by mixing the kick drum far too loud was Cerrone, a French guy."

Laurent Garnier 1997

He's been called everything from the godfather of French Touch to Mr Disco himself. To many, he is the James Brown of the disco world, a one-time drummer who defined disco's kick-drum heavy groove. To others, he's quite simply a musical guru whose back catalogue is ripe with gems for sampling, looping and turning into filtered disco.

Marc Cerrone was more than aware of his status. It hit you when you walked into his record company offices, Malligator, which sat in an upmarket mews close to the Eiffel Tower. As I walked into the offices in 2002, the first thing that faced me was a huge poster advertising his comeback album *Hysteria*. All around the waiting area were carefully positioned reminders of his status – magazines with his face on the cover, posters advertising a showcase for Radio FG, copies of his CDs tastefully placed on a table and gold discs everywhere.

Wander through into the meeting room and it was the same story. Posters, gold and platinum discs and all kinds of Cerrone based paraphernalia dwarfed the smoked glass meeting table. If the intention was to give the visitor a sense of the man's greatness, then it worked. Within minutes of being there, I had a sense of being bludgeoned by the artefacts of a legend.

Self-confidence oozed from Cerrone. It was the self-confidence of a man who believed in every last bit of the legend he had created. When Cerrone talked, his eyes had the glint of a man consumed with both his music and legend. He was a charming conversationalist who would

31

happily turn the conversation back on to his interviewer to put himself in a position of power. It's a skill he'd perfected in close to thirty years (on and off) of life in the spotlight.

"Have you heard my new album?" he asked with a disarming smile. "What is your favourite track? If you're not sure, that means you probably haven't listened to it properly yet?" he continues when I fail to come back at him with an immediate answer. "So what is my favourite track? Me? I love them all... of course."

Jean-Marc Cerrone was born in Paris in 1952 to an Italian immigrant father who had fled his country during the Mussolini era and a Parisian mother. He described himself as a naturally inquisitive child with a hyper-active disposition. Perhaps because of this he quickly developed an urge to beat out rhythms on anything until, at the age of 12, his mother bought him a drum kit. He soon discovered a natural talent for drumming and became a regular feature at local bars and cafés, playing along to old rhythm and blues records. By the time he was 18, he had won his first post as the orchestra leader in a Parisian club. However, it was short-lived as soon after he left Paris for the warmer climes of St Tropez, where he joined the seminal Afro-Rock band Kongas as their percussionist. Kongas became the house band at the leading St. Tropez club Papagayo, where they were spotted one night by French producer Sound of Barclay record label owner Eddie Barclay.

Between 1971 and 1974, Kongas constantly toured Europe, releasing two albums, including the highly respected *Africanism*. With many of the Kongas tracks becoming heavily sampled years later by producers such as Masters at Work, they have gained something of cult status in the years since their demise. However, what was most interesting about Kongas was that it was in this group that Cerrone first started exploring the symphonic elements that would feature so heavily in his disco work.

Kongas came to an end in 1974 thanks to the duel forces of Cerrone's increased desire to be at the forefront and the age-old excuse of musical differences.

"Kongas were actually the first French group who were released outside of France. I signed my first American contract in 1971 with Buddah

Records for Kongas," exclaimed Cerrone with justifiable pride. "We had a lot of success over three or four years but then the band tried to be a little bit more commercial and pop. We lost the original sound of the band, so I left because I didn't want to be in a pop band."

He didn't turn to a solo career immediately. Instead, he opened a record store specialising in imported US dance music. Soon he owned numerous shops all around the suburbs of Paris and was deeply immersed in the American sounds of funk and Philly soul that he was stocking. In 1976 he decided to record his own version of these styles. His intention was to marry the upfront kick drum and symphonic strings of the Kongas with a sexually charged female vocal chorus. He left Paris for London and entered Trident Studios in September and October 1976 and came up with the album that was to define the disco sound *Love in 'C' Minor*. Not that anyone was interested in it at the time.

"My first LP wasn't popular music at all. Nobody wanted to play it. It was so strange. Sixteen minutes of sexual moaning with the beat right up in your face and a bass line of two chords. The radio was like, 'what the fuck's that?'. Nobody wanted to release it either. I was told to cut the track down to three minutes and I wouldn't do it."

In an act that would mirror the punk movement also rearing its head at the time, Cerrone decided to create his own company to release the records and independently distribute them throughout his own stores.

"So I had to start my label Malligator," he continued. "Not because I'm a manager or anything like that, but because nobody would release my records. I went back to the UK and got Island to press up 5,000 copies of the vinyl. They were the only company at the time who would accept to manufacture it for me. I had to put the Malligator label on it, so I could manufacture it. When I received my copies, which I'd paid for in advance, and then I sold copies into the shops. Just like the house kids of today. But that was 27 years ago.

"Then one shop in Paris sent back as a return 300 copies to New York. It was a mistake. The guy was supposed to send back Barry White records, but he sent mine instead. When the guy in New York opened the package and saw the record sleeve with a nude woman on it he was like, 'What? A sex record?'. So he played it. And the guy was a DJ, who then started to play '(the song) 'Love in C Minor' in the gay clubs he played at. Two weeks later, we got a massive reaction."

Whether or not the guy who made the mistake in the record shop was actually Cerrone is not clear. Either way, it was an act that turned the Parisian producer into a major recording star. Not, however, before he had visited MIDEM music conference in the South of France and discovered that Casablanca Records had released their own version of the album's title track in the US where club reaction had been incredible. Naturally, everyone wanted a copy of this underground gem by this unknown artist. With many of the dance labels feeding off club hype, it wasn't long before A&R scouts were clamouring for information about Cerrone. The cover version was the obvious option when no one could find anything more about him or simply discovered that he lived in another country.

"Casablanca Records did a cover of the track as the Heart of the Soul Orchestra," he explained. "It went right up the charts. So I was like, 'it's me, that's not the real version'. I went to New York and met the people at Atlantic who thought the story was so funny. I signed with them and they killed the cover off. Which was pure luck for me."

Pure luck that translated to sales of over five million! *Love in 'C' Minor* brought together all of the different musical and cultural facets that would mark out the hypermasculinity of the disco era. A macho adventure in a world of willing and grateful women, the album opens with a group of girls – Cerrone's Angel's – discussing the merits of the men they were eyeing up. Essentially this came down to size. Whether that was a bank account, height or the bulge in his trousers, the girls discuss their prey with a voracious appetite while downing champagne like its water.

When listening to the track in conjunction with the cover image, the target of their desire (for these women really are hunting their man in a full-blown, hypermasculine fantasy) is obviously Cerrone. Here he is pictured lounging in a bathrobe as a naked woman drapes herself over him. She may have been the hunter, but the image says he is the true victor. Explore the image more closely and you notice the clothes of more than one woman strewn all over the floor. The back image shows three women fully clothed dancing around Cerrone for his pleasure. With this in mind, it's what's not shown on the front image that tells the entire story. Cerrone, the love God has, we are encouraged to imagine, just had sex with three girls. Two of which are too exhausted to pose next to their man. The only remaining girl is clearly ready for more.

There is also a racial undertone to this image. Of the three angels, only the remaining girl is white. It is, therefore an image that plays with racial stereotypes of the day by suggesting that Cerrone is the sexual master over all races, while the final twosome inadvertently displays the 'natural order' of white-dominated same race, heterosexuality. Furthermore, the cover image held a connotation that disco was a musical playground where the white man was supreme – thus echoing Rickey Vincent's concerns outlined earlier.

Musically the album moves in similarly macho waters. Opening with the title track, you are immediately faced with the object of Cerrone's macho pride – and the one thing that he will continue to claim as his contribution to the dance music lexicon – the pounding kick drum. From here, he combines sixteens with an on-then-one bass line, which revolves around two chords. It is rhythmic simplicity, the depth and structure of funk and soul stripped back to its immediate, physical core. Over the top of this, strings borrowed from Philly Soul intertwine with chicken grease funk guitar, horn and string stabs, simplistic keyboard motifs and congas. The separate parts all play their own simple melody based on the overriding string motif that gradually builds towards the main verse. Here the girls start to sing "love me" in a pleading, submissive chorus as the funk guitar is driven by a wah-wah pedal as the string refrains swell towards their climax. Then the strings disappear and stabbing horns strut, and the girls all moan in full-blown sexual pleasure in unison.

The remainder of the track finds strings exploring the various themes individually while Cerrone pounds his percussion instruments in a show of chest-beating victory until a sax brings a climactic crescendo. He is the master of the bedroom, the master of his women and the object of every woman's dreams. And it all takes 16 minutes and 17 seconds!

After this wanton display of macho posturing, the remaining tracks – a cover of 'Black is Black' and the more melodic 'Midnite Lady'- seemingly blur into insignificance. In 'Love in 'C' Minor', Cerrone had already told the entire story of disco. He'd taken the guitars from 'Shaft', the strings and the ladies' man image from Barry White, the rhythms of The Trammps' 'Disco Inferno' and added his own kick drum.

"Because I'm a drummer, the main peculiarity about my music was that I put the kick right on the front – like nobody else," he said. "If I was a saxophone player, I would have put the sax to the front, but I'm a drummer, so it's the kick drum that is upfront. People played that beat like I played it before me, but I was the first to make that kick strong. Like it is for house music today, for example.

"When I started to do my music it wasn't labelled disco. It was my music. For the media, we cut the words discotheque. We said 'this nighttime music is for the discotheque'. And then we just left the 'theque' out and said it's disco music. Really there were two or three artists at the time like that; Giorgio Moroder, Nile Rogers (of Chic fame) and me. We were the three main guys. Because we had a lot of success, we started to see a lot of productions from younger people which was more pop music arranged as a disco soup.

"Then in 1976 when I arrived with 'Love in C Minor' and Giorgio arrived with 'Love to Love You Baby', and then the movies arrived. *Saturday Night Fever* exposed the world to disco, which was good, but on the other hand, it was bad because many record companies produced a lot of fucked songs with a disco beat and disco arrangements. Today the younger generation never have any confusion of this. They know what pure disco is, but back then, people didn't. That's why my back catalogue has never been out of the shops.

"But it was because of the success of me and Giorgio and a couple of other guys that Billboard created a chart for disco music. Before that, it was like 'dance music, what is this?' so we helped create a new media for dance music. And not only the magazines – in the TV, in movies, everywhere. We can see the importance of this today with dance music becoming a real media."

A year later, Cerrone returned to London's Trident Studios to record the second instalment in his disco vision. Called *Cerrone's Paradise*, it would prove far less successful than its predecessor. However, it is now largely considered one of his strongest recordings. Ironically this album's success actually predates the wider acknowledgement of *Love in 'C' Minor*, which had been mainly a club hit at the time. It was *Cerrone's Paradise* that won him respect among people outside of the disco market in Europe and the US. Which in turn, sparked new interests in his previous record, resulting in huge sales. Furthermore, *Cerrone's Paradise* also saw the cementing of the songwriting partnership that was to bring him his biggest success – the melodies of Alain Wisniak, who had previously collaborated on 'Midnite Lady' from the previous album, and the lyrics of Lene Lovich.

The arrangements on the second album were far more complex with the rhythmic interplay between keyboards and strings becoming a continual presence. On the title track, the main thrust comes from the call and response of horn stabs and string arpeggios. Guitars are brighter, with less funky 'wah wah', while melodic themes are based on sharp, stabbing string refrains. Cerrone himself is able to run riot with percussive gymnastics.

Although the sexual aspect of the album was less obvious than with *Love in 'C' Minor*, *Cerrone's Paradise* did contain a subtext that again placed the main man in the dominant position. Once again, the album opens with women discussing the merits of their men. This time, however, they all argue over Cerrone. The cover depicts Cerrone crouching by a fridge, which has naked women draped over it. The message is simple; Cerrone now has women on ice as well as on fire!

Musically themes are just as macho as before. All instruments thrust and strut. All melodies are simple and direct. It's music that is all about direct response. Again there is no foreplay, just action. Followed inevitably by post-coital saxophones – surely an instrument invented by a man in the aftermath of self-satisfying sex. As if to acknowledge the critical comments of the length of *Love in 'C' Minor*, Cerrone included an edited mix of the track 'Cerrone's Paradise' on the album. Ever the businessman, he would have realised the commercial impact of limited radio play. By having two versions, he was able to explore his full vision on the 16-minute original and supply radio with the three-minute version. It is an act of an artist with one foot in the musical underground and another in the commercial mainstream. A position that would mark out his work over the next few years.

Elsewhere on the album 'Take Me' introduces walking octave bass lines to the equation, where once again women moan with pleasure and strings, brass and funky guitars out strut each other for sonic dominance. Melodically it remains one of his most successful tracks, with the interplay between strings and vocals showing Wisniak at his best. The remaining track, 'Time for Love' finds Cerrone in slow groove territory, introducing for the first time in his music, the so-called language of love, French! It also features the man himself on seductive, breathy vocals as his angels spin out a chocolate box melody. It is Cerrone as deep in cliché as he would ever descend as he acted out the sensitive side of the macho man.

"I used a lot of female backing vocals and because I created albums with atmospheres that sounded better at night. It was obviously sexy music. When we did music for discotheques, we were much more excited to look at each other. Men to women, women to men. Men to men, woman to woman. The night… we are more interested in sex at night. That doesn't mean I don't like to have sex in the morning; I don't say that. But of course, at night, like the rest of the world, I am more excited about sex. My music is for the discotheque, which is a sexual environment. That's why my music is sexual."

When asked if the overtly masculinised sexuality of his music has a place in the society of the early 2000s, he was quick to offer an argument against contemporary stars.

"My first LP was censored. I don't think there is more sex on this cover than what I see on the videos of Britney Spears or Christina Aguilera. They're close to pornography. I'm always surprised when people ask me about why sex is so important to my music."

The difference, of course, is that in the videos of an artist like Christina Aguilera the woman is portrayed as being in control, dominating the path of the fantasy. Even today, with his latest album, Cerrone's vision puts women in the subservient role. They are perpetually passive, but for the manhunt. Or, to be more accurate, the Cerrone-hunt.

As disco music became the commercialised pop music of the day, Cerrone increasingly felt the need to react. In many ways, he saw that the industry appropriated his trademark sound. By June 1977, only three months after he'd recorded *Cerrone's Paradise*, he was back in Trident Studios to record album number three, *Supernature*.

The title track would become his most successful recording yet, selling more than eight million copies and gaining Cerrone a Grammy Award in 1978 for best New Male Artist (among four other awards on the same night). What made this track stand out on the surface was that it embraced the possibilities of the synthesiser in a way only previously explored by Giorgio Moroder.

"We sold eight million copies of *Supernature*, which means you're on a promotional tour for years," he recalled. "I remember I used Lene Lovich for the lyrics, and when we received a Grammy Award, for the lyrics and for the music, for best LP and best new artist. And when we were in New York to receive the Grammy and I was like, 'this must be a mistake'. After 25 years, I realised how big it was, but at the time, I was in the middle of it all and didn't have time to stop."

The creation of *Supernature* in the first place was a direct reaction to his own success and to the growing commercialisation of disco.

"When I was 20 I was more provocative," he explained. "My first two LPs had a lot of orchestration and a lot of brass, and of course, I don't do the arrangement. I have people to do that. I was like some of the track is not me and if the critics think so much about someone else doing it, then maybe I should do the whole track myself."

Interestingly, however, despite any claims for this to have been his own work, Alain Wisniak was once again credited as co-songwriter on the record label and Lene Lovich was once again on board as the lyricist. However, the cover clearly displays the words' Music composed by Cerrone'.

"I was tired of the brass stabs and the strings which were everywhere by then, while I was so influenced by Kraftwerk at the time," he continues. "I also received some synthesizers like the ARP Odyssey to use in return for printing the names of the synths on my LP. So I used it, and the first thing I did when I switched it on was like 'de-de-de-de-de', so I used it. And I composed one track like that I called 'Supernature'."

With 'Supernature' he created a track that at once exemplified the electronic music that was starting to take hold at the time. His take on Giorgio Moroder's Eurodisco groove nestled closely alongside Bowie's Berlin-era *Low* album, and Kraftwerk's ongoing success. *Supernature* is often viewed as the one true classic Cerrone track. It quickly became the soundtrack to London punk at lesbian club Louise's before becoming a regular new romantic tune in DJ Rusty Egan's Blitz Club sets. Perhaps inevitably, given her love of disco, Madonna would include 'Supernature' in her live sets throughout the 90s. The song was a cultural phenomenon.

With 'Supernature', the uniformity of the horn and string stabs were replaced by unrelenting synth arpeggios, thus creating a rigid groove that would exaggerate the emphasis of the kick drum. Suddenly the free-flowing percussion of Cerrone's rhythm was stripped to the metronomic beats of the machine. Only the very present vibraslap remained as a reminder that this was a human rhythm.

Musically the 'Supernature' journey was similarly reliant on simplistic melodic refrains. However, with the string and brass interplay replaced by synth motif, the effect was of a further simplification of the Cerrone sound. Ultimately it was a bleak sound compared to his earlier works. Even the vocals of Cerrone's Angels were imbued by a chilling ambience, thanks largely to the lyrical science fiction theme of genetic engineering creating a super race.

The album itself could be split into two clearly distinctive themes; the 'Supernature' side and the 'Give Me Love' side. The former found the lead track seamlessly mixed into 'Sweet Drums' (a Cerrone solo production), in which Cerrone gets to run amok with his percussion while the synths continue on the 'Supernature' theme. This is followed by the almost ambient version of the main track 'In the Smoke', which echoed the work of fellow French producer Jean-Michel Jarre who was at that time enjoying international acclaim for pioneering symphonic electronic music piece *Oxygene*.

The flipside of 'Supernature', however, revealed Cerrone back in his better-known territory of combining simple funk b-lines with sweeping strings, brass stabs and female vocal chorus. Perhaps the most interesting development is the increased reliance on Stevie Wonder style jazzy keyboard fills and rocky electric guitar displays.

Taken on their own, the three tracks on this side, 'Give Me Love', 'Love is Here' and 'Love is the Answer', are among Cerrone's finest disco tracks. They depict him and his dream team actively pursuing the original music ethos of disco while exploring fresher territory without descending into the pop mire, which had come to mark out disco music. Here was the Cerrone sound at its deepest, a sound which would go on to have a huge impact on the house and garage generations over ten years later. However, the 'Love' side of this collection is completely overshadowed by the 'Supernature' themed side.

"Originally, it was meant to be on the B-side of the album," he explained. "The rest of the tracks were more like the other stuff I'd done, but then it was so successful that it became the A-side. The first single was supposed to be 'Give Me Love' but 'Supernature' took over."

The dual themes of the album were also explored on the album cover. The front image finds Cerrone standing in an awkward pose before a hospital trolley on which a body is stripped of its flesh down to the muscle and sinew stretched as a representation of the stripped bare sounds of the lead track. At his feet are dog and pig-headed doctors grovelling on the floor. The back cover shows Cerrone, the musician, surrounded by his timpani drums while women grovel at his feet. Although, just like the doctors, these women have the heads of a dog and a pig. So, no longer just the sexual master of women, Cerrone is now depicted as a superhero saving the world from the mad doctors intent on creating a perverted race of manimals. While he is also shown to be the master of the females of this new race. Once again, he is intent on saving the 'natural order' of things.

As we discussed the merits of 'Supernature', Cerrone's assistant interrupted with a reminder of a recently discovered picture of Cerrone to add to the already impressive library. This time however it was from *Kurt Cobain's Journals* in which the young Kurt drew a cartoon of Cerrone saving the world. The image he used is from the front cover of *Supernature*.

"When I first saw this, I felt like… wow," he exclaimed, a look of pure excitement taking over from the polite enthusiasm that had underlined our conversation so far. "I remember that in the period that Kurt was big, I was a bit frustrated. Everyone thought disco was has-been music. So when the guy's diaries were published, I discovered that back at that time I was thought of as a has-been; this guy who everyone loved was doing a cartoon of me. I was like… wow!"

Such interest from Kurt Cobain does, however, serve to underline the cultural impact of both Cerrone and 'Supernature'. The release of this record coincided with a growth in electronica as outsider's music. Traditionally disco had also been the nightlife sound of the outsider, so he could once again be seen to be exploring beyond the periphery of pop. It was a track that would have an immediate influence on the late 70s electronic music explorers and ultimately a massive impact on the post-punk futurists and new romantic artists like Visage, Ultravox and Japan, all of whom would release singles that would closely assimilate the *Supernature* electro-disco sound palette. Surprisingly, despite the success of *Supernature*, Cerrone didn't pursue the style in future recordings.

"When the style you do in the underground is taken by everyone, you have to react. 'Supernature' is something that I could never do again," he said. "It's something you can never repeat. The proof of that, I got maybe fifty remixes of it – William Orbit, Tenaglia, Todd Terry, Morales – everybody tried to do it, but nobody improved on the original. I would be happy if someone did. I even tried myself but no, it wouldn't work. Grace Jones tried to cover it, but it wasn't any good, so she didn't release it.

"And nobody has sampled the track except two or three sounds that have been lifted by a French rapper, Rohf. Oh, and Ozomatli sampled a bit of it as well. Universal has told me that I am in the top three artists to have the most samples of them. It may be true of the other tracks, but nobody ever used 'Supernature' in any substantial way. I like that."

The album that followed, *Cerrone IV – The Golden Touch*, was issued a year later in 1978. By this stage, Cerrone had ditched Alain Wisniak and Lene Lovich was merely credited as a translator. The resulting album was much softer, lacking in focus and featuring his weakest arrangements to date. Despite spawning the medium-sized hits 'Je Suis Music' and 'Rocket in My Pocket' the collection was a relative failure. However, it has had an impact on dance culture that goes deeper than the record itself, with 'Rocket in My Pocket' containing one of the single most sampled drum loops.

"I don't care about being sampled. I don't care because I know there is much more on the original track. I do care when someone takes eight bars of my music and then edits and loops it for six minutes, and then adds a new beat, and that's it. And then the guy says he's the composer, publisher and so on. The minute I hear that, I send my attorney and we stuff it. When I accept, it's like Modjo, or Bob Sinclar with 'I Feel For You', or Daft Punk, or Groove Armada. These tracks are done with creativity and with this kind of deal I always ask for 50% of everything – masters, publishing, writing. I am surprised the way they use the samples and create a new piece. Some of it is bullshit, but some of it is good, good. Modjo was really good. Daft Punk not so…

"Paul McCartney sent me a CD last year to ask permission to sample the track 'You Are The One' (from *Cerrone VII – You Are the One*). He's taken five samples, and edited it to six minutes and added the vocals of 'Goodnight Tonight' by Wings and it's great."

Interestingly the cover of *Cerrone IV – The Golden Touch* found the musician now presented as a modern-day Roman Emperor, driving his disco chariot across the appreciative audience. His semi-clad angels metaphorically pull the chariot, as Cerrone himself holds their reigns in one hand, and a record in the other and spotlights pick out his white suit. No longer the saviour of the natural order, he is now the conqueror of winged women and willing subservient fans. He has become the natural order.

The albums that appeared in the last two years of the decade saw Cerrone's grip on the charts slipping even further. The OST to the Brigade Mondaine movie *Striptease* featured various Cerrone produced artists to varying degrees of success. Full-length artist album *Cerrone V – Angelina* followed an even more lightweight and directionless path than the previous artist album, while *Cerrone V1* found him at an all-time creative low. Only the return of a naked woman on the cover hinted at the Cerrone of old.

As with the disco scene he had grown up with, at the turn of the 80s, Cerrone faced diminishing interest. Disco had been superseded by punk rock in the hearts of the kids, electro too was coming through and only the synth arpeggios of Giorgio Moroder and 'Supernature' found favour with the post-punk futurists and new romantics.

In 1980 Cerrone moved to the US, where he has lived in West Hollywood, close to Valley Hills since, only returning to Paris a few times in the intervening years. His first US production *Cerrone VII – You Are the One* was recorded at New York's Power Station (home of Chic, among others) and represented a style shift towards mainstream disco. No longer did Cerrone attempt any kind of experimentation; his sound now echoed the commercial US soul ventures of recent years. The album was notable, however, for the way he heavily featured the vocals of Jocelyn Brown, who would go on to score huge international hits, including 1991's 'Always There' with Incognito.

From here, Cerrone continued to release albums with varying degrees of success, never again reaching the same levels as experienced in the period of those first four albums. Indeed, when questioned about his 80s and 90s output, he is particularly evasive.

"I am not a big fan of the 80s," he explained. "The legacy of the 80s is not very good. Not like the 70s. I stopped releasing records between 83 and 89. I composed with Earth, Wind and Fire; I passed a lot of time touring with a couple of guys from the group Yes. It was a period of performing rather than creating. I did produce Colonel Abrahams, the first record of Latoya Jackson. I also produced Laura Brannigan and Joceyln Brown."

It was the only time in the interview in which he appeared to be slightly agitated. Partly due to my lack of knowledge of this period of his work, but also because it represents a time when Cerrone, the musician, had been forced to take a step back from the spotlight.

It wasn't a period of inactivity, however. During this time, he claimed to have discovered the British act Art of Noise, although it's more likely that his time working with members of Yes brought him to Art of Noise through Trevor Horn. Not only had the former member of Buggles started producing and performing as a member of Yes but he also used the band as his session players on records by Frankie Goes to Hollywood, among others. Art of Noise was the work of Horn and ZTT record label colleagues engineer/producer Gary Langan, programmer J.J. Jeczalik, keyboardist and arranger Anne Dudley and music journalist Paul Morley.

Cerrone recorded several movie soundtracks and even produced a movie starring Alain Delon and Patrick Dupont. Furthermore, he composed the rock opera *The Collector*, which was performed on Trocedera Place in Paris and broadcast worldwide by over 40 TV stations. He also produced something of an extravaganza in support of the launch of the first satellite TV broadcast in Japan. Once again, the spectacular show was shown throughout the world.

Another show of which he is particularly proud was in support of the Dalai Lama and the plight of his native Nepal in the face of Chinese oppression. Cerrone scurried back into his own private office and returned clutching a framed photo of him with the Dalai Lama at the mention of the show. It is one of the few moments of humility that he has shown throughout the interview. Perhaps because he started to follow the Buddhist faith in the early 90s, but also out of simple reverence for someone he sees as a great man. Indeed, Cerrone was not slow in extolling the worth of those great people he has known or worked with.

In the post-house years, Cerrone took on near-legendary status. His records were sampled by so many major players that is hard to ignore the legacy of the Frenchman's early output. However, in early 2000 an unlikely Parisian ally came through from the French jazzy trip hop underground. His name was Chris Le Friant (aka Chris the French Kiss), who had released music under the aliases of the Latin funk inspired The Reminiscence Quartet and abstract beats outfit Mighty Bop. Together with Alain Ho (aka DJ Yellow), he had created Yellow Productions, one of the key Parisian labels of the 90s.

In 1996 Le Friant launched a house project under the alias Bob Sinclar after the main protagonist in the famous French detective movie *Le Magnifique*. The first album under this name followed a year later. In a direct reference to Cerrone, it was called *Paradise*. Then in 1999, Le Friant approached Cerrone for permission to use a sample on a track called 'I Feel For You' for his forthcoming album.

"Cerrone had a reputation for not wanting to clear anything," recalls Le Friant in total contradiction to Cerrone's own claims. "He was completely into his music and didn't want to be sampled. But I talked to him and found it really easy. The sample was cleared within four days. And then he asked me out to Los Angeles to work with some singers in a studio out there. And that is how 'I Feel For You' came about."

"Bob Sinclar called me and asked to use a sample," explains Cerrone of the collaboration. "So I heard the song and I said 'there's not one sample, there's three'. He laughed and said, oh, so you recognise it. Of course, I did. So I asked him what he wanted to do with it. He said he wanted to put a melody on it and I was like, OK, you want to have my sound? He said yes. So I said come to LA, you can have my girls, and we'll work together. So we did 'I Feel for You' 50/50, and it became a club smash."

If this nod of respect for the work of Cerrone wasn't enough, then on *Champs Elysees*, the Bob Sinclar album that followed, Le Friant opened the vinyl version with a pastiche of the intro chat from the first two Cerrone albums. Tellingly Cerrone's Angels had a new object of desire – Bob Sinclar. After the success of 'I Feel For You', a number of labels pursued Cerrone for a compilation. However, he decided to develop the relationship with Le Friant further and offered him the chance to create a DJ's perspective of his back catalogue. Le Friant was invited to trawl through Cerrone's songs and create a mix from them using contemporary DJing techniques.

"I had three record companies ask me to do a compilation album. I thought that was crazy, so I decided to do something a bit more creative," recalled Cerrone. "I came to Paris and asked Chris if he wanted to have his name on my new record? So I gave him all of my records and gave him the freedom of choice to programme a set from them, simply as he does it in the club."

The resulting mix *Cerrone by Bob Sinclar* spans the high points of his 70s albums and even draws on Kongas material and productions for long-time Cerrone friend and collaborator Donray. Furthermore, the way Le Friant edited and mixed the selections gave the album a powerfully contemporary feel, removing the disco-isms, which hadn't stood the test of time and in their place, he extended those passages that had been heavily sampled by house producers. In every way possible, it is a compilation that could only have been created in the musical climate of the early 2000s. Le Friant's skills in the mix were paramount to the album's success.

"It took a day and a half to complete. We released it and sold 800,000 copies," exclaimed Cerrone, pointing to the gold disc on his wall for added effect. "That woke me up to the idea of a brand new LP. Because I'm tired after 25 years of talking about 'Supernature'."

That new album *Hysteria* was released in November 2002. A 12-track affair, the album found Cerrone attempting to come to grips with the house scene that had adopted him while retaining the sounds that were his trademarks.

"New album is me, my sound. I tried not to be like the house people. I think there were two easy mistakes I could have made on this LP. Try to be myself 25 years ago. Or try and play the young DJ. But it's not my fault if the young generation copies so much from me! So I tried to do an acoustic sound with real drums, bass, brass and strings, and real guitars from Nile Rogers. And then when everything was recorded, we put everything on the computer to make the groove more mechanical. This way, we stopped it from sounding old and retro. I tried to be in the middle, electro-acoustic. For example, I tried to mix it on SSL but it sounded too much like pop. So I went back to mix on Pro-Tools, which makes it sound like house. But when it's real instruments, no matter if you use Pro-tools and make it metronomic like house, it's still acoustic."

Despite his protestations that the album contained no attempts to aim at the house crowd, the opening salvo of 'The Only One' came in like the golden era of the French Touch, aping Stardust and Modjo, before opening out onto a Chic-esque uptempo disco-pop song. It was the sound of two worlds colliding with only the surface level tricks of each surviving the battle. The beats and bass lines were outdated while the vocal effects and occasional flourishes of production were directly from 2002's studio lexicon. Similarly, the aspect that made Cerrone's old sound great, the interplay between brass, strings and vocals, were lost in favour of immediacy. The story was the same on the entire album as Cerrone-style melodies were joined by vocoder effects, Nile Rogers' trademark guitar sound playing counterpoint to 2000's style synth washes. Cerrone's drumming was also quantized out of all humanity by the programming techniques.

The main problem with *Hysteria* was that in attempting to assimilate the two worlds, Cerrone had lost the things that were great from each era. Thus the production on this album wasn't contemporary where it should have been, and the song arrangements weren't classic, where they could and should have been. However, the songs themselves were all strong, with the title track, 'Love On The Dancefloor' and 'Funky Love' standing out thanks to the typically understated hook lines in full flow. Sadly they are smothered by the schizophrenic and bland production. On this evidence, neither his son, DJ and producer Greg Cerrone, nor mixmaster David Sussman was up to the required level of skill.

Hysteria was released to a mixed response, with many people feeling he had lost his own sound to the house arrest of Pro-Tools. Others, like Bob Sinclar himself, felt that the production was too rooted in the past for the album to have any relevance at that time.

"He is a producer of the past. You can see that on his new album," Le Friant said when we talked a few days later in his basement studio. "The production is really old. It's from the past and I'm not into that kind of production. But he believes that he is still of today. He didn't really understand that on our collaboration, it was the mixture of old tracks edited and mixed in a new style, and the combination of my name, which is quite strong, that gave it success. The hits were from the past, but my edits and production, and the Bob Sinclar name are from now. And that's the collaboration. You know the album is in the shops under the Bob Sinclar section. Which is very good for me. But I have no wishes to do a new collaboration."

Ironically the third Bob Sinclar album, called *III* in another cheeky nod of respect to Cerrone, featured what was perhaps the most perverse form of Cerrone collaboration of them all. Le Friant took on the role of Cerrone himself and teamed up with the Cerrone dream team of Alain Wisniak and Lene Lovich! He even used Cerrone's Angels on vocals. The first results of which 'The Beat Goes On' were as close as house can get to being Cerrone without actually sampling his music. Furthermore, Le Friant's underground house project Africanism also borrowed its name from Cerrone's history. It was the title of the second Kongas album.

So was Bob Sinclar stealing the Cerrone sound?

"Um, yes, a bit… in a way. Without wanting to sound pretentious, I am the millennium Cerrone sound," admitted Le Friant. "I could be Cerrone's son in the production. It could be the evolution of his music. *III* is a kind of a Cerrone cliché. I should have been *Cerrone 15* but he didn't produce *Hysteria* as he should have produced it – with his head turned to the future. You know what? I will be completely obsolete in ten years, and new guys will come to say, Chris, you have to work in this way now. But with Cerrone, he lives large and his ego is strong, so he doesn't have the intelligence to go with a younger guy. He didn't come to me and offer a 50/50 to let me mix his tracks to get a modern sound. To know about beats and production, you have to be strong, and he wasn't. So with taking his dream team, I think I was trying to create Cerrone's

49

millennium sound. Because I do love his music. And he hasn't taken it into the new millennium."

Not that the man behind Bob Sinclar was anything less than complimentary about Cerrone.

"I think it's so cool that he didn't play anything but drums and he managed to create this music," he said. "Wisniak tried to create something on his own but it failed, so Cerrone must have had something special."

Back in the plush offices of Malligator, Cerrone contemplated his future. Clearly fired up by the experience of producing a new album, he talked about other possibilities.

"I would like to work with Moby," he said, strangely opting for one of electronic music's least sexy people – despite the New Yorker's claims to the contrary. "Moby interests me a lot. He's got a really creative way of working. Really interesting. He's technically a smart guy. On *Hysteria*, I asked the engineer to get a sound like one on (Moby album) *Play*. The engineer said that it was an orchestra in reverse. So we did an experiment and sampled a sound from Moby and reversed that. And it was an orchestra!"

That Cerrone considered Moby's skill to be rare in conjuring this sound only supported Chris Le Friant's claim that the man behind 'Love in 'C' Minor' was out of touch with beats and production. Such tricks were commonplace at that time. However, what is likely is that what Cerrone recognised in Moby's sound was the New Yorker's love of disco!

"You know what?" concluded Cerrone as he leant back in his chair for effect, a look of pure satisfaction on his face. "It feels so good that 25 years after being treated like an impostor by the industry that so many youngsters sample me, that a member of The Beatles has sampled me and that I'm still producing new music. Five years ago, the door was completely closed to me to do something like this, but then when people started sampling me and mentioning my name, the time came for me to write a new track again."

Not quite as relevant or groundbreaking as he was in the 70s perhaps, but Cerrone remains Europe's leading exponent of the disco dream. He gave us the paradigm of the sound and has subsequently inspired many of the leading names in contemporary house culture. Furthermore, his sound was a key component in the creation of French Touch.

Cerrone continues to release music with *DNA* (2020) exploring synthwave to startling effect and showing a new breed of Daft Punk inspired synth artists how it's really done.

BEFORE DISCO THERE WAS MUSIQUE CONCRETE

Discotheque culture may have had a significant bearing on the sound of contemporary French dance music, but many musical explorers also helped create the electronic music aesthetic. Perhaps the most influential development in late 20th Century composition was musique concrete, an approach to music that would hugely influence the sampling generation and how they perceived music.

Just as many people claim that everything is art, the musique concrete school believed everything to be a source of music. Through a combination of brilliant tape editing and imaginative musical structuring, these composers would create stunning pieces from the most wayward of sound.

"'Concrete music' is a kind of style of music, realised with different concrete sounds (not only from regular instruments). Very often, the work of many composers – like Pierre Henry for example – is a mixture of regular and traditional music instruments," explained the self-styled humoristic-easy-listening-electro-pop-musician Jean-Jacques Perrey to me in 2002. "The concrete sounds they use are sounds from nature, industrial sounds, animal sounds etc., as well as strange sounds made by original synthesisers."

The term musique concrete was first coined by Pierre Schaeffer to describe the new form of music he had been developing. A style in which composition was based upon the acoustic manipulation of found sounds. Schaeffer, a Frenchman who lived through the Nazi occupation of France, wasn't actually a musician. He was a telecoms engineer. However, it is possible that this job did give him an insight into the sonic possibilities found in all objects.

His compositions were largely viewed as being inferior and as such, he was unable to convince the classical music elite of the worth of his concept. However, Schaeffer soon found a classically trained composer as a musical ally (Pierre Henry, another Frenchman), with whom he would enjoy his few moments of contemporary critical acclaim for the piece "Symphonie pour un Homme Seul" ("Symphony for a Lonely Man"). Henry had been drawn to the unique opportunities that musique concrete opened up to the traditional composer. He didn't, therefore, find Schaeffer's work to be unskilled, as others had. Instead, he considered them to be groundbreaking and ultimately intriguing.

"Symphony for a Lonely Man" corresponds to my first step toward concrete music," Henry told Iara Lee for her film *Modulations* in 1997. "Before that, I did some tryouts with equipment, with instruments of sound search. When I met with Schaeffer again, we composed this piece. It's not research. The search had already been done. It was continuity. We wanted it to be like a spokesman, with an aesthetic approach. And the aestheticism was a symphony of voices, instruments with noise. 'Symphony for a Lonely Man' was composed by two lonely men."

Pierre Henry was born in Paris in 1927. As a child, he was unhealthy and was unable to go to school. As a result, he had a series of private tutors who would encourage his musical tendencies. He started to show talent as a rhythmist very early on by hitting furniture, tables, anything he could in order to create a beat. He quickly graduated to drums, and here started a musical journey that would take him to the forefront of experimental composition. In explaining what Musique Concrete was years later, Henry would claim that as a child his head was filled with sounds, which couldn't be interpreted literally. This imagination for unpresented sounds lay at the creative core of Musique Concrete.

"... fairly quickly I realised that for me it was music – Music," he told John Dack in 1999 for his article 'Pierre Henry's continuing journey' in *Diffusion* vol.7 (1999). "It was neither music called electroacoustic, concrete, nor electronic. It was a fusion of all musics, and there was a sense of "will" of "globality". I believe that it was one music containing everything but, naturally, having recording as a medium. That is to say, music that will not be played but which will be inscribed on a medium. Recording is indispensable. I do not compose to be played; I compose in order to record and diffuse the music myself."

The first research into musique concrete involved manipulating phonograph records. However, tape technology became more available, and with it, the possibilities of splicing and pasting parts together.

Musique concrete was, Henry maintained, a music that was timeless. It neither came from interpretation nor performance. Subsequently, imaginary sounds became linked to a functional way of formulating these sounds. Fundamentally it is a fabrication of music both in its conception and composition.

"Many composers, artists, writers, painters imagined that one day music would transform itself into a vast opera of new sounds, unprecedented sounds, sounds that have never been heard of," Henry has said.

In 1944 Henry enrolled at the famed Paris Conservatory, where he was taught by some of the twentieth century's most influential musical figures. Lessons were with Olivier Messiaen and Nadia Boulanger, who taught him theory and composition, respectively, while his piano and percussion teacher was Passeronne.

In 1949 Pierre Henry was commissioned to compose the music for the television documentary *Seeing the Invisible*. Like most of his early work, it had been created through the use of traditional instrumentation and barely hinted at the directions the young Parisian would take in the future. During this period, he started to capture the sounds of everyday life on the 'disque souple', the writable record. The tape recorder was not yet available in a practical model.

"When I decided to keep all my sounds, it was to build a kind of – as Borges said – a library of Babel that makes everything exist like a pyramid, like a memory," he continued in his 1999 interview with John Dack. "It is like having a library full of the books that you treasure. It is also a collection of all sorts of things – noises, voices, animals, instruments... and all this was planned a long time ago, a long time before sampling appeared. I decided to keep my sounds. There are sounds, of course, which don't satisfy me anymore, that have to be thrown away, that have to be sacrificed, but apart from that, sounds are a part of what I like around me. They are my family circle."

Around the time of *Seeing the Invisible*, Henry first met Schaeffer. He was already aware of the man's work and the works of Cage and Stockhausen with whom Schaeffer was most commonly associated. Later in 1949, Henry and Schaeffer began to work together on "Symphonie pour un Homme Seul". All of the sounds for the piece emanated from the human body, thus introducing a theme that would be taken up by future generations of musicians, from Pink Floyd to Herbert. 'Symphonie pour un Homme Seul' itself was divided into ten movements that were intended to conjure up the sounds and atmospheres experienced by someone walking alone at night.

Interestingly Henry himself never considered his music a reaction against the traditional form. But an extension of it.

"Why did I suddenly want to start to work with a new musical universe?" he said to Ios Smolders of *Vital* magazine, 1995. "This was at practically the end of my formal musical studies. I have said it many times and I will tell it again now: I started to listen to the world around me, outside and in my parents' garden, inside the house where I had started my musical studies at the piano and vocal scales. Well, all of it must have been due to my fondness for noises."

"There weren't any reactions against any school," He further explained to Iara Lee. "We came from a musical cell. Before, I was a normal music composer. I wrote for instruments. I studied at the academy of music with Olivier Messiaen. I played percussion. The classical approach to music led me to connect this new music to tradition. So there wasn't any opposition to atonal music nor to serial music.

"The idea was to find a new form of music, a new writing style instead of just imitating and being stuck in a trend. We essentially wanted to bring out a new music. It had nothing to do with the other kind of music. It was meant to be a revolution in connection with the state of being a musician, to the musician's function and to listening. We are different from other musicians but we are not opposed to any music."

By the end of the decade, Schaeffer had received funding from the state to further explore musique concrete in his studio Radiodiffusion Francaise. Henry eventually joined the Groupe de Recherché De Musique Concrete in 1951 and the two composers immediately set to work on another major composition, *Orpheus* – an opera for voices and musique concrete. The debut performance of *Orpheus* in 1953 at the Donaueschingen Festival in Germany was met with public outrage.

Through his research and development, Schaeffer created the Phonogene, an early tape recorder. It was a development that would actually lead to the invention of the Mellotron keyboard some years later. Also heavily used in the Paris studio was the Morphophone, which was a specialised loop deck containing ten playback heads and an adjustable filter to allow the creation of timbre effects.

Among the various methods of tape manipulation pioneered in Scheaffer's studio were innovations in which tape would be cut and spliced at different angles to create different attacks and decays. Tape looping involved the precise splicing of the ends of a recording that would literally be stuck back together in a loop. Other effects mastered through working on the tape included echo, feedback delay, changing pitch and backward masking. The latter of which would involve turning the tape over and recording sounds backwards.

The Groupe de Recherche de Musique Concrete created many of the recording techniques that would be adopted by rock musicians in search of the avant-garde sometime later. These included the Beatles, whose 'Revolution #9' from *The White Album* experimented greatly with cuts and loops.

In the book *Paul McCartney: Many Years from Now*, John Lennon describes the creation of 'Revolution #9'.

"It has the basic rhythm of the original 'Revolution' going on with some twenty loops we put on, things from the archives of EMI. We were cutting up classical music and making different size loops, and then I got an engineer tape on which some test engineer was saying, 'Number nine, number nine, number nine.' all those different bits of sound and noises are all compiled. There were about ten machines with people holding pencils on the loops – some only inches long and some a yard long. I fed them all in and mixed them live."

Henry was director of the Groupe de Recherché de Musique Concrete between 1952 and 1958. During this period, he also scored the music for Astrologie, which was the first commercial film in France to have an electroacoustic score. It also represented his foray into audio/visual compositions that would follow later in his career.

Henry grew increasingly interested in musical techniques beyond those presented by the Groupe de Recherché de Musique Concrete. He wanted to incorporate synthesised sounds with other musical techniques in an attempt to create hybrids of Schaeffer's theories and the growing new technology. Indeed his compositions of 1959, 'Entity', 'Coexistence' and 'Investigations' combined synthesised sounds with the found sounds of musique concrete.

It soon became apparent that Henry was almost the opposite of Pierre Schaeffer. The two Frenchmen may have had their curiosity for order within sound in common. However, Schaeffer was far more academic in his approach, more interested in concrete sounds from a theoretical point of view. As a result, he was far more intent on defining the pure form of musique concrete than Henry, who was interested in the potential for a fusion of all sounds as a means for composing new music. As a result of this dissatisfaction with musique concrete, Henry broke away from Schaeffer in 1958 to form his own cell, Studio Apsome. Famously this was the first private electronic music studio in France.

In the years that followed, Henry pioneered the use of the synthesizer (his first entirely synthesized project *Le Voyage* came in 1962), while also marrying the synth with a combination with found sounds and tape editing. Henry's first major commercial success arrived in 1964 with his album *Jerks Electronique* which sold over 150,000 copies. In 1967 Henry combined forces with Michel Colombier to compose a piece entitled *Messe*

Pour Le Temps Present for a ballet by Maurice Bejart. Henry commissioned Colombier "to recreate the sound textures and violent atmosphere of certain American films." The resulting combination of Colombier's psychedelic rock and Henry's additional off-the-wall electronic effects has subsequently achieved legendary status and has been sampled heavily in recent years. The album has been described as a beat-heavy Moog masterpiece. Crazy bell sounds, electric piano, choppy overdriven guitar, clean jazzy guitar, wicked jazz-based drumming, all overlaid with bizarre Moog-style sounds. Superb and highly recommended.

Following the success of both *Jerks Electronique* and *Messe Pour Le Temps Présent*, Henry was persuaded to explore a collaborative venture with 60s rock group Spooky Tooth. The resulting album *Ceremony* was a happy experience for Henry.

"The great success *of La Messe Pour Le Temps Present* and *Les Jerks Electroniques* with Michel Colombier gave my editor at Philips the idea that I should work together with an English group to make a thematic album, based on the idea of the Mass," he told Ios Smolders. "When this started, I didn't know these people at all, and I accepted for a number of reasons which would not interest me now, but to me, this enterprise was totally without any result for years."

Over the years that followed his hugely successful *La Messe Pour Le Temps Present* and *Les Jerks Electroniques*, Henry continued to compose music for films, ballet and advertisements. His work gradually moved from the confrontational tones of his early works to a quieter, more reflective sound. And yet, despite the quieter tones of his more recent work, Henry remained respectful of the confrontational aesthetic. For these reasons, he admired much of the punk rock canon. To Henry, there is no such thing as noise; there is only sound.

In 1997, Henry's French label Philips Music Group commissioned a set of remixes of pieces from *Messe Pour Le Temps Présent* by the likes of Fatboy Slim, William Orbit and Coldcut. It was eventually released as a double CD album, with the single 'Psyché Rock' purposefully aimed at the club crowd. The song was also licensed as the theme to the animated series *Futurama*.

Henry was less than impressed by these modern reworkings of his compositions, subsequently refusing "to be associated with the remixes".

It is of little surprise that Henry aimed to distance himself from the remix package. Most of the new versions lacked the originals' depth and humour and imposed a linear structure on Henry's fluid themes. In the case of Fatboy Slim, at least, the new track was more interested in the immediate hook lines than the deeper nuance. Furthermore, with Henry's vision of music, the composition should be enjoyed or experienced anywhere. These remixes were solely aimed at the club floor. It is a criticism that he has for the contemporary dance music scene.

"I'm interested by all kinds of rhythm, irrational rhythm and arithmetic... syncopation, jazz, rhythm, beats," he told Iara Lee for the 1997 film *Modulations*. "There is always a beat in my music. The beat is what I find more interesting than something asymmetrical. Everything has to be natural for me. It's a music that comes from nature. There are rhythms in nature that can be qualified of elementary, surprising that come and go. I don't like codified music.

"We've been recently talking a lot about techno music, in reference to the mass of the present that sort of initiated not so much rhythmic music than music of the rhythm. It's a music that must be drawn from technique and be connected to what I'm trying to do that is inspiration, to the body, some sort of cerebral trans. Though I think it's unfortunate that it is for the moment too much connected to the place it is listened to, to high volume listening where bass is powerful. It's music far too much connected to physiological reactions and not enough to mental reaction. It has no sensitivity, it's not surprising enough and it lacks poetry. I feel music should keep its share of poetry.

"And it's easy now for youngsters. They can get for only a few thousand francs, a box, an amp, something that makes sounds. There is no longer a formal sensitivity, meaning that music comes out. I prefer music that stays inside of us, that allows us to dream, to imagine and even perhaps to love. The music I'm referring to is one of communication. It's a language more than an art. Now it's no longer a language. It's some sort of tam-tam constantly present. I'm not convinced by current music, the way it is done. But there are some possibilities. Its form is similar to the one of beginning of music in the Middle Age in France where it was not only just a form but it was also very boring. I don't particularly like cave music. I prefer vocal music starting with Bel canto and then with Melesande and Pelleas. Music of yesterday was linear and white. When Renoir spoke of white, he meant with no colours. And music of today has no colours. That's why I try to add a little spatial effect and colours in my music."

It was Henry's belief that the main problem with contemporary electronic music of the early 2000s lay with the standardisation of technology. With the electroacoustic music he created, the main aim was to search out new possibilities. However, with the increased automation and standardisation of technology, the area of musical aspiration was removed from the composer, with the subsequent evolution of music moving towards convenience.

Using an argument that echoes Adorno's concept of the 'eversame', Henry argued: "Now we can't imagine any other kind of music… current music is constantly invented over and over again, it has become like the sound of the sea, constantly renewed, but always the same. That's why I fear that sound will be the same everywhere, on the radio, in films."

His disinterest in popular music especially extended to popular electronic music that he felt was standardised and sonically unchanging, leaving the listener nullified into a position of unquestioning, passive consumption.

"I think this music becomes more and more polluted … this music is absolutely disgraceful on the radio, at the cinema, in adverts. And I see that at the moment there is one sound. Not sounds. One single sound, everywhere. It's a sound that has been standardised. It's a sound that is produced digitally, and it all comes down to the same sound, which is a painful thing at this end of the century."

JEAN-JACQUES PERREY –
THE GODFATHER OF ELECTRO-POP

"I am not 'the' pioneer, but perhaps 'one' among many others in the electronic music domain doing a new style."

Jean-Jacques Perrey, 2002

If Pierre Henry remained scathing about the area of pop music, then at least one artist to have flirted with the tape editing of the musique concrete school of composition would appear to have been almost diametrically opposed to him. Jean-Jacques Perrey took his experiments with found sound, combined them with synths (and most notably the Ondioline and the Moog) and then edited the sounds into fantastically surreal pop minuets. Indeed his mastery of the sound he described as humoristic-easy-listening-electro-pop, but more often is called space-age pop, had a huge influence on the works of artists such as Air, Kid Loco, Beck and the Beastie Boys. Indeed, the Beasties even named one of their albums after a Jean-Jacques Perry release, *The In Sound From Way Out!*

Jean-Jacques Perrey pushed the boundaries of electronic music for over four decades. From his earliest experiments with the Ondioline to his Moog snapshots of the 60s, he explored a unique path within the avant-garde. A path that found him nestling in the pop charts just as comfortably as the classical and rock charts. Like Pierre Henry, he became the target of 1990s dance producers who sampled his back catalogue with a voracious thirst.

Spurred on by the developments in electronic music and the respect awarded him by DJs and producers throughout the world, he continued to work. Indeed, his early 2000s releases were among the finest in a consistently high-quality body of work.

When I interviewed him in 2002, Perrey, then aged 73, showed no sign of letting up from his musical quest. Indeed, when this interview took place, he was in Paris recording a new album with leading French producer Chazam – at that time considered to be a leading exponent of the methods evolved by Perrey.

Perrey's home was in Evian (near the Léman Lake). Our interview was conducted via e-mail for over a month. During this time, I found him to be almost disarmingly courteous, and profoundly enthusiastic.

Born on 20 January 1929 in a small village in the north of France, Perrey received his first musical instrument as a Christmas present in 1933. That instrument and he quickly "became possessed by a 'little demon of music'." As a child, Perrey admits to having a great thirst for learning. He would devour books and became a huge admirer of science fiction writers like Isaac Asimov, H.P. Lovecraft, Aldous Huxley, A.E. Van Vogt, Arthur C. Clarke and Ray Bradbury.

Following World War II, he attended Lycée d'Amiens (Somme), where he attempted to study music at the Amiens Conservatory, but was expelled for performing in public, an act that was against the school's rules.

"I was playing the accordion at small local events and the director gave me an ultimatum: cease these performances, or leave the conservatory. I knew that performing in public was very important for me – already I had a taste for the stage, so…"

So he then went to medical school in Paris for four years. In 1952, while at medical school, he would hear a record that impressed him sufficiently to make him want to make music again.

"I must tell you that I have been influenced very much by a record I heard in the 50s when I was 24 or 25 years old," he explained. "I was at this time studying medicine, and when I heard this record, I decided to quit the medical studies and discovered at the same time the first French synthesizer called the Ondioline, made by a man whose name was Georges Jenny. This record which decided my musical career was composed and realised by Tom Dissevelt and Kid Baltan. But I also started to be interested in sound manipulation when I heard the records of the fabulous guitar player Les Paul working with a 'multi-tracks system' (re-recording)."

Soon after dropping out of medical college, he met one of the French pioneers of electronic music, Georges Jenny, the inventor of the Ondioline, who would profoundly affect Perrey's life. The Ondioline is now considered one of the instruments that led to the invention of the synthesizer.

"I already knew Maurice Martenot, the inventor of the Ondes Martenot, which could produce only very limited sounds. I preferred the Ondioline, which on its small keyboard allowed one to produce new and original sounds as well as sounds from existing instruments such as the violin or flute. I was fascinated by the Ondioline and felt it had a great future."

Georges Jenny created the first Ondioline in 1938 whilst undergoing treatment for tuberculosis in a French sanatorium. Following his full recovery, he set up a company in Paris called "Les Ondes Georges Jenny" (later known as "La Musique Electronique"), where he continued to develop the instrument until his death in 1976.

The Ondioline was intended to be a low-cost instrument in order to keep it within reach of people with a passing interest, rather than scholars with a calling to create music. Each instrument was individually built by Jenny himself until they proved too popular for him to keep up with demand. At which time they launch a version in kit form. One of the trade-offs in his aims to keep the Ondioline inexpensive was the quality of components. As a result, the instrument needed a lot of care and upkeep to avoid it falling into a state of total disrepair.

The Ondioline was "a monophonic vacuum tube instrument, consisting of a single oscillator and a small eight-octave touch-sensitive keyboard (switchable through six octaves and tuneable via an octave transposer)". Essentially, this meant that the Ondioline was able to create complex waveforms via a series of filters. The sound waves could then be altered and shaped using a touch wire. By using a vertical finger movement, the user could alter the sound's attack, while a horizontal movement would add glissando or modulation.

Within a few months of leaving medical school, Perrey had taught himself to play the piano by ear well enough to impress Georges Jenny into giving him a job as a demonstrator for his invention. Out of these demonstrations, he developed a cabaret act, thanks to his continued desire to create music. For the act entitled 'Around the World in 80 Ways', Perrey played piano and Ondioline simultaneously. The show was a success and Perrey toured throughout Western Europe.

Through working the nightclub circuit, Perrey joined forces with singer/songwriter Charles Trenet and jazz guitarist Django Reinhart to record several songs. The most famous 'The Soul of a Poet' became a major hit in Europe.

In 1959 Perrey appeared at the Olympia Theatre in Paris with Edith Piaf, who was hitting an all-time career high. Piaf became a huge supporter of Perrey, even helping him gain access to recording studios and tape machines – this even though the general public in France had not taken to Perrey and his Ondioline music at all. In the process of using the studio organised by Piaf, he met with Musique Concrete creator Pierre Schaeffer. Sufficiently inspired, Perrey started looking into the possibilities offered by tape manipulation.

"With Edith Piaf as with Charles Trenet, I did what I felt with the Ondioline. They just gave me a few directions during the repetitions. I used my very good musical memory, and one day, Trenet advised me to never learn music because it will distort my ear! At that time, I showed the Ondioline in big European fares, and everywhere people were enthusiastic, except in Paris where they didn't like hearing some banjo or saxophone sounds coming from a keyboard," he once told Ya Basta Records and Gotan Project manager Arnaud Boivin.

With Perrey's music held in enormous respect everywhere in Europe, except France, he started considering moving abroad. His good friend Jean Cocteau advised him that he would never be accepted in France and suggested he look toward America. Perrey had met Cocteau in 1958. According to Perrey's own press autobiography, it was an encounter that would have a profound effect on him

He wrote: "…chance (if chance exists!) brought me a meeting with an extraordinary individual who said, "You are a pioneer. You must continue. But like all innovators, you will have difficulties, and in France, you will often feel yourself misunderstood. You should try to become well-known across the ocean. You have a mission on this earth because you were born to create. Thirty years after you're dead, you'll be able to retire rich!" This person – this giant of the arts whom I profoundly admire – was Jean Cocteau."

Today it is hard to understand why Perrey failed to have any huge impact on his own country. His suggestion is a simple one: "I'll answer you with a French proverb: NOBODY IS A PROPHET IN HIS OWN COUNTRY". It is a proverb that will be repeated by French musicians over the decades that followed Perrey's departure to the US, as everyone from Jean Michel Jarre to Daft Punk had to find their audiences abroad before their own country would accept them.

Edith Piaf herself became extremely involved in the development of Perrey's career. Not only had she organised the studio time for him but she also helped in choosing the right recording to showcase the Ondioline to its fullest effect.

"When she had decided that the tape was 'almost perfect,' she told me, 'Now you must mail this to a person I'm going to give you the name and address to in New York. I will write to him as well to let him know of your forthcoming correspondence. You'll see; he will answer you.' Piaf was impossible to debate with… one always had to do as she decreed!

"It was three weeks later that I received an envelope from America. These two friends of mine, the writer, sculptor, painter and film-maker Jean Cocteau, and the unforgettable French singer Edith Piaf helped me to find a sponsor in New York City. Thanks to them, a man called Carroll Bratman welcomed me in his place and gave me my chance in the music field, helping me to get a Musician's Union Card, an immigration Green Card and a complete fully equipped studio. He was very much involved in the music business in renting all kinds of instruments for TV and radio shows."

Perrey received an envelope from America containing a round-trip plane ticket with an open return date. Only one word was written in a big felt tip pen on the envelope: "COME!". It was March 1960 and Perrey flew to New York, where Caroll Bratman, his US sponsor, met him at the airport. Carroll Bratman was the director of Carroll Music Service on Ninth Avenue in New York, which rented musical instruments to recording studios, theatres, music halls and TV studios. A long-time supporter of innovative music,

Bratman had also hosted a historic all-percussion recording session in 1957 led by arranger Jimmy Carroll. The session was released on the Cook Laboratory label under the title Hi-Fi Bull in a China Shop.

Bratman set Perrey up in his own studio and arranged for his green card and union membership. Perrey then arranged to become the US sales representative for Ondioline, subsequently getting guest appearances on several television shows to play the curious French instrument.

"I stayed in New York City for ten years working in the studio he arranged for me," recalled Perrey. "I was producing music for films and commercials and also made four records at Vanguard Music Record Company. I had the luck to co-compose with Gershon Kingsley a tune that became the theme of the Main Street Electrical Parade in 1972 in Disneyland-California (it is now used in Disneyland Parks all over the World) and also a tune called E.V.A. which is on the charts and have been sampled by many musicians. It is still a hit nowadays."

During his last few months in Paris, while compiling his demo tape, Perrey had become increasingly interested in the tape editing techniques, which had been shown to him by Pierre Schaeffer. Although interested in the possibilities for serious compositional experimentation, he was more excited about using the techniques on more humorous, commercial music. He had no intention of following the same path as Schaeffer or Henry in pursuing serious contemporary music.

While in New York, Perrey set about developing his own system of sounds through intricate tape editing and looping. This involved the mathematical measurement of the tape in relation to tempo. Through his research, Perrey invented a new process for generating rhythms through utilising musique concrete sounds that included the noises of machines, animal cries, insects buzzing, etc. Once the sounds were captured, he would chop them, run them through filters backward at twice the speed (or half the speed), eventually rendering the original sound indecipherable.

In an act that would predate the sampling generation by some 25 years, he built a library of sounds stored according to the various parameters of frequency, attack, envelope, tonality, etc. He would then structure these sounds "…rhythmically according to well-determined, calculated patterns using repetitive loops and sequences. The result was astonishing. I had discovered an incredible goldmine, until then unexplored."

Talking to Dana Hollywood (who Perrey considered to be one of today's more interesting musicians working in the electronic music sphere) in 1998, Perrey explained how he succeeded in creating his intricate loops without the aid of computers:

"It was very easy. First, you have to determine the timing – the tempo. When you have the tempo, it corresponds to a certain number of centimetres and millimetres. For instance, a quarter note equals a certain length. I had a special unit to cut exactly the length. For instance, a half note was double the quarter, a full-note it was four times, an eighth note it was half of this. Then I cut the tape with a special ruler… The sounds were pre-recorded, and of course, I recorded them for making a loop at the same volume. It's very important because it has to be exactly the same volume on the VU meter; I recorded everything with the needle right at zero. I think it is a very important part of my life as a musician. It was really a kind of an invention of a sampler, without the sampling machine being invented yet!"

Around this time, Perrey took his Nagra tape recorder to Switzerland, where he recorded thousands of miles of tape capturing the sound of live bees. After 46 hours of cutting and splicing minute pieces of the recordings, he eventually created only two minutes of music – the melody of Rimsky-Korsakov's *Flight of the Bumble Bee*.

Soon after, he met musician Harry Breuer, with whom he struck up a lasting friendship. Together they composed and recorded numerous radio and TV jingles with the new sounds of the Ondioline and Perrey's tape manipulation working on Breuer's recorded percussion parts. They were a runaway success and eventually recorded an album for Pickwick Records called *The Happy Moog*.

Perrey also worked with arrangers Andy Badale (later known as Angelo Badalamenti) and Billy Goldberg. He recorded incidental music for an off-Broadway production of Ray Bradbury's *Dandelion Wine* with Goldberg. In 1962 Perrey played New York's Radio City Music Hall across four shows a day for six weeks to more than 6000 people at a time! During the course of the shows, he was invited onto the Johnny Carson Show, where he met Walt Disney, who invited Perrey to go to California to provide some Ondioline music for some of the Disney cartoons. He subsequently made arrangements with his staff of musicians in Hollywood, with whom Perrey spent one week recording the music while watching short film clips. Ironically he didn't even know the cartoon title.

However, it was to spark a friendship between Perrey and Disney that would last until the latter's death in 1966. Together the composer and animator talked for hours about their own separate search for the perfect creation. It was an inspiring time for Perrey, who even today says he tries to follow Disney's advice on the importance of developing his artform.

In 1964 Perrey met musician and composer Gershon Kingsley, with whom he would create some of his most renowned works. Their first album together, *The In Sound from Way Out*, appeared that year. Consisting of original tunes and a few tracks originally intended as jingles, the album subsequently became a major sampling source for 1990s/2000s producers. A year later, they released a follow-up album, *Kaleidoscopic Variations*. With this, Perrey introduced another innovation with which his name would become synonymous over the years, the Moog. Perrey was using the first big Moog, which was a bit temperamental, so creator Robert Moog would go into Perrey's studio to put any problems right! He occasionally changed modules with improved electronics, changing internal parts to improve the sounds. In many ways, then, the recording of *Kaleidoscopic Variations* also charted the development of the original Moog.

A blueprint space-age pop album, Kaleidoscopic *Variations* included 'The Savers', which would soundtrack a TV commercial which, in 1968, was awarded the prestigious Clio Award. The creative team at Disneyland would also use 'Baroque Hoedown' for their traditional 'Electrical Parade' on Main Street Disneyland. It has subsequently been adapted for similar attractions at Disneylands in Japan and France and has been heard by over 100 million visitors.

Following the second album, Kingsley started his own career working solo with the Moog while Perrey joined Laurie Productions to compose radio and television advertisements. He would go on to record two more albums during this period: *The Amazing New Electronic Pop Sounds of Jean Jacques Perrey* and *Moog Indigo*. Again both albums proved to be hugely influential, 'E.V.A.' from *Moog Indigo*, would later become a favourite for hip hop and rap artists and dance DJs, including Ice T, DJ Premier, and Fat Boy Slim. It is something for which Perrey declares a huge sense of pride.

"I feel very proud. However, many of them didn't ask for an authorisation from the publishers, except a few of them (among about 55) who gave credits to the original creators."

In 1970 Perrey returned to France. Upon his return, he became director of a ballet company, wrote and recorded music for many French cartoons and released several albums. Furthermore, he spent a huge amount of time working on a therapeutic music project utilising recordings of dolphins. His "top secret work" is how he described the project.

In the mid-90s he was encouraged to play live again by a young French electronic musician David Chazam. Together they also recorded an album *Eclektronics* in 2000. In a move that echoed Perrey's introduction to Caroll Bratman some twenty years earlier, Chazam first made Perrey's acquaintance by sending him a tape of his own compositions, suggesting a possible collaboration at the same time. Perrey was into the idea as soon as he heard Chazam's tape.

Perrey subsequently joined Chazam in the studio, bringing his prepared tape loops, which he was by now digitally loading into his Kurzweil synthesizer/sampler, and "several cine-reels in my head". These 'cine-reels,' were imaginary pictures and conceptual ideas Perrey wanted to orchestrate with music. The resulting album was a stunning fusion of Perrey's trademark melodies and contemporary rhythm.

Another interesting collaboration occurred in 1997 between Perrey and Parisian duo Air, who were long time admirers of Perrey's work. Given the fact that the shadow of Perrey's Vanguard albums (*The In Sound...*,

Kaleidoscopic... The Amazing New Electronic Pop Sounds... and Moog Indigo loomed large over Air's debut *Moon Safari* album; the collaboration was perhaps inevitable.

"This group is VERY TALENTED and I was happy to do a tune with them called 'Cosmic Bird'", he said in 2002. "They are young and I learnt a lot from them (Jean-Benoit and Nicolas), and they have a wonderful feeling in music, contributing to the evolution of the actual music."

'Cosmic Bird' found Perrey's trademark Ondioline pop sounds picking out a bubblegum western refrain over Moogs, occasional cut up loops (featuring the sound of children shouting 'Hey!') and of course Air's own brand of future-retro space-age synth swells. At only three minutes long, the track barely gives a taster of what could have been achieved between the two parties. Here there is a sense of compromise in the Air additions to the track. However, 'Cosmic Bird' is interesting enough to warrant a full album collaboration. Perrey died of lung cancer at the age of 87 on 22 November 2016, but his deep impact on music can still be heard in contemporary pop and dance music, hip hop and sound design experimentation.

The legacy of the musique concrete and electroacoustic schools – both in the serious works of Schaeffer and Henry and in the humorous style of Perrey – is hugely important to all contemporary electronic and sampling artists. Not least of all in their home country where producers have taken many of the techniques and translated them to the contemporary setting.

The editing systems are of particular note as they allowed people to understand the possibilities of manipulating sound sources. This translated to the sampling and sequencing technology as producers wilfully overrode certain limitations of the programme to forge new sounds.

Indeed, in this way, many of today's producers can argue with Henry's claim that all electronic music is now standardised by what are essentially factory settings. In the history of post-acid house music every major development has occurred through an artist pushing machinery to do what it's not supposed to do. For example, the burbling noises of acid house were created through the misuse of the Roland TB-303 bass sequencer. What had been intended as a digitised rhythm section machine to accompany guitarists and singers in small venues was turned into the sound of ecstasy captured, mutated and returned to the dancefloor.

A French artist Mr.Learn has also added to the pantheon of technology abusers with his own music. He actively created viruses that he introduced to sequencing and sampling software. The end results were a chaos of jittery rhythms and obtuse sounds.

However, Henry's argument is supported by the contemporary dance producers' need to follow the sound of the moment. This was especially critical in the growth of French dance music during the French Touch era of the late 90s. Here a paradigm was created that producers willingly followed. The resulting filtered disco music may have created numerous worldwide hits, but they also seemed to fade into each other. From the arrangements to the sonics, they were all cut and pasted from exactly the same sound source.

Like Perrey, Henry's greatest legacy lies in the way he showed that the fusion of styles was the way forward in creating new music. Both combined their own tape loop styles with the electronic medium to forge something far more than the pure vision of musique concrete. This eclectic approach has been taken up by the post-acid house generation with a passion.

And so, through French artists like Cassius, Air, Etienne de Crecy, Alex Gopher, Mr Learn, Mighty Bop, Rubin Steiner, Le Tone, Grand Pop Football Club etc., the ideas and techniques of the musique concrete vanguard are kept alive via update and regeneration. They may not have been the sexiest composers on the planet; they may not have been a part of discotheque's beautiful people, but without the works of Schaeffer, Henry and Perrey, electronic music may have sounded quite different.

2: AFTER THE PARTY – FRANCOIS K TO MIRWAIS

Following the creative adventures of France's electronic music forefathers Henry and Perrey and the global commercial success of the French disco innovators, the scene was set for France to develop into a musical tour de force during the 80s. However, somehow, despite the momentum gathered in the final year of the 70s, things just started to die. Suddenly the younger generation was uninterested in making groundbreaking music while the established frontline just seemed to sit back and live on the past glories.

"For me, it's still a big mystery why at the end of the 70s and the beginning of the 80s, the whole process stopped. All the people like Morali and Belolo, Cerrone, Patrick Juvet. I mean, there were tons of French artists being hugely successful worldwide. And then during the 80s, they stopped," said F-Communications founder Eric Morand. "I don't know if it was a pure business thing. These people made so much money during the 70s that they didn't want to spend much time and energy working in a new direction. Or maybe there was a severe lack of inspiration for the producers. All I can say is that it was amazing that people like Ottowan or the Gibson Brothers stopped. Why? I don't know. I did my first years in the music industry in '88 at Scorpio Music and even then, they weren't producing. They were just licensing tracks from other countries to France. Suddenly they were only thinking about the French market. They stopped producing as an international activity."

There are several possibilities why this might have been the case. By the time of the 80s, most of the disco generation had moved to the US and thus stopped being impacted by the grassroots influence of the younger generation of musicians. When in the case of Morali and Belolo, they returned to France, they stopped producing music on a global scale. Obviously, there were health issues for Morali but as Eric Morand points out, Belolo's Scorpion Records existed merely as an import business. It didn't actively produce and market French music for worldwide consumption.

The most successful of the other small labels that emerged during the disco era was Cerrone's Malligator. However, this was tied to a major label and only dealt with productions by Cerrone and his close family of musicians. Furthermore, if the initial success hinted at the beginnings of an independent infrastructure being put in place in France, it was certainly an opportunity missed. In truth, for Cerrone, it was enough that his record stores were independently distributing his own debut album. He had no interest in creating a distribution network for other small labels that might have come along.

All of this might seem to back up claims that all of the French disco producers of the era were more interested in fame and money than the music itself. However, there was another obstacle that faced everyone in the French industry. The major labels controlled every aspect of record production and distribution. Note that Cerrone had to go to English label Island to press his *Love in C Minor* album. Despite the multitude of pressing plants in France (many of which would have actually have been employed by English labels to press up their product), the stranglehold that the major labels held over these plants meant that independent production was almost impossible. On an A&R level, the French labels showed a total lack of interest in developing domestic artists and writers, despite global success for some. They were only really interested in their own chanson artists, which put many people off from chasing a deal. This situation remained true until the late 90s when French Touch forced the labels to alter their attitudes to dance culture.

Another significant factor in the failure of France to consolidate on the success of its 70s artists was the effect that the radio had on people. Until the beginning of the 80s, the radio stations had been state-controlled and, as such, gave maximum airtime to homegrown artists. However, with the creation of a free radio service, the French airwaves were suddenly open to music from all around the world. This inevitably meant Anglo Saxon music. Subsequently, the French Touch scene who had grown up through the 80s would inevitably claim the US and UK artists as their biggest influences. The French producers are rarely mentioned.

This event had a huge effect on record production in the decades that followed, with many French Touch and post-French Touch producers showing a shameless love of Michael Jackson, Cameo, Shalamar, Prince and the rest of the 80s dance stars. Where the US and the UK may have gone through numerous extreme permutations to get to house culture, France's producers took a straight line from the 80s tech-funk – a musical style which interestingly the French called disco while the rest of the world referred to it as tech-funk, jazz-funk etc.

"Until 1981, all the radio, TV and so on were controlled by the State. In 1981 we had the free radio which was allowed to air American music," confirmed Olivier Ruel from tech-funk house act Dax Riders. "Until then, we only had Johnny Halliday, or if there was an American track, we would get a version of it redone by a French singer. All the records coming from America were suddenly available to us and for me, the first music I really heard and loved was like Prince, Michael Jackson and all that stuff. So our generation was brought up with American music. And we were the first."

If the introduction of free radio brought with it an unhealthy obsession with the 80s funk sounds, then it was also responsible for introducing music such as electro and hip hop. The 80s saw a huge development in French hip-hop that would eventually be considered a serious global musical force in the 90s. The main influences were, almost inevitably, from the US until MC Solaar found success in other countries at the end of the 80s. French hip-hop was sidelined as an interesting quirk in French culture, although Wu-Tang Clan member Rza explained to me that the French sound had a powerful impact on their breakthrough album *36 Chambers:* "Man, these crews like NTM and Iam were big for us. We took it all back from them French brothers. They took hip hop, so we took it back."

Throughout the tail-end of the 70s disco years and on through the 80s, there was one French DJ and producer who would come to be regarded as one of the single most influential people in dance music. Not only would he A&R Prelude, one of the world's leading disco labels, DJ at some of the most famous clubs in the story of house, but he would also employ the tape editing and found-sound sourcing of musique concrete to create his own unique remixes of tracks he was spinning in the clubs. His name is François Kervorkian – the French giant living in New York, whose very presence on the foundation years of house culture was to have a far more direct influence on French Touch producers than many of the Paris disco elite.

FRANÇOIS KERVORKIAN – THE DANCEFLOOR CONTROLLER

"I was thinking about this a lot, and I realise that the first person that appeared to me as someone to follow was François Kervorkian. He was the remixer and producer I liked the most. I didn't know where he was from, but he definitely had a French name. I didn't know anything about Cerrone but François K was so influential to dance music today by way of the remix. François' touch can still be heard today. We know now that he took his influence from Jamaican dub. Still, he's a French guy from Strasbourg who created half of what we know today. For me, disco was so remote. It was not a French thing. But then I saw this French guy and I thought if this French guy can be doing this, then so can I. Maybe music wasn't such an inaccessible thing to me. Thanks to this guy being French and so far away, I found my link to dance music."

Dimitri From Paris

François Kervorkian was born in Rodez, France, on 10 January 1954. His mother and father separated when François was young, so he stayed with his mother, a dentist, until he was thirteen. Then he lived with his father, who worked for the French national radio and broadcasting organisation, the ORTF. In 1972 François graduated from the Montheron Lycee and progressed to study for a biochemical engineering degree in Lyon. After only a year of study, he was expelled for instigating a general strike. Despite the protestations of his parents, he decided not to continue with his studies. Instead, he opted to pursue his love of music. Naturally, his parents were mortified. So, to placate them, he moved to Strasbourg to study pharmacy. Again he dropped out. His love of music had got the better of him and, rather than spend time studying for his qualifications, he started playing drums for various local bands. He quit in his second year. It was 1974.

François decided to stay in Strasbourg because he loved the city's cosmopolitan vibe. He worked in a bar for a year just enjoying the psychedelic hippy scene, which had gained popularity there at this time. While working in this bar, François enjoyed his first DJing gig, playing chill-out hippy music like King Crimson, Mahavishnu Orchestra, Yes, Soft Machine and perennial favourite Hendrix.

"There were two turntables, but there was no mixer," he recalled in Jonathan Fleming's book *What Kind of House Party is This?*. "There was no cueing because you just changed decks when you wanted to change records, so you just put the record on, put the volume up, and that was it."

His DJing career for real started a year later after he moved to New York. It was September 1975 and he'd moved there with his aspirations of becoming a professional drummer. His earliest gigs were with R&B covers bands. One of the first people François met took him along to a club where he was DJing to show him his turntable set up. This included two decks, headphones and a mixer. Primitive by today's standards, but for Kervorkian, it was incredible. It was the first time he'd ever seen a mixer. And when his friend started to show him how to slip-cue records in order to create a seamless blend, he was blown away.

In February 1976, he was hired by the promoter of underground club Galaxy 21 to provide live drums while the resident DJ spun the discs. That DJ was the legendary Walter Gibbons, who at the time was New York's hottest property. The club also featured other famous names like in-house lighting engineer Kenny Carpenter, who would mix Loleatta Holloway's 'Hit and Run' and create the first commercial 12" single 'Ten Percent'.

Although it has often been claimed in print that this fusion of live drums and DJ was a happy experience that only came to an end because of the club itself closing down, the reality shows a picture of pure friction. Walter Gibbons hated the fact that he was working with live drums. As a result, he would drop in loads of recorded drum solos to try and catch Kervorkian out. Unfortunately for Gibbons, François knew all of the drum solos by heart.

"... at the same time, it was like an enlightenment for me, 'cause while I was playing drums to the music, I could hear what Walter was doing with the records," he told Fleming.

By now, Kervorkian was completely hooked on disco, his drumming experience with Gibbons opening up the intricacies of the sound to him. At the same time, the ever-growing attraction to DJing helped him hear the sounds as a part of the club experience.

"The excitement about disco was incredible," he recalled in 1997. "Clubs like The Flamingo or The Gallery were amazing. The Loft was like a fucking religion – I saw people crying on the dancefloor because they were so moved by the music. There was a total communion with the music. And even when it became popular, that energy was still there. There were door policies like at The Paradise Garage, which was members only, where guests could only get in if they'd been recommended by a member before-hand, which, to an extent, helped the music to sustain an underground feeling even while the whole world was jumping on the bandwagon. And when the backlash against disco hit, the underground was still separate and independent so it survived to develop and push the music forward. There were parts of the scene that were like it is now – places like Infinity where Jim Burgess used to play, or The Funhouse when Jellybean played. It was something very special."

When Galaxy 21 was closed down, François found a job at another club, Experiment Four. However, his position was slightly less fulfilling – he was the kitchen porter and toilet cleaner! Still, he was determined to become a DJ and quickly struck up a friendship with the resident. His name was John 'Jellybean' Benitez.

Benitez had his own basic studio, which he gave Kervorkian access to and the Frenchman started to experiment with tape editing. Inspired by the few medley cut-ups that were doing the rounds, like the very popular Hollywood Medley, he started splicing different tunes together. However, his trademark addition was the inclusion of sound FX and found sound that was inspired by his love of reggae. Among these early productions was a version of Rare Earth's 'Happy Song and Dance', which was a New York club staple for years afterwards.

"There was a place called Sunshine Sound where you could go to get acetates cut," he recalled. "It was really interesting because, for $10 or $15, you could buy a slate of re-edits that other DJs had done. They'd edit up the big hits of the time in their own style, put it onto acetate and you'd be able to pick up a copy and figure out what everyone else was doing. That inspired me to go back home and try it out. I recorded little snippets of tracks onto tape and then, with a pair of scissors and some Scotch tape, I made up my own edits. Eventually, I found out about edit blocks and razor blades and splicing tape – all these conveniences which made the process really easy – but being able to edit allowed me to make up my own versions that I could use to put together demo tapes for clubs. I'd record onto one channel of my Revox, figure out the delay between the playback head and the record head, and then record on the other channel as I mixed the next record in. I'd master the whole thing to a mono cassette, so you couldn't tell that I didn't have two decks. The tapes ended up being very individual and they gave me a head start as a DJ because after all that, mixing live was a piece of cake."

Kervorkian would give his creations to Benitez to play. However, despite the popularity of these plates, he still couldn't get a DJing gig of his own. Then one night, Benitez was tired and decided to take a night off. He called in sick and sent Kervorkian in his place. It was to be his first real gig.

Following this gig, he started to audition to DJ at the new clubs that had started to open in New York in 1977. He eventually came across a drag club called JJ Knickerbocker, which had a DJ contest every month. He won a few times thanks to his already skilled technique and those special dubplates and came to the attention of some of the key African American underground club promoters of the time. The people behind the infamous Chase Galleries.

These same promoters rented out a club called The Flamingo during the summer. The rest of the year, it was the biggest white gay club in New York, but in the summer, the clientele went to Fire Island. This left the venue open for hire and it went from being a white gay club to a strictly black crowd. In the summer of '77, they called it Sesame Street and gave François Kervorkian his first taste of paying to a real underground club crowd. He loved it.

Among his biggest tunes of that summer were Barry White's 'It's Ecstasy', Salsoul Orchestra's 'Magic Bird of Fire' and Morali and Belolo creation The Ritchie Family, with their 'African Queen' classic. Sonically it was the black and Puerto Rican extreme of the disco sound.

After the summer, the club moved to 43rd Street. However, the promoters went into partnership with another group of businessmen and after the third week, arguments raged about money and Kervorkian decided to walk. Although he did give the DJing job to Benitez as a thank you for giving him his first DJing break!

In the summer of '77, two new clubs had opened in New York, which had attracted the fashionable celebrity elite – Studio 54 and New York New York. Kervorkian auditioned for a DJ job at the latter and got it. He quickly found himself spinning to people like Andy Warhol and Grace Jones, although the music he was required to play was commercial disco, so he continued to search out gigs in the underground clubs in order to play the stuff he liked as well.

"At New York New York, I was playing to thousands of people every week, all of whom were completely enamoured with the idea that disco was the hottest thing that had ever existed," he says. "It was amazing. That was the year that both Star Wars and Saturday Night Fever came out and there was a real excitement about the music. You'd show up at the club and you'd start putting music on and people would start screaming. There was this energy going on which I've never ever seen since then amongst the straight, general population."

Kervorkian was by now building quite a reputation and as a result, Prelude Records approached him in 1978 to be their A&R man. His first job was to remix the track 'Push Push In The Bush' by Musique. It became a huge global hit. "That song would have been a hit anyway," he says. "It was a hit as soon as it was written. It didn't need my involvement, or anybody else's, to make it that way."

He would subsequently create successful mixes for Prelude act D:Train's 'You're the One for Me', 'Music' and 'Keep On'. Suddenly Kervorkian was the number choice of remixer for acts looking for club hits.

"Although I understood the concept of mixing, I had no previous studio experience whatsoever. Because I was so inexperienced, I figured that the only way to do it would be to go into the studio ahead of time for a listening session. I would make myself tapes of just a couple of elements of the track at a time – one take might be the drums on the left and the bass on the right, another might be the guitar on the left and the keyboards on the right. Then I'd take those tapes back to the office and listen to them. I'd draw very detailed song maps (a lot like the kind of thing you see on the screen of Cubase or Logic today) and doing that helped me to digest everything that was on tape. So by the time I got into the studio, I was able to tell the engineer exactly what I wanted in terms of what we were going to use for an intro, where the breakdown was going to happen, which sections we were going to extend, where we were going to edit and so on."

What followed for Kervorkian was a few years in which he never stopped working. Whether DJing the underground circuit or remixing and A&Ring for Prelude, 1983 found Kervorkian working alongside

Arthur Baker and John Robie on Planet Patrol's 'Play At Your Own Risk', which helped to establish the electro sound worldwide. He was subsequently asked to mix Kraftwerk's 'Tour de France', although he prefers to call this "a collaboration" since the band came to New York and worked with him in the studio on the project.

Despite his numerous remixes, he still hadn't produced a solo project from the very beginning. Eventually, the chance came with the seminal experimental dub 'Snakecharmer' EP with ex-PIL bassist Jah Wobble, U2 guitarist The Edge and Can skinsman Holgar Czukay.

"I had been involved in production through my A&R duties at Prelude and I'd done additional production on a lot of the records that I'd worked on but I hadn't had the opportunity to steer a project from beginning to end until Chris Blackwell at Island Records asked me to produce Jah Wobble, The Edge and Holger Czukay for the 'Snakecharmer' EP."

The 'Snakecharmer' EP was not only important in the process of establishing his own abilities as a producer, but it also represented something of an aesthetic shift in rock music. Here a group of rock musicians, albeit predominantly from the extreme leftfield, came to terms with the duelling legacies of black African and white European ideologies. The marriage ultimately found its niche by combining the tape edit techniques of dub and musique concrete.

"If there is one medium which constantly reinvents itself, then it's dance music. Rock music was never an option. On a cultural level, for me, rock music means 'the music of the land of white people'. Dance music is something different which is democratic and ethnically-mixed. Rock music isn't like that. There are so many things within dance music – it addresses the issues of tribalism, where people share together and engage in some kind of communal activity – and it has become such an important sociological phenomenon that it would be hard to underestimate its value. People have been dancing since the dawn of time and I don't think that our genetic baggage has changed all that much since then. People have always wanted to enter a trance state or put themselves into some kind of alternate reality. Modern dance music – whether it's house or disco or jungle – offers them access to that."

Kervorkian stopped DJing in 1984 for a period of five years, despite being a part of the New York DJ frontline alongside Tee Scott, David Mancuso and Larry Levan. He'd even been collaborating in the studio on tracks such as Sparque's 'Let's Go Dancing' and 'Body Music' by The Strikers with Levan.

"I felt like I'd done a great deal in so few years and I had been right to the top of my profession in so few years, so I quit while I was ahead. Before it got dreary and boring while I had all of those incredible memories in my head," he said.

Over the course of the 80s, Kervorkian became remixer to artists as diverse as Paradise Garage darlings of UK synth-pop like Depeche Mode, Yazoo, Kraftwerk, Eurythmics, Pet Shop Boys, Erasure, Yazz and Thomas Dolby, and guitar bands The Smiths and U2, along with funk and soul stars Diana Ross and Ashford & Simpson. With his remix output for early 80s UK electronic pop bands, François K produced the work which was to have the most impact on the French club culture of the time. By taking the brittle bones of the originals and adding a rich disco-fied sauce, he delivered plates that were as huge in the Parisian discos as they were in New York's Paradise Garage. Essentially, he gave these very British tracks a US feel, which was able to sit comfortably next to Cameo, etc.

In the US, the Kervorkian magic touch helped to break some of these bands thanks to their heavy play at the Paradise Garage. Yazoo's 'Situation' was a great example of this. Already a huge hit in the UK, the duo of ex-Depeche Mode synth player Vince Clarke and blues chanteuse Alison' Alf' Moyet, had been unable to translate to the US. This remix, however put them right into the heart of New York's hip crowd. A hit was soon to follow. In 1987 Kervorkian set up his own Axis Studio as a home for his own production and remix work. The studio also offered the perfect set-up for the likes of C+C Music Factory and Deee-Lite, as well as becoming a musical home for Wu-Tang Clan, Madonna and Mariah Carey. Appropriately the studio was located in a building with its own special significance for dance music. Originally a theatre, part of the site on West 54th St. was later refitted by CBS for use as a television studio before being converted by Steve Rubell and Ian Schrager into its most famous incarnation, Studio 54.

In 1990 Francois K returned to DJing after an offer from Larry Levan to tour Japan on the Harmony tour (Levan's last) proved too much of a chance to miss.

"I stopped DJing for a long time. But I realised I was missing it so much. It's what's inside me. I love funky, groovy music. There's so much to be played and so many good things to be shared with others that I can't see when I'm ever gonna stop!"

In the few years that he'd been away from the decks, disco had mutated into tech-funk, Chicago had delivered the house sound, Detroit had done the same for techno, the UK had created raves and DJs were now on the rise, taking over from live bands as star attractions everywhere.

Since the Harmony Tour of Japan, he continued to DJ the world over. In the mid-90s, he set up his own Wave imprint through which he has released a number of his own productions alongside high-quality work by other producers.

"I held off on starting a label, even though I had the production facility at Axis, because, for a long time, I didn't feel willing to take the step of becoming someone who was involved in marketing and distribution. But a lot of what I'm interested in just didn't seem to cut the cake for major labels. There's a lot of great music out there which needs an outlet, and, because I have the facility, I decided the time was right. Already, we've got a tremendous amount of stuff ready to go. But I don't want the label to be just another New York house track label, so, as my plans to put the label together were coming along, I decided that we needed something different to put out as the first release."

That debut release was Floppy Sounds' superb debut album, *Downtime*, conceived by Axis engineer Robert Rives with partners Will Soto and Lane Craven.

Perhaps his most influential record to emerge in this era was the 'FK-EP', which blended mid-tempo house beats with moody keyboards and trancey synth motifs. Clearly inspired by the 1994 productions of Danny

Tenaglia, Kervorkian's own version of that sound would go on to be copied wholesale some years later by the progressive trance scene.

"There's a world of difference when you compare 1977/1978 and now," he said in 1995. "The music has evolved so much. There's been a big change in the aesthetic of dance music because there's a whole new generation of producers who make music in a very different way. People have done with song structure completely, for example. In effect, they're concentrating all the elements which make dance music so powerful and eliminating all the superfluous elements.

"There are such exciting things happening right now. For me, music is a motivation to get out of your body and into your mind. To travel to unknown places. To see planets and galaxies colliding. It's a joy and a special thing. A way to reach new landscapes. And dance music has become purpose-built to accommodate that. It's addressing a fundamental need in people's lives. It relates to something that's both years old and thoroughly modern, providing people with a way to communicate and share experiences. These things don't change. What's special about now is that, while rock music dominated everything, we had the cult of the band, now it's the people in the crowd who are the stars. They make the party happen. What good is a DJ without people to listen to him?"

Perhaps the best example of his DJing style came with the *BBC Radio 1 Essential Mix* in 2000, which featured a heavy blend of early house, tech-funk and even later 80s New York hip hop.

"The style of music that I'm into is always a very eclectic one where I'll not play anything that isn't truly awesome music, not just one specific style of up-tempo 120-122 bpm kind of music, all night long, with the same kind of fucking chords and, you know… I'm sorry but if I'm DJing, it's not because suddenly there's twenty tracks that all sound the same that I'm gonna play all night long. I'm DJing because I heard some new tracks which I felt were all so different that they excited me enough to want to play them in a club situation," he told Jonathan Fleming,

"You know, it's like when you see a spectrum of light… you see all the colours from infrared to ultraviolet, but it's like they're all deciding just to play one of those colours of light, whereas I like the whole spectrum, full bandwidth."

His Essential Mix set was a soulful blend that told an alternative story of the early development of house than the usual Chicago tale. This was all about the New York influence on global dance music. An influence that is often forgotten in all but the contemporary garage scene.

"The excitement of making music and then being able to share it with others is something that makes me feel very privileged and lucky," he concluded. "I feel very thankful to have been in a position to do that..."

MUTANT DISCO, ELECTRO POP
AND A MAN CALLED MIRWAIS

The full influence of François Kervorkian may not have been acknowledged in his home country until long after the house explosion but his remixes of the 80s electronic scene did bear some similarities with numerous French artists during the 80s. As with the UK and the US, some French artists underwent a disco catharsis in the ten years following punk. Where this started as a creative marriage of the two different camps, the sound slowly transformed into electro-pop. In this world, the gauche tendencies of new romantic met the cold technological grooves of Kraftwerk and the melodies of Motown bleached white.

To see the journey from punk to disco, it is necessary to look back to the late 70s when a French punk band called Marie et Les Garçons were causing a stir with their abrasive post-punk sound. It was an era when the raw energy of punk joined forces with an increased love of funk, disco and Afro-Beat and groups increasingly started to incorporate these elements into their sound. The results were typified by the punk-funk contortions of groups like Pop Group, A Certain Ratio, early Shriekback and 23 Skidoo. In 1978, however, Marie et Les Garçons were still very much in the punk camp. Soon after their debut album release, Marie left thanks to a disagreement over musical direction. So the remaining duo of Eric

Fitoussi and Patrick Vidal became Les Garçons and moved to New York. Here they set to work enlisting some of the city's top disco musicians and producers to create what remains one of the finest mutant disco/no wave albums of the era.

Ironically, Marie et les Garçons had released an EP, 'Attitudes', which featured Velvet Underground member John Cale, on New York label Ze Records before their split. Ze was the home of no wave and mutant disco. It is possible that the band was being steered in the direction of disco long before Marie finally quit.

"People into underground disco were the trendy people who were also involved in punk – a little like in New York where you had trendy rock bands like Blondie who were just as much into disco as punk," says Micronauts founder Christophe Monier. "We had the same in Paris. For instance, there was Marie et les Garçons, who had Patrick Vidal in them. At first, they were an intellectual punk band and then they went to New York and did a disco style album."

The no wave/mutant disco movement emerged in the late 70s as the dual forces of punk and disco found a mutual space. However, the sound not only drew upon these two genres. It also pulled in influences from jazz, funk, electro, Afrobeat and even the layered guitar and subliminal rhythm layers of Krautrock bands like Neu!, Faust and Can. As a result, the New York scene became a melting pot of sounds all gelled together by the energy of punk and the rhythms of black music. Indeed they drew a direct line from James Brown, through Chic, the Sex Pistols, Brian Eno, Kraftwerk and finishing with Afrobeat legend Fela Anikulapu Kuti.

Among the many artists working in this area, the most notable were James White and the Blacks (aka James Chance and the Contortions), who married blistering jazz with punk-funk grooves; Defunkt who featured Lester Bowie's brothers Joseph and Byron (and occasionally acted as the backing band for James White/Chance), a group that created full force, horn-heavy street funk at high tempo; Material, the electronic post-punk brainchild of Bill Laswell (who would later set up a studio in Paris to employ some of the city's African musicians), and Liquid Liquid who created abrasive low slung funk. At the heart of all of these artists were the supposedly oppositional forces of the late 70s – punk and disco.

"In 1979, Les Garçons released an album called *Divorce* recorded at Blank Tapes Studios in NY with the greatest black disco singers and musicians of the time. How does it sound? Well, think of Happy Mondays, really, and replace Es by Quaaludes and coke," adds Monier, who would go on to work with Vidal on dance projects in the 90s. "It wasn't an electronic album; it was played in the disco style. Patrick was more into salsoul kind of stuff. He tried to marry a white voice and lyric with black style."

Like most of the bands from this scene, Les Garçons created a sonic mismatch of funk guitar, stabbing horns, disco sixteens in the rhythm and punk-ish vocals and melodies. The record, as with the no wave scene, was misunderstood at the time, so they split. At the end of the 90s, *Divorce* was reissued by A Man Called Adam's label Other Recordings. While labels like Soul Jazz set about reissuing many of the other key records of the era.

"Les Garçons were something of a mythical band for the French scene. They weren't at all successful, but they are still respected," continued Monier.

With the demise of Les Garçons Patrick Vidal became a DJ exploring very similar sounds to those being played at New York's Paradise Garage disco (from Sylvester to Montana Sextet, West End to 99 records). He held a residency at one of Paris' premier clubs Les Bains Douches (where James Chance and the Contortions recorded their legendary *Live Aux Bains Douches* album in May 1980). Les Bains Douches was, along with Le Palace, the favoured haunt of the so-called beautiful people – showbiz types, models, jet setters, pop stars etc. It was a club that typified Paris in the 80s.

However, after a while, Patrick started to miss creating his own music and longed to get back into a recording studio. He had developed a deep love of garage and was increasingly excited by the growing dance culture. A chance meeting with Christophe Monier would provide him with the key to returning to music-making.

"This guy who I was in a techno-pop band with in 1987 met Patrick and asked him to produce us. But it never happened," recalls Monier. "At the same time, I discovered acid house, so I didn't want to hear about any other kind of music. I was very radical. Then I met Patrick again in a record shop in the house import section. I was surprised to see him there because two years before he hadn't been into acid house. But because he always preferred the real black stuff and the underground disco stuff, he was more into garage and not acid house. But I'm a great fan of garage and disco as well, so we decided to do a song together."

Together they formed Discotique, their first record 'Sexe' becoming one of the most important in the story of post-acid house French dance music. Not necessarily because of the way it sounded, but because it was the first release on Manu Casana's Rave Age Records, which itself was the first independent dance label to have emerged in this era. A few months before the arrival of Eric Morand's FNAC dance imprint.

'Sexe' featured two distinctly different sides. The mixes on one reflect the duo's love of Chicago house, featuring a deep sound with wild pitch bass drones. The other had a UK flavour, its sound collage mirroring the early work of Nightmares on Wax and many of the other Warp Records artists. All of the mixes were held together by samples lifted from the Montana Sextet and Ice T.

In 2002 Monier compiled a collection of tracks from this era for Belgian imprint Quatermass. Called 'Rockers Delight', it featured one of the mixes of 'Sexe' from the debut single. The 'Sexe Dur' mix offered a punk house meltdown, featuring guitars to the fore and Vidal's, which sounds remarkably current today.

As Discotique, Monier and Vidal went on to record numerous tracks together which ranged in style from the pulsing dark techno of 'Vie, Vida, Life' – starring Vidal intoning the words "rock and drugs" over a synth washed groove that Underworld would echo a couple of years later – and 'Le Moment' that contained ringing telephones with startling swingtime horn blasts and the piano theme from television show *The Outer Limits*.

Around this time, Monier also co-produced some solo Patrick Vidal tracks. "A Winter Morning in NY", which featured Monier's band Les Claques 2 Velours, betrayed Vidal's love of Lou Reed, while 'Salinas' was startling simply for the fact that it was a cod-reggae meets techno tune.

While working together, Monier introduced Vidal to Thomas Bourdeau. Vidal and Bordeau hit it off immediately and formed the band Sutra. A couple of years later, they would find themselves recording an album (*Suicide*) with Mirwais Ahmadzai in the producer's seat.

"I introduced them to Mirwais, who produced their first album," recalls Monier. "I knew Mirwais because his studio was in the same street as mine in the 11th district of Paris."

Sutra's gothic electronica failed to ignite the public's attention and Vidal returned to his DJing. In 2002 his main residency was at the monthly KABP parties in Paris. He also did a series of parties called Disco Not Disco, Wave No Wave covering the ten year period from 1977 – 1984, pre-empting a revival in the sound a few years later.

MIRWAIS – MADONNA'S PRINCE OF ELECTRO

The coming together of Mirwais and Patrick Vidal for the Sutra album was perhaps inevitable. Both had received critical acclaim for their work over the years. Both had explored pop and rock's leftfield. However, there was one major difference; Mirwais had enjoyed huge commercial success. This had been with his first band, Taxi Girl.

"Taxi Girl were very different to Les Garçons. They weren't using disco at all. They were into The Doors, Velvet Underground and Iggy Pop, but they did it in a very different way because they were using synths, which made them sound more modern. They liked to fight and stuff on stage; they were really extreme at first." Christophe Monier, 2002.

Mirwais Ahmadzai was born in 1961 in Switzerland to an Italian mother and Afghanistani father. The family moved to Paris when he was only six. By the time he was 12, he had discovered the music of Jimi

Hendrix and the Stones, encouraging him to learn to play guitar. As the first waves of punk energy started to be felt in Paris, he was moved to form his first band.

As with many of the French punk musicians of this era, Mirwais didn't listen exclusively to punk. His influences were wide-ranging. In fact, and almost inevitably, punk purity was far from his mind by the time he started looking for musicians to form a band.

"For a teenager, the late 70s were a strange mixture of disco music and punk. And it was OK to like them all," Mirwais has said.

At 17, he met Daniel Darc and together, they hatched a plan for a band. The others had to be like-minded people who were fans of both The Stooges and Kraftwerk. However, they also had to want to capture the "energy of disco" in their music.

"We met with the college," explained vocalist Daniel Darc on their 1984 press release. "Opposite the college, to be more exact, at a cafe where we drank beer while listening to Bob Dylan tracks lost in the jukebox between fifty disco music tracks. I studied literature but punk rock demolished most of the enthusiasm that I threw at it."

Eventually, in 1978, they finalised the band's line-up and set to work writing their first batch of songs. The name, however, had already been discovered thanks to the café owner's porn collection.

"The owner of the coffee had hidden a porn magazine behind the counter," recounts Darc. "Between its centre (pages) was written the title in Gothic letters TAXI GIRL. I found that funny. I even thought that it would be a good name for a group."

Despite their use of synths, the earliest incarnation of Taxi Girl was actually closer to punk in spirit. They were renowned for their wild live performances and had more in common with Iggy and the Stooges than the disco energy they apparently aimed to capture. Slowly the style of the band started to change and by the time of their first single, 'Mannequin' in 1981, they had developed a fine line in new wave synth-pop. Soon after, they delivered their second single, which would provide them with a huge hit, 'Cherchez le Garçon'. Both singles were collected together as a mini-album called *Cherchez le Garçon* later that year.

In 1982 they released their only real album (many compilations have followed), *Seppuku* (Samurai's suicide), produced by The Stranglers bassist J.J. Burnel. Although Burnel didn't play, he did write some of the choruses for the songs. Other Stranglers connections on the album included drumming by Jet Black, under the name Jet the Black, while The Strangler's sound engineer Steve Churchyard also worked on the album.

In a 1989 interview with French rock magazine Inrockuptibles, Daniel Darc offered his point of view on the work of Burnel, who he maintains ruined *Seppuku*: "In the long run," he said. "*Seppuku* allowed us all to break from the past and build a new foundation to show who we were really. We could have made another 'Cherchez le Garçon', but that did not interest us. You would be astonished to hear the demos before the work of Jean-Jacques. He wanted a unit in the sound but brought only one style. Moreover, it accentuated the dark side. It was to be an album of guitars, but the sympathy which had been created between Laurent and Burnel privileged the keyboards. Burnel was harmful commercially and artistically, but I do not have anything against him, even if I do not like this record."

Keyboards player Laurent Sinclair left the group after *Seppuku* following increased tensions with Darc and, in particular, Mirwais. The combination of Sinclair's friendship with the album producer and the subsequent dominance of his keyboards created a rift that couldn't be healed. Perhaps unsurprisingly, Sinclair worked with Burnel again on his 1986 single 'In Front of the Mirror'. It was a commercial failure.

Now stripped to a duo, Mirwais and Darc didn't move towards a guitar sound as might be expected. With Mirwais doing all of the drum machine programming, keyboard and guitar playing, he ploughed a more dance-floor-orientated sound. They enjoyed a couple more sizable hits between 1984 and 1986, most notably 'Paris'. However, they decided to call it a day in 1987.

Mirwais has described his time in Taxi Girl as a nightmare: "It was a very tragic band". However, they remain one of the most influential bands to have come from the synth and electro-pop era.

Perhaps their most effective obituary came from Darc, who summed up Taxi Girl in three succinct sentences: "TAXI GIRL loves James Brown and Marc Minelli. TAXI GIRL likes Bruce Lee and Grandmaster Flash. TAXI GIRL does not like Michael Jackson."

The legacy of Taxi Girl could be seen throughout the 80s in the French charts as techno-pop became a staple of Gallic music. It was a sound that was to subsequently have a huge effect on many contemporary dance producers, especially in the years immediately following French Touch, when many people started to return to 80s electro sounds through the electroclash scene.

Among the more interesting and influential to a degree were people like punk rocker Jacno, who combined rock with electronica and found great commercial success. Pascal, aka Dijon based producer Vitalic, explains another phenomenon of the time in France:

"Indochine was a French version of the British new wave in a less dark way but very dancefloor friendly. The songs were about third-sex people or subjects like this that were hype in the 80s. The tempo was fast, the drums in the front and easy to remember lyrics made for some songs ever-lasting tunes in the French club culture."

Finally, an artist of note was Desireless.

"Her 'Voyage, Voyage' is another example of French electronic dance music. It was very successful in other European countries, too," adds Pascal. "Based on the Indochine recipe and dancefloor orientated, it brought a very feminine touch to the club scene. This track is still a standard in many clubs and particularly at Pulp in Paris, as a lesbian hymn."

'Voyage, Voyage' was a huge hit in Europe, even reaching #5 in the UK charts. A rare achievement for a French language record. It was an achievement that always alluded Taxi Girl, who, despite their love and respect for the UK scene, failed to score any hits in Britain.

Following the Taxi Girl's demise, Daniel Darc released three solo albums, while Mirwais' first post-Taxi Girl venture was Juliette et les Independants, which he formed with his girlfriend. Perhaps as a direct reaction to Taxi Girl's reliance on synths, Juliette et les Indépendants were an acoustic folk duo! They would release one album *14 Juillet*. Mirwais reappeared in 1991 with a self-titled solo album. However, it was still far removed from contemporary electronic music, this time revolving around a power rock axis.

When Christophe Monier met Mirwais in 1994, he was far removed from the electronic culture of the day.

"He wasn't connected with dance music at all then. He came back little by little as he met people into dance. I met him in 1994 because he was working in a studio which was next to mine."

It was after hearing a drum & bass tune in 1994 that Mirwais was truly bitten by the electronic music bug again. Suddenly he recognised a spirit and energy he had known as a teenage punk and decided to pursue his own productions. In order to release his tracks, he set up the Naïve label and, in 1999 secured a deal with Sony. His 2000 single 'Disco Science' proved to be a huge club hit thanks to its combination of sultry guitar layers, burbling 303s, slowed down Daft Punk style beats and a commercial leaning.

"It isn't a normal speed for dancing in a house club," explained Mirwais. "It's a reference to the tempo of late 70s disco."

As a result of this, Mirwais recruited Giorgio Moroder to remix the track, thus bringing the loop full circle back to disco.

"Both me and Daft Punk share a huge influence in Giorgio Moroder," he explained in 2002. "I think that what Daft Punk are doing is great, but you've got to remember that I'm quite a lot older, and Moroder was an influence for me the first time around."

The video for 'Disco Science' saw Mirwais employing the services of a friend from Taxi Girl days in the director's seat – fashionable French photographer Stephane Sednaoui. The resulting film, based loosely on the Japanese movie *In the Realm of the Senses*, which blurred the lines between art-house and porn. Naturally, it was banned from daytime viewing. However, it perfectly suited the overtly sexual nature of 'Disco Science'.

The next part in the Mirwais story reads a little like a fairy tale. Sednaoui passed on a copy of 'Disco Science' to Madonna, who was at that time on the prowl for a producer to work on her latest venture. She had already been working with French producer Fabian Lamont (who was regularly working with Nellee Hooper at the time). However, the early recordings weren't going in the direction Madonna wanted and she quickly dispensed of Lamont's services. It is often suggested that Madonna was determined to get the French filtered disco sound for her project and when Thomas Bangalter allegedly turned her down, the arrival of Mirwais was seemingly a godsend.

In the end, Mirwais produced six of the tracks from her *Music* album. His pop sensibility enabled Madonna to work with great effect in this area of electronic dance music. More than her previous producer William Orbit, Mirwais helped Madonna reach an underground audience as well as her traditional pop following, thus gaining her all-important credibility. Mirwais would subsequently work on the follow-up album and the theme tune to the 2002 Bond film 'Die Another Day', which combined orchestration and acidic 303s to an 80s electro-pop groove.

Madonna's *Music* was released almost simultaneously with Mirwais' *Production* album in 2000. Featuring a version of the standout track from *Music*, 'Paradise (Not For Me)', this collection found Mirwais picking up on many of the stylings of contemporary French dance music. However, his particular additions to the electronic lexicon were strong enough to give the album its own distinct identity in an increasingly homogeneous environment. From the scattered electro beats to the richly hued strings, the 303s to the vocoders, there is no mistaking Mirwais' deft touch in the production.

"I truly believe that this man's a genius," exclaimed Madonna when asked about her producer. "He is so incredibly smart and visionary. I listen to his stuff, and I think this is the future of sound."

3. RAVE REVOLUTION OR HOUSE ARREST?

WHOSE HOUSE IS THIS ANYWAY?

As the house explosion gripped much of Europe at the end of the 80s, so too in Paris, a small group of people caught the bug. However, the first few notable events in France, like Pyramid at Le Palace and The Jungle at The Rex Club, were run by UK promoters like Glasgow's Slam/Soma crew. Largely the clubs in Paris were still hung up on the commercial dance music being presented by artists like Madonna. This underground sound didn't represent enough of a commercial attraction for established clubs to embrace it. Furthermore, the affluent clientele of these clubs were very resistant to change. They were doing well, and they didn't want anything to change.

The first night dedicated to house sounds (with a few electro-funk and go-go beats thrown in for good measure) was in 1988, when Jerome Pacman and Laurent Garnier hosted their Discomuzak party at the now infamous Locomotive club in Paris. However, this was a one-off night that had little impact on the rest of the Locomotive's programming. However, the first club to embrace house music was, perhaps unsurprisingly, a gay club called Le Boy. Indeed, even in Paris, it had always been the gay clubs that introduced the new styles to people. House, and then techno, were no exception.

Le Boy was located in the basement of The Olympia and was the first to play house and techno every night," explained F Communications' Eric

Morand. "It was the place where I discovered house. Some friends literally pulled me into the club and I was like, 'what's this?' The DJ was a guy from Belgium and he was spinning a mix of Italo House, Nu Beat, psychedelic things like tracks from Serge Gainsbourg or Pierre Henry, hip house stuff, and Inner City. The club closed in May '92, but for two or three years, it was the club where everyone heard everything. It was open from Wednesday to Sunday."

Le Boy quickly gained an avid following among the cooler gay and straight crowds, attracting a regular crowd of around 300 people. The other clubs in Paris, like Le Palace and The Rex, took notice of this reaction and started playing host to occasional parties such as DJ Deep's Zoo parties and DJ David Guetta's Rex events. However, nothing substantial occurred until the rave explosion of 1991.

"Things shifted very quickly into rave in 1991 and '92 in Paris and the surrounding area," explained Morand. "In '92, the music got very hard and fast and the clubs like Le Palace stopped doing techno nights and Le Boy closed down. So suddenly, there was nothing apart from raves where people like Lenny Dee were spinning a lot. The only club was The Rex on a Saturday. But there was a general energy from a few hundred people in the clubs and raves and we all knew each other. So there was so much energy. We all really felt that this was going to be the main movement of the 90s."

Rave culture encouraged local people like Luc Bertagnol, Pat Cash and Manu Casana (who would launch the first French techno label Rave-Age in 1991) to start putting on free parties in ever more unusual places. These ranged from mushroom farms to multi-story car parks. Anywhere that could house a soundsystem and a few hundred ravers was up for grabs.

Among the best known of these parties were the Mozinor events between '91-'93. They were hosted by Luc Bertagnol's The Cosmos Factory group in the Mozinor district of Paris and played host to numerous international DJs. These included Francesco Farfa, Mikki, Roby J, Joy Kitikonti, Blake Baxter, Eddy de Clercq, Sven Vath and local house guru Jerome Pacman.

RYTHMiX Records' Benua Carles remembers Mozinor fondly: "A high quality party, nice people, crazy look, high, high," he said.

"Mozinor was fantastic," added techno DJ and producer Manu Le Malin. "It was on top of a car park on the edge of Paris. This place was a legend. All of the Paris scene would be there. Inside it was amazing. I played maybe twice, but I was always there as a raver."

Another Paris-based DJ to feature regularly at Mozinor events was Liza 'N' Eliaz, who had carved her name out as a hard trance and techno champion. Such was the regard held for her that she was considered one of the spiritual leaders of the free party movement in France, even though she was Belgian.

Although 'N' Eliaz only started DJing in 1991, she had already spent a decade in music with electronic groups such as Krise Kardiak, Divorce and The Honeymoon Killers. By 1985 she had developed a one-woman performance featuring an array of synths. An untitled CD from this period displayed her as a unique talent that married the dystopian robotic ambience of early industrial groups like Front 242 and the melodic inference of the electro-pop groups of the era.

At the end of the 80s, 'N' Eliaz moved to Amsterdam, where she discovered acid house. And, after hearing DJ Eddy de Clercq on Radio 100, she felt inspired enough to take up DJing herself. Her rise to prominence as a DJ was almost immediate, while her productions under the alias Bonzai and Atom (among others) placed her at the forefront of the hardcore scene.

Sadly Lisa 'N' Eliaz died in 2001. However, her memory lives on among in the worldwide family of free party and techno people

"She was actually from Belgium but she was like God in Paris," recalled Le Malin. "She was working for Technotrance who were big organisers. They were really into the music, not cliched. So the atmosphere was just really colourful. It was a huge loss when she died. Not just to the techno scene, but to music."

Between 1991-1993, many free parties emerged on the outskirts of Paris, although Luc Bertagnol, Manu Casana and several UK promoters had put on parties as early as 1988. French promoters Fantom played host to Spasmes and Nostromo with DJs like Juan Atkins, Njoi and Armand. The events were renowned for their extravagant decoration and massive sound.

Echoing the UK's response to rave culture, French parties suffered at the hands of a draconian, authoritarian regime with laws quickly passed to govern the dance events. *Libération* newspaper held one of the first legal parties at La Villette in 1992. It attracted 5000 people for featured guest DJs Paul Van Dyk and Sasha alongside UK legends LFO and internationally renowned French DJ Laurent Garnier.

It was during this period that the South of France first developed its foothold on French rave folklore. Borealis in Montpelier was *the* big event. "The first one took place in 1993 in a suburb club," recalled Benua Carles. "They had house inside with DJ Per, hardcore outside with Liza 'N' Eliaz and then after on the beach with different DJs."

Borealis grew to enormous proportions, settling in a regular site and attracting upwards of 300,000 people to each event. However, the parties had to stop after a storm destroyed the place in 1998.

Another huge party at the Aqualand water theme park at Gif Sur Yvette near Paris took place in 1992. Benua Carles recalls the event: "A big swimming pool with waves. Music was from Paul Jay, Dimitri from Holland, Jack de Marseilles. On the flyer, their names were written – and PAUL JAYser, DIMITRIdent and JACKuzzi It was incredible. Everybody was in bathing suits and it was February! 10,000 people! We all get a cold after... And the rarity of the night? Dry cigarettes and rolling papers! Fantastic!"

Throughout this period, the events were organised by, or with, certain key people who would become important figures in the growth of the French dance scene. David Guetta was one of the first people to set up parties at the Rex club with Laurent Garnier. Indeed, in direct reaction to the growth of rave culture over club culture, Garnier and Eric Morand launched their now infamous Wake Up! Paris nights at the Rex in May '92 with international guest DJs and residents Garnier and DJ Deep.

Coda magazine was getting more heavily involved in the scene at this time while local Parisian radio station Radio FG took the decision in 1992 to only play house and techno. It subsequently became an important stopping off point for visiting DJs who would provide exclusive live sets for the station. B.P.M. record shop was also important to this period. One of the people at B.P.M., Olivier Lacourt, would go on to set up the Discograph distribution company in 1998, itself a highly respected distribution hub for artists internationally.

Among the leading French DJs of the time were the aforementioned Liza 'N' Eliaz and Manu Le Malin on the hardcore techno and trance tip. Also notable on this scene were Antoine Kraft and his Impakt-Teknokrates collective and Laurent Ho, whose weekly trance and techno sessions for Radio FG as early as 1991 were essential listening.

However, on the house front, DJs like Jérôme Pacman, Eric Rug and DJ Deep were becoming hard to avoid. Indeed these three names would be essential to developing the French profile abroad.

Jérôme Pacman discovered house music at the age of 17 in Ibiza. It was the summer of 1987. He was already known as an electro DJ, but he swiftly moved to house and by 1998, he was a regular DJ at some of the biggest free parties in Paris. Parties like the aforementioned Mozinor by *Cosmos Factory* and the *Libération* newspaper rave in 1992. From here, he went on to become a well-respected DJ throughout the rave world. He became a resident in the UK, Holland, Germany (being a regular at the *Love Parade*), Italy and Spain. In the late 90s, he also started to spin regularly in Hong Kong, where he was a resident at the French Kiss events. He also became a resident at the Magic Garden parties in France from their first event in 1995. This association led to the hugely popular mix set *Jérôme Pacman's House Café*, which sold 12000 units in the French territory alone.

In 1993 Pacman started to release his own productions on French label Omnisonus. He debuted with the heavy duty 'China Chicks', which gained critical acclaim in the UK press at the time. In 1996 he released the *Mouvement Perpétuel* album on Obsession, which featured in that year's albums of the year charts in UK dance magazine *Muzik*. His deep sound encompassed an uncompromising early house aesthetic alongside heavy percussion. Indeed, the music he created was so unique that the style became known as "the Pacman sound" in his native France.

Another of these early DJs was Eric Rug. Considered to be the true legend of French house in many quarters, he was present in the earliest days of house parties in France. An enigmatic figure who has shunned the spotlight in favour of his underground beliefs, he was not only a regular DJ throughout Europe but was also responsible for Parisian radio station Radio Nova's Saturday night show. This programme featured the entirety of the up-and-coming and frontline players in the late 1990s French Touch scene. Subsequently, he was a key player in creating the infrastructure that took French dance music to an international audience. His *French Fried Funk* compilation in 1998 brought together all of the main producers in one essential mix that remains a perfect snapshot of the era.

Rug also became known for his stunning production. Recording under the alias 2 Frenchman, Waxwork and Daphreephunkateers (with Dimitri from Paris), he delivered numerous club floor fillers such as the 10" white label hit 'Psykotic Phunk Reaction' as Daphreephunkateerz Vs Aleph. He also released genius house cuts such as 'Cut a Rug' and 'Don't Fuck With My Shit' as Dirty Jesus.

Finally, DJ Deep. In 1996, when Daft Punk finished what was to be their debut album *Homework,* they invited only six people to the first playback. Among them was DJ Deep, so important was his opinion to them. DJ Deep, aka Cyril, started DJing at the Boy club in 1989. From here, he moved to Le Palace for their Zoo Parties. By 1992 he was a resident at Wake Up! Paris, which introduced him to the international DJing fraternity.

His activities soon went beyond club DJing and in 1994, he launched a career as a radio DJ at Radio FG. His show was broadcast daily from 12 to 2am. Around this time, he also produced his first track 'Deep Contest' in collaboration with Ludovic Navarre, DJ Cam and Gilb'R. He also delivered his own production, 'Sweet Summer Vibe'.

In 1995 he moved from FG to Radio Nova for the Saturday night show, further enhancing his reputation. His productions that followed displayed a deep understanding of house music. Not so much a Parisian producer as an international one, his records were picked up by legendary DJs like Louie Vega. Indeed Deep's 1997 cut 'Fire' was a regular in Vega's sets. Other releases have included the 'Playing for the City Meets the Deep', 'Funk Force Project' on Straight Up Records and the 'Earth' and 'Colours' EPs on BaseNotic.

If the early 90s saw a huge growth in the parties, DJs and producers coming out of France, the period was also notable for the development of the media surrounding the culture. As has already been mentioned, Radio FG had developed a house and techno only policy as early as 1992, while Paris station Radio Nova had an eclectic policy that embraced hip hop, African music, and the new dance sounds emerging.

On the magazine front, however, Coda attempted to cover the scene but had to remain partisan to their main readership. As a result, although they were heavily involved early on, this actually amounted to very few printed pages. The Liberation newspaper was also very vocal in its support of the whole scene, most notably Didier Lestrade, who would go on to found *Magazine*, *Têtu* and *Act Up Paris*. Another magazine that launched during this time was *Eden*, a pocket-sized fanzine that featured all of the events on the French underground.

Launched in May 1992 by Patrick Vidal, Thierry Pilard, S. Legland, Alain, Adelaide Dugdale, Vix and Widowsky, Eden quickly became an essential link between ravers and promoters while presenting a solid overview of the global culture. Furthermore, it created cohesion between France and the rest of the world, locating domestic DJs and producers within the international spectrum. In itself, this was an important factor in creating a solid and productive scene in France. Something which required the development of a dynamic sense of national worth among ravers, DJs, producers, promoters and media alike.

RAVE-AGE, FNAC AND THE TECHNO REVOLUTION

French producers weren't slow in reacting to the sea change brought about by the house and techno revolution. However, they were forced to look overseas to release their productions on labels. Germany, Belgium and Holland were the first to sign French musicians with Hexagona on Djax up Beats, Vigipirate on Tresor, Mental Overdose on Dance Opera in Belgium. Even Laurent Garnier was forced to deliver his debut slice of vinyl on a foreign label. In his case, however, that song ('Who Cares' under the pseudonym French Connection) came out on Manchester's Eastern Bloc Records in 1990. Manchester was Laurent's home at the time.

The first label to emerge in France was Paris' Rave-Age Records in 1991, headed up by local promoter Manu Casana. The debut release came in the shape of Discotique's previously discussed 'Sexe'. Casana faced the same problems that beset Cerrone over a decade earlier in setting up an independent label. It was almost impossible to get vinyl pressed up in France if you weren't a major label. Distribution too was limited by the big companies who controlled the network. Radio airplay for contemporary dance music was out of the question on all but Dimitri's NRG radio show. His shows were far more firmly rooted in the house sound and Rave-Age was most definitely a techno label.

The final obstruction in the way of Casana's progress was the perception of French people themselves. As has already been mentioned, mainstream France considered this music to be a soundtrack to drug addiction. More than being a part of underground culture, as had been experienced in England and other countries in Europe, rave was considered an act of pure subversion in France. As a result, the task that faced Casana and his contemporaries was the complete creation of infrastructure – from production through to distribution and on to promotion – without support from established businesses. Little surprise then that the first Rave-Age releases sold mainly in the UK, with France only accounting for a negligible amount of sales.

Soon after Casana launched Rave-Age, support for the scene came from a surprising source – department store FNAC, which had also launched a record company. Despite being mainly focused on French vocalists and highbrow releases, one of the label's staff, Eric Morand, constantly pushed for the launch of a dance arm to the label. In his capacity as A&R man, he had already licensed numerous house and techno projects from abroad, but he believed that the only way to create a real dance market in France would be to nurture domestic producers.

"At FNAC, when I started in A&R, the first things I signed for license were LFO and Warp Records," he said. "Then I signed Speedy J and things like that. But it was a nightmare. In 1991 no one in France gave a shit about LFO or Speedy J. To them, it wasn't music. So we thought that the only way to really develop the scene in France was to have French artists being successful outside of France which has the boomerang effect of everybody saying, techno music is great, you know? So having successful French artists would be good for everyone around the world who were releasing techno records in France."

In 1991 Eric Morand was rewarded for his persistence by being invited to head up the creation of the FNAC Dance Division.

"It was a great challenge for me because, at the time, nobody thought that it was at all possible. When in late '91, or even '92, I said I wanted to give international exposure to French artists, everyone was laughing. They thought I was a crazy old fool. Everyone said I should move to London, or go to Amsterdam, but here in Paris, I was wasting my time. They said it would never work. But I just couldn't see why it was possible everywhere else, why not France. Especially when, if you go back to the roots in the 70s, France was one of the leading countries producing disco."

Throughout our interview, Eric Morand had the air of a man in control. His conversation was relaxed but forceful, his mannerisms gentle but strong. The combination of dark thinning hair, close-set eyes and blemished skin provided him with a ruggedness that betrayed too many nights spent in the darkened corners of clubs the world over. And when he fixes you with his commanding yet friendly gaze, you are given no room to doubt his integrity. Eric Morand was a businessman, for sure. But his heart still beats with an honest and passionate rhythm. It was an overwhelming attitude that came from being a pioneer in his chosen field for so long. An attitude that comes from years of self-belief, belief in the dance culture and above all, the tenacity to hang on to his ideals.

At times his quest may have seemed to be a case of being led by blind faith, but proof of the validity of his ideas and strategies have been present in the French (and worldwide) dance scene ever since he first walked into the offices at FNAC as an A&R man.

Perhaps one of the reasons that he developed this almost perverse tenacity came from the fact that in the early days, it was quite literally a case of him and a couple of friends against the entire history of the French music industry. For Morand and his friends were truly trailblazing through virgin territory in his home country.

"In a way, in the whole process, I've been very lucky because I was able to use the power and infrastructure of FNAC to start," he admitted. "The first years are very hard for any label, but especially with this because we had to do everything that other departments took for granted. We had to build everything. We had to find the right studios to do the cutting and the mastering. We had to experiment on how to record and mix the music because there hadn't been a structure before. We also had to spend a lot of energy and time just setting up the licensing and export. It was like a year to start to have a bit of faith from the UK or Germany just to buy our records. In a way, I was very lucky, because if we'd had to do everything by ourselves with our own money, we would have stopped after twelve months. So the sales were shit at the beginning but around '93, we started getting the following in the media."

FNAC launched with a series of singles by French producers who would become mainstays of the scene. Laurent Garnier delivered more work under his French Connection alias. At the same time, Ludovic Navarre launched a career that would culminate in the worldwide success of his St. Germain guise a few years later. Another huge talent snapped up by Morand's FNAC was Shazz, while he also invested in the techno outfit Lunatic Asylum.

"It was all just like a question of faith," he continued. "When I started the process in August '91, I said to Laurent and a few others, 'you know you should really produce some stuff'. I was also meeting people like Ludovic Navarre and Shazz and I was getting this feeling that things they were doing in terms of music were interesting and slightly different. For me, I didn't see any reason why we couldn't do it."

Any hopes Morand and friends had for a slow build were quickly blown out of the water as their records started to sell really well. They had respected dancefloor hits with the classic 'Acid Eiffel' by Choice (aka Laurent Garnier and Shazz) and then enjoyed a huge European hit with Lunatic Asylum's 'Techno Sucks Vol. 1' and 'Techno Sucks Vol. 2'. However, 95 per cent of their sales were still outside France.

One of the problems, they felt, was that France didn't have a real club culture. The free parties and raves were still strong, but club culture remained locked in the past. Except for Le Boy and the regular sessions at The Rex and La Palace, there was nowhere actively playing techno or house in the club environment. There was nowhere when Le Boy closed in May '92 and other clubs shut their doors to techno and house because of the shift towards harder rave culture.

"At this time, I was really depressed when I was going to England at the weekends, and then coming home where nothing was happening but the free raves," confided Morand. "We all felt the same, so it gave us a real passion to build the scene. It was like being in a virgin jungle where you have to create all of the methods of working. But at least you can do things the way that you feel or want it, rather than having to do things the older way. So it was difficult and very exciting.

"One day, on the way back from London with Laurent, we were just so depressed. After a great weekend, there was nothing at home to go to. So at this time, we decided to start up a club night called Wake Up! Paris at The Rex Club. It ran from May '92 to June '94."

Wake Up! Paris remains one of Europe's legendary club nights of that era. It was the first club night to introduce a truly global policy where huge DJs from around the world would play alongside local DJs Laurent

Garnier, Eric Rug and DJ Deep. It was at this club that you could see the seeds of the mid-90s boom as, for its lifespan, it became the most important meeting ground for techno and house DJs, producers and organisers.

"I think Wake Up! Paris was very important in the creation and inspiration of the scene in Paris because the idea of the club was to bring the energy of raves and the idea of booking some foreign premier DJs to a club," continued Morand. "The first party we did had Laurent spinning. Derrick May came along and he loved it. After that, we closed down for the summer and then reopened in September with Derrick May and Kevin Saunderson on the same night! Which was incredible for the time. It felt like the real start. From here, we brought in everyone."

"Wake Up! Paris was extremely important to the dynamic," adds Laurent Garnier, who arrived an hour late for the interview. He looked tired, thanks to his exertions the night before, where he delivered one of his famed marathon DJ sets at The Rex.

"It was the weekly meeting place for everyone," he continues. "It was important for the label because all of the artists would spend time together every week. And it was important for the scene because it was the place where people would exchange emotions and ideas about things. And, as Eric said, it was the first party in a club which had guest DJs."

The popularity of Wake Up! Paris saw queues stretching along the road all night as people begged to get in. The buzz that surrounded the venture encouraged other clubs to bring in guest DJs to try and capture some of the Wake Up! flavour. Furthermore, no fewer than four domestic techno and house compilations were put together during this time. A true sign of a burgeoning market.

The first and most important compilation to arrive in 1992 was the *FNAC #1* collection. The album featured two tracks licensed from Rave-Age (Electrotete's 'I Love You' and 'Le Temps' by I Fly) alongside FNAC staples like Shazz with the stunning tracks' A Corner Called Shazz' and 'Moonflower', Laurent Garnier's techno noir classic 'Storm' and Choice's epic 'From the Arch'. Also present were cuts by Kat Kall, Deepside and Impulsion, while Christophe Monier and Patrick Vidal's Discotique project was included through the gorgeous 'Love Dub'. And, just to add to the historical tone behind French electronic music's first compilation album, 'Psyche Rock' by Pierre Henry was also included.

The other compilations released during this period were the *PUR Collection*, which included tracks by Jerry Bouthier, The Pat Cash Soundsytem and Erik Rug & Jerome Restre. Rave Age delivered their set *Tekno Nostrum*, which included artists like Archimede, aka Mederic Nebinger, an early associate of Guy-Manuel from Daft Punk. The final collection was the less inspired *Ravelation* set which aimed to represent the less inspired aspects of the rave scene. However, it was the FNAC set that proved to be the true landmark album. Not only did it capture the essence of Wake Up! Paris at its most poignant, a meeting ground of underground talent, but it also showed FNAC to be a domestic label with truly international appeal.

However, just as things seemed to be unstoppable, two major events took place. First up, FNAC closed down all of their record companies, and then Wake Up! Paris shut its weekly residencies.

"After two years, we had brought everyone to Paris that we wanted to put on, and it was a lot of work doing a weekly club," explained Morand. "So basically, after two years, we decided to stop. Also, by this time, there were a lot of clubs booking guest DJs. We'd done it, but it was time to do something else."

"After that, I carried on The Rex on my own," continued Garnier. "The Rex has always been my house. So, at that time, I just thought fuck it, I'll do it on my own. I had no guests and had a monthly night with just me."

And as for FNAC?

"Around the end of Wake Up! we moved on from FNAC and got on with the new label," explained Morand. "The whole company was kind of weird. I knew from the beginning that it wouldn't last because I've been in the music industry for a long time and I'm used to record labels opening and closing departments. The dance department was actually going very well but the rest of the company was making huge losses. Also, at the beginning, there was a guy who asked me to join FNAC Music who thought the idea of developing French artists was strong. But he left after two years. The rest of the management didn't really understand what I was doing and for them, it wasn't a priority. So I just thought, OK, I'm leaving. And they let me go quite easily. They didn't even try to keep any of the artists."

It was February 1994 and rather than let the grass grow under their feet, Morand and Garnier joined forces to create the F-Communications label. This imprint would build on the notoriety already achieved by FNAC Dance before becoming an internationally acclaimed stable of talent.

"F Comm were of a great importance," stated leading techno producer Vitalic a few weeks later. "Great artists emerged from this label. St Germain, Shazz, Mr Oizo, Lunatic Asylum... It was the time of the first exportation of French techno and house. This label was very open-minded, and even if it was an eclectic label, it sounded homogenised and was the first proof of a French sound."

"We started F Comm quite quickly in April 1994," says Morand of the transition from FNAC to the new project. "We already had a reputation with our artists. We had St Germain, Shazz, and we had Lunatic Asylum, who was absolutely huge in Germany. We'd done Wake Up! which came out on Warp as well and was very big. We did 'Acid Eiffel' with Choice, which also came out on Transmat in the USA. Carl Cox was a huge superstar at the time and was doing remixes for us, so FNAC was already kind of big. But the funny thing is, we became big outside of France and then came back to France. France was not the country that gave us our reputation. It was Germany and England."

Once again, any plans to build slowly were forgotten as F Communications scored immediate dancefloor hits with St. Germain and Shazz. The latter especially had Europe-wide success with a trance track called 'Milky Way', released under the moniker Aurora Borealis.

Despite the success of these records abroad and the achievements of Wake Up! Paris, Eric and Laurent were still a long way from their goal of creating a strong marketplace for techno in France. Their domestic records sales still only accounted for five per cent. The ongoing efforts of *La Liberation* newspaper to cover the culture and the increased exposure on Radio FG created minimal interest in the general public, and France was still resistant to the dance phenomena. This was when the rest of Europe (especially the UK and Germany) were experiencing a deluge of chart-dominating dance acts.

"People still didn't know anything about techno in France," explained Laurent Garnier. "When you went in to record shops, they didn't know what this music was and didn't give a shit about it. So we were faced with the choice between spending all our energy convincing people in France to listen to our music or spending the energy in England and Germany talking to people who understood what we were doing. So we did the latter and people here started to say, 'what's happening with these French people getting all the attention?'. This finally made people more confident with the sound. That was just how it worked in France. If we had reviews in *Melody Maker* or *NME* or *Mixmag*, then people took notice."

And F Communications got plenty of reviews in UK weekly music papers *NME* and *Melody Maker*. Indeed they were regular features in their dance sections Orbit and Vibes. They also received enormous support from magazines like *Generator*, *Mixmag* and *Melody Maker* off-shoot *Muzik*. Indeed the first few years of F Comm coincided with a golden period in dance music journalism, with magazines thriving on and encouraging the pioneering attitude of the better labels, DJs and producers.

The net result of all of this attention abroad was that the French media started to cover F Communication's roster with greater regularity. However, the general attitude among the domestic press remained one of mild disinterest. As Laurent explains: "The funny thing about France and Paris is that it was very hard to find F-Communications records in specialist French shops; they weren't ordering it because it was coming from Paris. But you have to understand the thing about France is that it is not like England because here we don't support our own artists. In fact, if you have any kind of success, the French become jealous. So there was a kind of love and hate thing going on with us. The French media could not disrespect or disregard what we had done, but they weren't supportive of us compared to what happened with French Touch."

However, domestic sales did increase for the label, proving that even that little bit of attention from the French media was having an impact. That and the increased volume of people visiting England after the launch of the Eurostar train shuttle in November 1994!

"Gradually, it got bigger each September after people had been travelling over the summer," continued Morand. "'93 to'94, '95 it just got steadily bigger and bigger. And then around '96 it levelled off at the percentage of French sales being around 30%. This was when the market reached its maximum size. Which fits with the effect of the French Touch, the time when the scene in France matured."

Perhaps the defining moment for F Communication came in 1994 when they decided to move into the artist album market – notoriously one of the toughest areas for dance music. However, the decision saw F Communications change from a dance floor centric singles label to a development stable for an eclectic mix of production styles. The first album on the F Communications imprint was *Shot In the Dark* by Laurent Garnier.

"When Laurent decided to make an album, it was a weird decision because none of the other artists were doing them," explained Morand." So when he came back from the US and said he wanted to do an album, I thought, why not? Our expectations were quite low. We thought we'd sell between seven and ten thousand copies, which would be OK. These were the kind of sales Kenny Larkin was doing on Warp. Six months after the release of the album, it had sold 80,000 copies!"

With the positive reaction to Laurent's debut album, Morand encouraged some of the other artists on his roster to work on albums. Among them was Ludovic Navarre, who would create one of French electronic music's milestone albums in *Boulevard*.

Ludovic Navarre had been a mainstay of the French techno underground since the turn of the decade. A would-be sportsman who was forced to quit due to personal reasons, he soon took up the challenge of producing and DJing. His releases, first as Sub System (with friend Guy Rabiller), and then as Deepside, Soofle, Modus Vivendi, LNs and Nuages would set down a blueprint of Detroit-esque techno patterns over sparse rhythmical landscapes. His St. Germain project seemed to be heading in the same direction with the earliest releases, 'French Trax' and 'Motherland' in 1993 on FNAC.

Then in 1995, he dropped a series of singles that displayed an astounding new direction. Called the 'Boulevard' series, these singles featured a sublime fusion of jazz, blues, soul and languid techno, a combination of the club-friendly beats of 1990s house with the live musicianship of a bunch of jazzers from the St.Germain district of Paris. These singles were subsequently collected together as an album *Boulevard* – a richly textured masterpiece that provided the essential cool soundtrack to the long hot summer of 1995. It was a huge success selling over 400,000 copies in the first year of its release.

However, rather than bask in the glory of that album and deliver another set of similarly inspired tunes, Navarre withdrew from studio production entirely. He felt he'd achieved what he'd set out to do, and the notoriously shy producer had no intention of becoming an artist for whom quantity was more important than quality. He was, he claimed to me at the time, "against the industrial production of techno. Who says I have to produce another record now?"

Foremost on his mind at this time was the need to gain a greater understanding of how musicians work. His involvement with the musicians on *Boulevard* had given him an insight into an alternative way of working. One which didn't only involve the solitary process of programming. To come to terms with this new area of interest, he put a band together and took it on the road. The live band experience was new to F Communications. Still, they adopted the same kind of pioneering spirit that they'd always had with things – preferring to view this move towards the standard live show as a leap forwards rather than a step back. Inadvertently it was a move that beckoned the next development in the label.

However, the St. Germain live experience wasn't the runaway success that the album had promised. Writing for now-defunct UK weekly music paper, *Melody Maker* in February 1996, I was hardly able to conceal my disappointment at his LA2, London show:

"Playing a one-off show Ludovic and co's arrival to these shores has brought the club cognoscenti out in force for a jazz-in-the-house groove fest. Standing stage centre, behind his mixing desk Navarre surveys the audience with the smug look of someone in the know. His time has come and to add to the event, he's brought along a live band. Thus a percussionist who looks like an escapee from Womad sits next to a truly laid back ivory tickler on keyboards who is the epitome of Mr. Jazz. He sits next to the horn section – and thank you 'God of things to look at' for them. In a musical style which isn't normally noted for performance technique (no wailing Diva's here tonight), the St. Germain ensemble take visual boredom to a new extreme. With the obvious exception of the trio of horn players who shimmy to the grooves, strike Dizzy Gillespie poses and generally try to bring life into the proceedings – of course.

"Indeed 'life' is the missing ingredient to tonight's sonic recipe. Mixing their way through material from the album, the band never find that spark that this music needs. That spark which brought *Boulevard* to life in the first place. The energy behind the finest house, the on-the-brink-of-losing-it euphoria of the best jazz – only once in the entire set does it come together. With Navarre pushing the bass to the fore, the kick drum igniting the percussionist into a frenzy of salsa triplets, the trio of horns move into full swing with a series of brass hooks reminiscent of Defunkt's Bowie brothers, Joe, Byron and Lester. In this single moment, the atmosphere lifts and the crowd forget that they're in a venue more suited to rock music.

"Unfortunately, it's a case of the band climaxing too soon, as they never achieve this passionate state again. True, the grooves keep feet moving. After all, we've waited a long time for this carnival to come to town, but hearts are filled with disappointment and the ambience is heavy with the polite air of a crowd 'making the most of it'.

"Towards the end of the set, the horn section etches out a pastiche of a Charlie Parker track and it leaves you wishing that St Germain (the band) would just let go, spread their wings and fly like The Bird – like you instinctively know they can."

Navarre's strategy soon paid off despite my misgivings. In 1999 he signed a deal with legendary jazz label Blue Note. After an absence of nearly five years from the studio, he delivered the *Tourist* album. *Tourist* found Navarre taking those early live jazz excursions into far more satisfying terrain. Despite the fact that there were only four dancefloor tracks in the set. Among the standouts were 'Rose Rouge' and 'Sure Thing', which found the template of *Boulevard*, being stretched to include a deep, resonating soul ambience. *Tourist* would go on to become a global success.

Thanks to the initial impact of *Boulevard*, F-Communications was suddenly viewed as being an eclectic label. It was a chance which Morand and Garnier seized upon, encouraging their artist to explore wider terrain. Their output having visibly moved on from those early days in techno.

Soon their roster would include the ambient moods of A Reminiscent Drive (whose single 'Flame 1' was *NME's* Single of the Week at a time when the paper's writers still displayed the courage of their convictions). Also on the label roster were the dark techno of Scan X, the atmospheric house of Nova Nova and the tech-rock odysseys of Juantrip. While in 1997 Laurent Garnier would deliver his second album, the far more diverse *30* and Shazz would finally translate his languid house grooves onto a long-player with the *El Camino Project* set.

"Now F Comm has a strong back catalogue and a lot of strong artists," confirmed Morand. Perhaps one of the more interesting and colourful artists to emerge from France in the 90s, and one who is all too often ignored was Juantrip'.

Long before Juantrip' the artist was ever imagined, the Versailles born child of hippy parents was known simply as Basil. At the age of seven, his parents took him to live on a commune in the Pyrenees, an experience which Basil describes as being "a kidnapping, suddenly I was in this place where I just wandered free and everyone looked after me." However, it was here that Basil first became aware of the power of music. On his eighth birthday, he witnessed the entire commune hear the news of Elvis Presley's death at the same time. All who understood were reduced to tears. Basil's response was to pick up a guitar, pluck at the strings and spontaneously write his first song, which in turn brought the commune out of their depression. It was called 'Black Soap' and Basil was awoken to the world of music.

Basil returned to Paris sporting dyed red hair – unusual for an eight-year-old kid anywhere – and spent an unremarkable few years in formal education until he quit school at sixteen to become an artist. But he soon left to hang around the French alternative underground. In 1989, he and a few friends packed up their instruments and headed for the south of France. It was to be another life-altering experience.

Eleven of Basil's friends joined him in a huge jam in the mountains. They'd discovered this mountain shack which had an electrical supply so, armed with little more than their instruments, some wine and a plentiful supply of LSD, they embarked on a jam that was to last for four days.

"I got my name from here; it was a gift," explains Basil. "While we all played, I met this smoky spirit guy. He told me my name was Juantrip'."

And so Juantrip' was born. Stranger still was the fact that all eleven musicians seemed to have encountered the same vision at the same time. Acid ramblings perhaps, but for Basil and friends, the experience completely changed their approach to music. Many of them went off to become DJs and free party promoters, travelling around Europe with soundsystems. Basil continued to create music playing live at parties like France's Fantom Raves. By 1991 Basil was deeply entrenched in the endless possibilities offered by techno.

In 1993 Juantrip' released his first single 'Ecstasy's God', on Rave-Age Records. However, it wasn't until he met F Communications' Eric Moran that his recording career truly started. Initially signed on a one-off deal for the single 'Louie's Cry', the label saw huge potential for creative growth in Juantrip'. Over the next few years, Basil worked hard on his production to find his own voice.

With each new release, the Juantrip' sound became more unique, moving away from its techno base into a wider, more inclusive sound. 1996's 'Interstone EP' edged towards a sound he described as "psychedelic techno rock'n'roll", with Basil drawing on a lifetime's experience in order to realise his own ideas. On 'Ble' from 1998 single 'Electronic', he delved ever deeper into those wayward psychedelic soundscapes and heady vocals, offering an insight into the direction he was travelling in.

In 1999 he released the album *Balmy Under the Stormy*, a culmination of one man's extraordinary journey through music and life. One of the most panoramic explorations into the eclectic to be heard that year, the album was best summarised by the inner sleeve artwork. Featuring a world map printed upside down and in reverse, it questioned all of those things we hold to be true. Who said North was up, that white isn't black and that techno isn't rock'n'roll? Who said that a communal hallucination couldn't happen and that the writing of 'Black Soap' wasn't a bigger event than Elvis' death?

With tracks like the brooding 'Fly to the Moon' with its contorted strings, lo-fi electronica and vocodered psychosis, or the dreamscaped ambience of the lysergically charged 'Downward Rush of Streams', the album introduced a new lexicon into the world of psychedelia. On 'Picture This Kind of Her Smile' and 'Waiting for the Train', he drew on Syd Barret era Pink Floyd and bands like Soft Machine but relocated them in a contemporary setting through the darkness of modern life.

"This album is all about how we would view the world if we were all a little bit mad instead of just boring," said Basil in conversation with me just before the release of *Balmy Under the Stormy*. "It's about what we think is true actually being a lie. In fact, the album itself is a lie."

A unique album from a unique artist with an equally unique life story, *Balmy Under the Stormy* not only introduced a full breadth of this under-supported artist's vision, but also represented a point when F-Communications could be seen to be taking a truly solitary path. Ironically, this was the French Touch era when Morand and Garnier's dream of domestically produced music being distributed all over the world became a reality. And F Comm wasn't a part of it – at all.

"We came from a different background to the French Touch," said Morand. "We'd come from the rave scene and the techno scene. A lot of the French Touch people came from hip hop and indie. More people arrived in the techno and house scenes in 93-94, but we're from the generation of '88-'89. The thing was that they were a new generation who wanted something new and we were old."

After years of pushing at the boundaries, the F-Comm posse was suddenly displaced by a new generation who were effectively benefiting from the work that Garnier, Morand *et al.* had put in in the first place.

"Sometimes it was a bit hard to swallow, but that's life," confided Morand. "You know, I like the fact that everyone can bring their own vision of the scene and that's what makes the whole scene interesting. But we just kept doing what we'd done for years. We never wanted to be a label of the month. Our vision was always more long term.

"You see, we were before French Touch, and we're still here after French Touch and things haven't changed for us, but that was a part of history," continues Garnier. "During this time, our artists and the label grew up. We were doing albums, which was a deeper experience. The twelves are created for a time and place: the dancefloor between 12 and 6am. But for albums, it is far less focused in this way. Of course, this helped our artists go deeper because they could do so much more than what excited them in the first place – which was the dance floor. So through the explosion of the French Touch, we definitely matured. But we didn't do this on purpose because we'd not been assimilated with the French Touch. It was just a natural progression."

Rather than sign up the first artist they could find doing filtered disco, F-Comm took an ever more perverse path – further defining themselves as an idiosyncratic label with designs of pushing at the outer edges of electronica.

Among their signings to emerge during this period was Frederick Galliano. His explorations into the fusion of jazz, African indigenous music and electronica found the label moving in a direction diametrically opposed to the French Touch sound.

"F-Comm was a techno label in the beginning. Then it was a techno and house label," enthused Garnier. "Then we had a lot of different kinds of music. Ready Made, for instance, gave a fresh turn to our music. Then we had Juantrip', which was kind of rock, so people started wondering what we were doing. Then we had Frederic Galliano, which was jazz and everyone was like 'fucking hell'. OK, St Germain was jazzy, but it was still dancefloor music, but Frederic was jazz. So, at the same time as the French Touch became targeted and narrow, we were getting very wide in our approach."

The sounds being explored by Frederic Galliano were just about as wide as you could imagine coming from a label with its roots in techno. With his first two albums, *Espaces Baroques* and *Live Infinis*, Galliano, who lived away from the hype and bustle of Paris in the south of France, followed a unique path in the electronic music world. His aim was to defend the positions of jazz and African music, rather than subsume them into the aesthetics of electronica, as had happened in the work of French artists Deep Forest.

In 1998 Galliano set up his own label Frikyiwa to further explore his love of African music. His live band Frederic Galliano Electric Sextet, further experimented with the sonic fusions of his albums, taking the concepts to an extreme. In the same year, he also began working on what was to become a mammoth two-CD set, *Frederic Galliano presents the African Divas*, a collaboration with over fifty African jazz musicians he'd met on his travels. An astonishing album that redefined the parameters of Afro-electronic music, it represented a giant leap for both artist and label.

The growing interest in jazz had also been present in Laurent Garnier's 2000 album *Unreasonable Behaviour*, in which he too explored the possibilities presented by the combination of live musicians and studio programming. However, this didn't mean that the label was necessarily moving beyond the world of the dancefloor. Indeed, in 1999 F-Communications found themselves being swept along by the unlikely success of an artist with talents as diverse as they were quirky. That artist was Mr. Oizo, who will be best remembered by the television watching public for his puppet creation Flat Eric.

Mr. Oizo was otherwise known as Quentin Dupieux, a young film director from Paris who had already directed eight short films for French

National television while still a teenager. In 1997 however, he was to have a fortuitous meeting that was to push him into the world of music. His father, a car salesman from a lot on the same road as Laurent Garnier's house, told him of his son's achievements while in the process of selling the DJ a car. Garnier suggested his son should drop a showreel off to him, which he duly did.

Garnier was so impressed by the director's raw and humorous style that he commissioned him to film a short for his 'Flashback' single. This then extended to a short film for Garnier called 'Nightmare Sandwiches', which starred Garnier on decks and featured the man's music. Through the course of the film shoots, Dupieux often told Garnier of his ambitions to create music to go with his films. Garnier encouraged him and in 1997, he delivered his first single '1' to F-Communications. It bombed. His second effort, the more dynamic 'M-Seq' fared little better. However, the self-directed video to that single did open a few doors.

A copy of the video was mailed to the ad agency dealing with Levi's non-denim range campaign. So enamoured were they with Dupieux's style that they commissioned him to film an advert for the clothing range. What Dupieux delivered, however, was beyond the pale even for Levi's. Here was a company that had sold its product through cool music and strange films for a few years. However, nothing could have prepared them for the sight of a yellow sock puppet headbanging to a driving, lo-fi techno track while sitting in the passenger seat of a Chevelle as the unamused driver observed him with a disinterested look set in stone on his face.

That puppet was called Flat Eric, the tune was called 'Flat Beats' and what followed the advert's launch was nothing short of a phenomenon. Flat Eric was merchandised, with soft toy versions of the mischievous puppet appearing everywhere. More adverts featuring the character were commissioned. Brighton based beats artist Ashley Slater even performed an autopsy on Flat Eric for the video to his single 'Cop In a Coma' as Dr Bone. The film was subsequently banned!

The knock-on effect for Mr. Oizo, the artist, was equally phenomenal. 'Flat Beats' would go on to sell over two million copies, hitting the #1 position in charts all over Europe. Not bad for a minimal techno track that was high on distortion and low on melody! The album that followed *Analogue Worms Attack* may not have had the same commercial appeal as the 'Flat Beats' single, but it did manage to benefit from the knock-on effect of the single. Thanks partly to the inclusion of 'Flat Beats' as a bonus track, the album was picked up to some extent by people who wouldn't normally buy techno records. The album's combination of humorous electronic cut-ups and TV jingles provided a hook for the uninitiated.

The album may have failed to reach similar peaks in terms of sales as 'Flat Beats' but it did represent something of a commercial revival for F Communications. Furthermore, the sounds were suitably underground for Mr. Oizo to be taken seriously by the techno fraternity. All they had to do was get past the concept of Flat Eric, which, by the time the adverts had stopped running a few months after their initial launch, had turned into one of the more annoying characters on television. Ashley Slater's autopsy was probably the kindest thing to do to the creature that certainly outlived his welcome.

Dupieux, on the other hand, proved himself to be a more than welcome addition to the global electronic music tapestry. And he continues to make films and videos (including the promo for Parisian musician Alex Gopher's 'Party People' single in 2000).

The F-Comm office of Eric Morand featured a testament to the success of Mr. Oizo, in the shape of a platinum disc set in a supremely kitsch nativity scene, all mounted in a glass presentation box. A beautifully surreal artefact to commemorate one of their most off-the-wall artists.

Throughout their entire career, both Morand and Garnier tirelessly promoted the thoughts and aesthetics of the techno underground to the greater public. And, despite their continued moves into less dancefloor orientated sounds, they were still active in this work right up until 2001 when they decided to take a step back.

"We spoke to different establishments to change their ideas on the music," Morand explains. "We met politicians and talked to a few ministers. We spoke to them, did a few TV shows, which made things change slightly. To me, this was what made us very different from the rest of the scene. We had to fight for years just to be able to say, 'I love techno'. We had to fight to have techno parties. So we've always been very active in fighting for the scene. Which makes us very different from a lot of the other labels and DJs in France. By the time people arrived in '94 -'95, things were getting accepted. We'd already done a lot of the fighting."

"I talked on a lot of TV shows because we feel that if you want the scene to develop and keep the credibility, you have to give something to get something," continues Garnier. "So we've been spending a lot of time just explaining the scene to people, fighting for the credibility of the scene.

"I have slowed down a bit now. Mainly because after ten years, the scene doesn't need to be defended any more. But also, I found that a lot of politicians liked to talk, but when it came to opening their wallets and investing in the scene, or changing the law about parties, or investing time and energy into the scene with educational stuff like the risk of taking drugs and stuff like that, then it never happened."

As the new millennium dawned, F Communications spread its creative net even wider, taking on an ever more perverse approach to its musical ideology. On the dancefloor tip, they released singles and albums by the Montpellier duo The Youngsters, whose self-titled album offered a rich and funky take on the brittle beats of electro. Parisian house producer Alexkid also delivered his stunning *Bienvenida*, which featured New York poet Ursula Rucker, Viennese downtempo producer Richard Dorfmeister and FComm label mate Readymade (who also released his superb *Bold* set of backroom lo-fi electronica, which included vocals by Japan former frontman turned avant-gardist, David Sylvian).

Other artists to deliver albums at this time included Brique Rouge label founder Ludovic Llorca whose *Newcomer* presented an obtuse yet soulful take on house, Edinburgh's *Aqua Bassino* with the jazz-funk meet Chicago house collection *Beat 'n' Bobs* and Belgium's Soul Designer with the Detroit flavoured *Walking on a Cloud*.

Clearly, F-Communications had benefited from their time in the shadow of French Touch as their roster displayed a rare depth, betraying a label that still had the pursuit of excellence at the core of their ideologies.

"A lot of labels aren't into music; they're into making money," argued Garnier. "They use marketing terms to make lots of money. So a lot of labels are more interested in signing trends. They didn't develop artists because you really have to be into what you're doing."

"Maybe it's because we've been around for a long time, but we think it's life, so we have to deal with it," continued Morand. "At the end of the day, all you have to do is have faith in what you're doing. All the fights we had setting things up back in '89, having the parties, building the label, you know we had a lot of fun, we acquired a lot of faith in what we're doing. Back in the beginning of FComm, we asked why are we doing this? Is it just because we want to bring French artists to the international market? Well, no, that wasn't it because we'd already done that with FNAC. We were doing it because we wanted to enjoy ourselves and express our visions, the things we like. If we like it and believe in it, then that's the main thing. We don't care what the other people think."

"For years, people were like 'OK Ludovic Navarre, he's cool, then suddenly in 1995 they were like 'ahhh St, Germain, he's the best'. We were like 'fine', but we knew it all along," exclaimed Garnier. "We believed the same with Mr. Oizo. At first, his first two EPs, the sales were shit. Then suddenly... bam! He took off. But we'd always had belief in him. As we do all of our artists.

"For us, the most important thing is the label and we think that when you have a successful label, with successful artists, then you also pull the scene forward," Garnier continued. "We always followed whatever we wanted to do. Never had a goal or a target beyond pleasing ourselves and being happy. We never had a game plan. That's why our first album was called *Shot in the Dark* because we didn't have a fucking clue what we were doing, really. I still think we're exploring, only now we are opening up to different kinds of media, which is all a part of growing up.

"Now that the whole house techno thing exists to the extent that it does, we're not going to be able to change things, and we are aware that house and techno had its time, but we can remain true to ourselves. Which means pushing new music. And what is house and techno but a digestion of different styles of music? So the thing is moving on.

"There's something we always try not to do as a label, and that's repeat ourselves. In the record industry, you have people who repeat the successful formula over and over. And you know what? I could knock out fifty (1997 Garnier track) Crispy Bacon's. It's not easy, but I'm sure I could do that. But what's the point of that? I couldn't do it. So we have to change, we have to move on all of the time. Which means some things are more popular than others are, but there's a saying, 'you can't make an omelette without breaking eggs.' And that's true of music. And we understand this. That's why we have to push things."

"Even though we know much more than ten years ago, we're still learning," Morand concluded, "We have to keep that freshness. We've been around for such a long time and of course, things are different now. The scene has changed totally."

In the decade following FNAC dance division's emergence, both Morand and Garnier had been the leading lights of the French electronic music scene. French dance music would certainly have been a far less attractive proposition without their unwavering tenacity. Sure, they were never the only people encouraging producers to make music. As with the rest of the techno and house scenes, the overriding influence was the sense of global community. Electronic music transcends nationality; it is a global phenomenon, of which the F Communications story is just one small part. However, Morand and Garnier managed to promote a self-belief among young French producers to succeed on the international stage.

France had been happy to produce music for international consumption for so long. Suddenly in the early 1990s, the views both within and beyond the country's borders were within people's grasp. Of course, the business infrastructure that FNAC and F Communications put into place was a major part of this wider vision. However, another story at work here was having a huge impact both musically and culturally. The story of an individual within the F Communications set up – Laurent Garnier.

LAURENT GARNIER – THE TEACHER

"Laurent Garnier is the one. The teacher."
Vitalic, 2002

Some nights of your life you never forget. They remain locked in your memory, rerunning at random, bringing back that untouchable sense of elation, that incredible *joi de vivre*. The exact date and time may have become blurred, but the actual experience is there for life, like a tattoo on the subconscious.

I can still remember the first time I heard Laurent Garnier spinning on the decks. I can still remember that feeling, the smell in the air, the sweat on my back and the dryness in my throat. It's all still there, a special memory. It was a February night in 1991. I was with a posse of ravers from Nottingham hitching a ride with the infamous DiY Soundsystem crew. There was nothing special about that; after all, it was a normal occurrence throughout that time. This trip, however, wasn't to an illegal site in the British countryside. It was to Paris for a party at premiere Parisian house and techno joint Le Boy.

Pulsing with unusual energy, the venue's heat hazed and smoke-filled air combined with a succession of mixing meltdowns to create a heady buzz that seemed intent on dragging the crowd upwards towards the glass ceiling. DiY built things to a frenzy, using the word of quality house to help transcend the language barrier until Laurent Garnier took over the decks and sent the vibe ether bound. His set was perfection, a blissed-out wander through the choice cuts of the underground – seamlessly mixed and chemically charged.

Over a decade later, Laurent Garnier's reputation as a spellbinding double-deck genius had spread to all corners of the globe. He was renowned for delivering extended sets that took you on multi-hued journeys. A dance floor trailblazer who fought the good fight in the name of techno and an experimenter who pushed the boundaries of sound with his own musical projects. If ever techno had a natural ambassador, it was Laurent Garnier.

Sitting in the sterile surroundings of London's Savoy Hotel in 2001, Laurent Garnier talks with almost childlike excitement about his introduction to music.

"When I was a kid, I was always obsessed with music," he exclaims, eyes shining in the spring sun. "I would always be listening to my Dad's hi-fi and imagining that I was making the music or whatever. Then when I saw a DJ for the first time, I knew that was what I wanted to do. So I got some decks and started doing parties for friends, which eventually led to doing a radio show. In the 80s, there were illegal radio stations everywhere in France. They were the only places where you could hear good import dance music, so they were really popular. But then the authorities really cracked down on the pirates and we had to stop. But I'd already moved on to the club scene anyway. I was very young but I was still DJing in the clubs."

When Laurent Garnier talks, he really talks. He opens his mouth and an avalanche of words tumbles out. Sentences run into phrases that in turn tumble through thoughts and ideas, with barely room for the occasional pause in between. And yet his conversation is always engaging, filled with passion, energy and absolute love of what he does. Qualities that have marked out his DJing style since his early days in Paris' gay clubs. Laurent Garnier launched his DJing career at gay club L'an-fer in Dijon and then pioneering acid house in Manchester in the late-80s as a French expatriate living and DJing.

"I feel very honoured to have been a part of those times," he says. "Especially playing at The Hacienda, which was the most important club at that time. DJing there was such an exciting buzz."

Born in Boulogne Sur Seine in February 1966, Laurent Garnier moved to London in the late-80s to take up a job as a trainee chef at the French Embassy. A job he had hoped would encourage him to improve his English and help him avoid compulsory national service.

"I was working in the catering business and if you want to do well in that business, you have to speak English," he says. "Anyway, I got offered a position at the French Embassy in London and I was told that maybe it could count as my military service. I found out later that that was a lie, so I left there to get a job in another restaurant. I got called up for the army in 1988!"

That restaurant was Tony Wilson's Dry Bar in Manchester. Given Wilson's involvement with The Hacienda, it was almost inevitable that Garnier would start hanging out in the club, getting into the house sounds being spun by Mike Pickering and Graeme Park. A sound that Park had first heard at a rare groove all-dayer in Nottingham when resident DJ Colin Curtis became the first UK DJ to play house.

During this time, Laurent was also introduced to the likes of Derrick May, Marshall Jefferson and Adonis, who he saw DJ. Suitably inspired, he decided to update the skills he'd learned as a kid and started to hassle for a DJing gig there. His eventual debut Hacienda set was drawn from the entire lexicon of contemporary dance music, incorporating Washington go-go, R&B, tech-funk and the house and techno records coming in from the US.

He immediately returned to The Hacienda following his national service, where he took up a six-month residency. He couldn't believe how much the music had changed in the year that he'd been away, a fact that only went to underline his feeling that France was lagging behind the rest of Europe culturally.

"Manchester gave me a hell of a lot," he says of his time there. "I remember you could just see this invasion of the white kids happening in front of your eyes! It was really, really funny. Before then, it had been a black club and it just changed over the course of three, maybe four weeks... So fast that we couldn't believe what we were seeing. The thing is, these rave kids were going to see the Stone Roses as much as The Stone Roses were going to the raves, and the whole thing just went off together. In fact, that was the vibe, all together. There was no VIP bars or any of that rubbish; there was a real sense of community about the whole thing. If you saw anybody you recognised from the club out... it was like a really big secret you shared."

After his six-month stint, Garnier decided to return to France. He hadn't been able to forget that sense of shock when he returned to the UK to discover how much the sound and scene had moved on, and he determined to try and push things a bit in his home country.

"When I came back to Paris in 1990, part of what I had in mind was to try and build the scene in France, but the clubs were in a really bad way then. There's actually a very long tradition of dance music in Paris. People think that the Parisians just discovered house very recently but for us, it's always been there. It was a natural progression from the disco scene. Paris was a real club capital then, and the people were very flamboyant. Transvestites everywhere – it was a really gay scene. And then it all just died."

Inevitably Garnier's interests started to extend beyond simply DJing towards actually creating the music as well. His debut release, 'Who Cares' as French Connection in 1991 on Manchester's Eastern Bloc Records, gained immediate respect from Britain's underground DJs of the time. However, with his second release as French Connection on the fledgling FNAC Dance Division label, he gained huge and voluble acclaim from media and DJs alike. This came during a time when a debate raged about whether or not DJs could make good records. Indeed with producers like The Orb, Orbital and Aphex Twin gaining huge support in all circles, DJs were increasingly accused of simply creating mixing tools to include in their own sets rather than making classic music. It's an argument that clearly still angers Garnier.

"What is this shit about whether or not DJs can make good records?" he exclaims. "It's a very English thing to say. Nobody ever questioned any of the Detroit guys about their music and those guys could DJ as well as make music better than most of the rest of the world at the time. But some people have this idea that you can only be good at one thing in life. But creativity is difficult to hold back if you have it."

Of course, it was his DJing that Garnier was best known for at this time. With the launch of Wake Up! Paris at The Rex, he really had the chance to add his own vision of the dance scene of the time. Inevitably this rubbed off on his music and with the release of the collaboration with

Shazz, 'Acid Eiffel' by Choice, his own sounds became a staple in the DJ boxes of people like Carl Cox. Garnier further refined his DJing style throughout this period, building a reputation for adrenalised sets drawn from disparate sources but hinged on the energy of techno. When Garnier and Morand launched F Communications, the DJ's blueprint style initially defined the label. The initial releases proved to be regular and worthy additions to Garnier's sets.

It wasn't until 1994 that Garnier really showed his own production prowess when he delivered his debut album, *Shot in the Dark*. An 11-track set of minimalist techno, dark trance and brooding ambience, it offered the perfect picture of the sets he was putting together as a DJ at the time. However, *Shot in the Dark* received more than its fair share of criticism, with people feeling that it was excessive in its need to present the club sounds. It was generally felt that the sound pool he was swimming in was far too narrow for the needs of an album. A criticism that Garnier himself would support when he delivered his second album, *30*.

Shot in the Dark may have been a DJ tools set, but that doesn't take away from the quality of the tracks it contains. 'Geometric World' is a contorted acid-trance monster dedicated to French hardcore DJ Manu Le Malin. It snapped at the synapses with its white heat intensity. 'Shapes Under Water' offered fizzing ambient swathes while 'Astral Dreams (Speaker Mix)' took Detroit on a wander through the darkside of Paris with its shuddering beats and rolling 303 sub basslines and crescendos that were built for the ecstasy drenched club floor. 'The Force' found Garnier repeating heavily vocodered Star Wars quotes ("may the force be with you, House force house force…") over a rumbling bassline and jittering techno beats, while standout cut 'Harmonic Groove' found scorching four to the floor beats built around discordant Japanese bells.

A year later, in 1995, Garnier was recognised by the French music industry for his work as an international DJ and producer with a growing reputation. He was awarded best new artist at the French equivalent of the Brits.

"Laurent Garnier has received a French award in 1995 Les Victoires de la Musique," explained Yann-Erik of Grenoble based Soul Shake Records to me a few weeks earlier. "Before that, the French public believed you had to use drugs if you wanted to hear this music! This award allowed everybody to hear electronic music practically without prejudice.

"Moreover, this kind of electronic music had originally come from the USA by the homosexual community and at the beginning of 90s, we had to go in homosexual clubs to listen to it. I'm not homosexual (it's important to clarify my point of view), but I think it's important to point out that it was they who introduced electronic music to France. So, after Laurent Garnier was recognised with this award, the media became interested in this music and we could hear dance music in a lot more public areas – I repeat, practically without prejudice!"

By 1996 Garnier's reputation had been rewarded with gigs at the biggest clubs in the world and appearances at major outdoor parties like Tribal Gathering. His extended DJ sets, sometimes up to seven hours, offered a sublime and inspiring journey. His skills behind the decks were subsequently captured on two compilations that year. The first and by far superior set was *Laboratoire Mix* on React, which remains one of the finest DJ mix collections ever captured thanks to the spiritual mix of classic Chicago house, hard minimal techno and a large amount of Detroit techno. Featuring a lineup of some of the underground's finest, Green Velvet, Fumiya Tanaka, Neil Llandstrumm, Robert Armani, Juan Atkins, Aux 88, Stacey Pullen, Rhythim is Rhythim – the list is endless as it is impressive. It was also a testament to Garnier's production talents that his own track, 'The Force', didn't sound out of place or inferior.

The second mix set of the year was the shorter *Mixmag Live!* release. Taking material from similar sources as the React album, what this set lacked in length, it more than made up for in sheer intense quality.

By 1997 Laurent Garnier returned to the artist album landscape with his second collection, *30*. A much more eclectic collection than *Shot in the Dark*, *30* found Garnier pushing way beyond the club floor and out to the very fringes of electronic music. From the submerged weightlessness of 'Deep Sea Diving' to the Robert Hood inspired minimalism of 'Flashback'; from the cinematic 'Le Voyage De Simone' to the deep techno of 'Crispy Bacon', *30* was an album of contrast and maturity that truly marked out the extent of Garnier's vision.

30 not only found Garnier exploring a wider range of musical possibilities but also showing a greater depth of understanding of the studio than on his earlier releases. However, much of this new depth was achieved more through accident than design. He had an unexpected break from DJing, which allowed him to experiment in the studio. Previously his DJing diary had been so demanding that a trip to the studio would leave him relying heavily on an engineer and pressured by limited time. As a result, he was rarely totally happy with the finished result. Early in 1996, however, he decided to cut back on his DJing activities, to record some music and perhaps get an old injury seen to.

"When I was younger, I damaged my shoulder pogoing to a punk record at a party in Manchester and as I got older, it started giving me a lot of discomfort," laughs Garnier. "I decided to have an operation to put it right again. But I had to take much longer off than I had previously thought."

Garnier, of course, isn't the kind of person who would waste his unexpected free time sitting around dreaming. For him, this was the perfect excuse to build his studio and learn the ins and outs of the technology. *30* was the result.

"Suddenly, I had all of this time on my hands, so I started working on the album," he confides. "It was important for me to make this album far more a part of me. *Shot in the Dark* was much more aimed straight at the dancefloor, but with *30* it had to be far more about me. Where I am now, growing up, turning thirty years old and so on. So I had to spend a lot of time learning about the equipment and just feeling my way around the tracks – making them work for me.

"The variation of styles on the album is far more indicative of my musical tastes," he continues. "At my age, I'm bound to have quite a wide taste in music. I mean, I've been into punk, disco, hip hop, house – all styles. So inevitably, my record, if it was truly saying something about me, had to be eclectic. I've had a lot of criticism about certain tracks because they're too ambient or not clubby enough. But I don't care. I'm not saying that this album is perfect. It's a statement about me now, at this moment in time. I know there's better yet to come."

Laurent Garnier is used to criticism. Some quarters of the UK press were less than positive about the release of *30*, criticising it for its obvious influences. To him, however, all criticism is worthy, unless, of course, it's obvious that the person doing the criticising hasn't made an effort to understand the full picture of what he's doing. "I've read really bad reviews about each of my records, but that's life. I've been around for a long time," he laughs.

Indeed the full picture is the most important thing to Garnier. He understands how one style of music is related to another. He sees beyond the barriers of category into the very essence; the soul of the post-acid house experience. This is why the DJ sets which followed the release of *30* found him seamlessly mixing drum & bass into his deep house and techno melting pot. This fact, unsurprisingly, brought with it massive ridicule from some circles. It has to be pointed out that, at this time, there was a huge divide between the techno and drum & bass scenes. Despite the fact that they both took inspiration from the same Detroit sources.

"Why did everyone get surprised when I played drum & bass?" he questions. "Like it was an amazing thing for me to be playing this stuff that isn't like house or techno stuff. But I've always played breakbeats as well. Back when I was at the Hacienda, I would always play the hip-house stuff and no one said it was weird then. It's not like I suddenly discovered drum & bass and thought, 'Hey, I better start playing this so I can keep popular'. That's just bullshit."

In 1997 Garnier's obvious love, knowledge and understanding of breakbeat based dance music transposed itself into the man's superb ability to pick up the finest drum & bass tunes and work them like the natural he is. In fact, it was an ability that didn't go unnoticed within London's close-knit drum & bass fraternity. He was even invited to spin to an all-star crowd at the city's legendary underground drum & bass club PM Scientists, to an overwhelmingly positive response. Furthermore, he provided a very positively received remix for the 1997 re-release of "Detroit" by Jazz Juice (aka Alex Reece and Wax Doctor), an underground classic from 1994 which fully documented the drum & bass scene's original love of the works of Juan Atkins et al.

Breaking new ground has always been the main motivation behind Garnier's musical pursuits. It's what brought him back to Paris in the early nineties. Where he could have developed himself as a household name in Britain, he instead decided to devote some of his energy into promoting house in his homeland.

In the couple of years that followed *30*, Garnier experimented with the live situation. Perhaps inspired by the acclaim his friend Ludovic Navarre was receiving for his live forays as St. Germain (the show got decidedly better after that ill feted London show), he went on the road with live jazz musicians in tow. The results were hit and miss at first, with Garnier struggling to find a true voice within this new set-up. However, he gradually adapted and soon he started to work on new material with the live band included.

"With the live thing – it's more organic," he says. "You're moving with other people. When you're DJing, it's a different world – you're just up there on your own. With a band, if you're not getting on together the crowd feel it straight away. So, what do I prefer DJing or playing live? Well, that's a difficult question to answer. If we're comparing a real, really good live show with a DJ set… the answer would have to be the live show because it's your own music. What it lacks is the feedback and communication that happens with DJing, where you can change direction and talk with the crowd.

"The thing I don't really understand is that when you play live and the machine fucks up, it's considered to be my fault,." he continues. "This hit home for me when I saw Daft Punk play and one of their machines broke down – everybody slagged them, I got really pissed off with that because if you're going to see an electronic act and don't have a fucking clue about the way things work, you shouldn't go out! Everybody's computer at home has crashed at some point, so people should understand. If you're a DJ and the mixer breaks down? It's not your fault."

In 2000 the fruits of his live labour, breakdowns and all, were released in the astounding set *Unreasonable Behaviour*. Drawing heavily on the ever-present influence of those 80s jazz-funk sounds that he'd originally started DJing with his post-teens discovery Detroit techno, *Unreasonable Behaviour* found him wandering through evocative electronic jazz noir, dislocated techno stylings and emotive jazz ambience. A far more idiosyncratic set than his previous albums, it featured only a few dancefloor tracks on the CD version – although the vinyl came with different versions of the tracks that were more club-centric.

Standout cuts included the bruising tech funk of 'The Sound of the Big Babou' and the abrasive shuffle, modulating synths and screaming saxophone of 'The Man with the Red Face'. While swinging electro groove of 'Communications from the Lab' and the fuzzy distorted sonics of the contorted jazz-fusion cut 'City Sphere' offer Garnier's tech-soul moods at their most expansive. 'Last Tribute from the 20th Century' is perhaps more indicative of the overall mood of the album. Its pulsing bassline playing counterpoint with sombre synth strings and distant flutes as a lone voice offers tribute to "New York, Detroit and Chicago – with much respect." Quite beautiful.

"This album has a lot more emotion in it than my previous ones," he says. "It has got three or four strong dancefloor-orientated tracks, then there are the ones based on more filmic themes, which is something I want to explore more. There were a lot of tracks that didn't make it onto the album in the end. They were really hard to put together to create the right sense of mood, to get any kind of comprehension. It's like a DJ set – it's so important to give these tracks a sense of light and shade. Here it's different, though… with a DJ set, it changes completely depending on feedback from the crowd; when they go home at the end of the night, there is nothing left. With an album, it is a completely different story – it will be listened to in a lot of different places rather than the dance floor."

One of the album's key tracks is 'The Man With The Red Face'. However, at the time of its release, it caused some consternation as to what exactly the title referred to. Laurent's answer was more obvious than anyone expected.

"'The Man With The Red Face' was called that because my saxophonist was working so hard his face was really red! Sometimes you create a tack and it's really difficult to give the track the name it should have; you've got to try and mix it up with the images you've got in your head while you're creating the music. Sometimes the most literal ones are the most appropriate. It's like when I was recording the B-side to 'The Sound of the Big Babou'; the drummer was hitting his drums so hard he got a blister. The track was the called 'Sore Fingers', of course."

And of the album's title?

"I think this world is pretty unreasonably behaved," he says. "There's too many people starting wars and hatred and not really understanding anything about anything – just being really stupid, especially in France. We're now the most corrupt nation in Europe – we even beat Italy. They all come from the same school, they're all scratching each other's backs… and they all know the dirt about each other, so no one will tell."

A few months after its release, *Unreasonable Behaviour* was reissued with an extra live performance CD. This version provided an insight into how Laurent had worked with the musicians to create the studio album, and, although it is not his best work, the live set is an interesting artefact. Constantly evolving exploring endless avenues in the electronica sphere Garnier's music embodies the ideology that drove F-Communications, where quality is a way of life.

"F-Communications is intended to a be a label for quality music," Garnier agrees. "Not just house or techno, but quality dance-related stuff. I'm the same. My music doesn't have barriers apart from the ones I put there. Sometimes this open-minded approach causes problems with people but I don't care. At the end of the day, we're putting out quality stuff, developing our artists – which is very rare for dance labels – and staying true to what we believe in. And I'm doing the same with my own records. Staying true to what I believe."

It's an ideology that could sum up the career of Laurent Garnier – staying true to what he believes in. Today he believes in his vision as passionately as he did all those years back, listening to his parents' records, DJing on pirate radio, and then later spinning records at 'L'an-fer in Dijon, The Hacienda in Manchester and The Rex in Paris.

"The thing is with Laurent, he is always moving on from what people know him for," adds Morand, who briefly joins us for orange juice and conversation at the end of the interview. "And people still want the stuff before because they have to discover the new music for themselves. *30* was different to his techno twelves, and people still asked about early tracks. The last *Unreasonable Behaviour* was different again, but then people had caught up with *30*. He's a musician that likes to move on."

"But people still want the old tunes," adds Laurent. "Last night, I had kids asking for 'Crispy Bacon'. People don't ask me for the new stuff, but in five years, they'll be asking me for 'Dangerous Drive' or 'Man With the Red Face'."

Since this interview, Garnier has steadily moved away from club orientated music. His 2005 album *The Cloud Making Machine* was a conceptual home listening techno album, while the 2009 set *Tales of a Kleptomaniac* found him exploring a myriad of styles to startling effect. He has moved more deeply into soundtrack work as well as becoming an author with his autobiography *Electrochoc* providing his unique perspective on his life in music and the music of his life. In 2021 he teamed up with downtempo breaks act Liminanas to create the wonderful *De Pelicula* album that offered a collision of vintage ambience, languid breaks, analogue punk and frayed techno.

HOLLOW VICTORY –
RAVE CULTURE AND THE TECHNO PARADE

"The French society is very castrating, inhibiting and paternalistic. So are the French politicians and laws. Previous generations hated youth and didn't want people to have fun, to enjoy life and to express themselves with new art forms. So even if the authorities are officially saying that it's possible to organise raves and parties, they have put so much legal, technical or safety obstacles in the way that, in practice, only huge commercial events put by well-established traditional promoters are possible. The main obstacle being the need to obtain the necessary authorisation from the local politicians and officials.

"It's a contradiction of the whole idea and spirit of raves (and of youth!). Of course, a lot of raves and free parties are organised but they are illegal. In the last years, they have been severely suppressed, with CRS (French infamous riot police) devastating or confiscating equipment and records, beating everybody, and putting in jail not only promoters but also punters if found in possession of drugs." Christophe Monier (Micronauts), 2002

The rapid growth of the free parties in France took the authorities by surprise. Just as with England at the time, the power of word of mouth quickly became apparent as parties grew from the initial few hundred regular faces to crowds numbering in their thousands. In the UK, the government's reaction to the illegal raves was to very quickly impose laws against aspects of rave culture. The first stage of this came with Graham Swift's relatively quick Entertainment (Increased Penalties) Bill. Aimed at the heartland of the rave, the Bill raised the maximum fine for unlicensed parties from £2,000 to £20,000 and six months imprisonment. This would be followed by the Criminal Justice Act in 1994, which outlawed everything from convoys of cars to collecting together in groups and dancing in public to music with 'repetitive beats'.

In France, the reaction from the authorities initially seemed to be less oppressive. Raves were occurring throughout France, especially in the south and west, and as they grew, so too did the hype that surrounded them. With the overpowering police presence and increasingly commercialised rave scene in the UK, many British based DJs and soundsystems saw France as a utopian environment for free parties. Indeed by 1992, France's rave scene was the closest to the original ideology behind the scene. No wonder techno free party activists Spiral Tribe decamped from their native England to the rave friendly environment of France. So too did Bristol band and soundsystem The Moonflowers. Again in search of the original free party atmosphere.

What they found was a country on the brink of draconian police measures against a rave scene seemingly hell-bent on standing up for their rights. In truth, however, only a handful of ravers were prepared to stand up against the authorities. The French public's almost overbearing sense of apathy blunted any weapon of opposition that the ravers may have had.

By 1993 the French Riot police (CRS) were regular visitors to the raves, breaking up the parties with extreme physicality. And they had the general public behind them as techno and house had been promoted in the wider media as drug music. In an attempt to get around these actions, Laurent Garnier and Coda Magazine joined forces in 1993 to put on the Oz rave in Amien. Permission was given and the organisers set to work putting together the bill and sorting out the amenities for the expected 15,000 people. Then only two weeks before the event was supposed to occur, the local authority banned the party. As there were no anti-rave laws in place that they could use against the parties, they used a public order law instead. All of the promoters, Garnier included, lost a fortune.

In reaction to this and many other events that were closed down, Spiral Tribe instead put on an illegal rave. The net result of this event was that illegal raves grew even faster as a few free party promoters stood defiant against the authorities. As far as they were concerned, the message was clear. They had no intention of giving up their rights to party. However, the government had different ideas, and in 1995 they outlawed all big illegal raves.

In 1996 many of the leading names in the techno movement joined forces to create Technopol, a forum for disseminating information about techno culture and creating a dialogue with the government. Members of Technopol included Christophe Vix, who had been the director of Radio FG in its earliest days. Other key figures were Eric Morand and Lauraunt Garnier. Technopol was created after the Polaris rave in Montpellier was closed. The main factor in the closure of this rave was the production of a dossier by the government that condemned both raves and the music. The dossier was sent out to all of the regional prefects and mayors. They, in turn, awarded the police the absolute power to stop the one-off parties and arrest anyone under suspicion of either being involved with drug use or being involved in the promotion of drug use. They were also given to authority to detain party organisers, DJs or even the musicians themselves simply for being involved in a scene that seemed to condone drug use.

Any suggestion that people should publicly speak out against the police would have been silenced by the draconian measures brought against French rap outfit NTM at this time. They had earned themselves a spell in prison for condemning police action while on stage.

"Music is political," stated Daft Punk's Guy-Manuel de Homen-Christo in 1999. "And the French techno scene was forced to see this."

Certainly, events like a small techno-trance party in Bordeaux in 1995 acted as a short sharp shock to anyone hoping to rediscover the summer of love in France. When 300 revellers started up the party motors, approximately 400 CRS descended upon the scene in a hard-hitting act of zero-tolerance.

"We had a dialogue with the Minister of Culture to try and find a solution because there was a big report saying that raves were very risky... they were also denouncing media like *Liberation* for giving out the information for raves," explained Arnaud Frisch of UWe in 2002. "Technopol started a few wheels in motion, but it took a long time a lot of work. With the socialist government of 1997, things got better, though."

The government change brought with it a body of people who were far more tolerant of the party culture. Among them was Minister of Culture Jack Lang, who gave public support to the arena of electronic music and techno parties, suggesting that these were areas in which people enjoyed themselves without prejudice. He also condoned raves as being places where people could escape from the pressures of everyday life without harming anyone. Enlightened perhaps, but they proved to be very unpopular words with the French public, who were still anti-drug music. Furthermore, Lang and his cohorts didn't have the government's full support, which created quite a lot of confusion.

"It was very strange here because we had the cultural minister encouraging rap and dance music but then you had government policies directly opposed to those styles," explained Daft Punk's Thomas Bangalter when I interviewed Daft Punk on the strength of their demo – a tape that I passed on to people from Soma, among others. "Music like rap comes from the suburbs where people are unhappy about their lives, they're unhappy about the police. So they rap about them. Then they are arrested. For the French police, the rave parties are very difficult to understand. This country is all into vocal music. We don't have all of the different little subcultures that you have in Britain, so with the one-off dance parties, the police just saw them in terms of drugs. And that scared them."

Despite the public and police opposition, the government agreed in 1998 to allow Technopol to stage a huge party right in the middle of Paris. The Paris Techno Parade was the culmination of all the talks between Technopol and the government. It seemed to give the scene, and the entire industry infrastructure set up around it, some legal credibility and seemingly opened the way for the culture to be recognised by the general public. However, despite government support from the Minister of the Interior, the event was still put in jeopardy by Paris' Mayor, who tried to ban it.

"The first Technoparade in 1998 was very difficult to put together because the mayor of Paris didn't want it to happen," explained Arnaud Frisch, who was heavily involved in the organisation of the first two Technoparade events. "But she failed because the government wanted it to happen. It was very hard to organise, but after the success of the Technoparade which got 200,000 people from all over France, people were very positive. And we had a better relationship with the Minister of the Interior.

"The Technoparade in 1998 ended with a big party at Place du Nation with Manu Le Malin, Laurent Garnier, Carl Cox, Kojak. It was very huge – like rock 'n' roll years before but very symbolic of the new culture now being accepted. All the media were saying, 'look, it's not only people taking drugs, it's people enjoying themselves'. It was at that time that the media started being very, very positive."

One of the most successful aspects of Technoparade was an associated festival of electronic culture called Rendezvous Electronique. Here a wider public had the chance to experience the works of artists, designers and so on. It was an attempt to show an entire culture at work, not just the desire to party.

A year later, the second Technoparade saw an attempt to assimilate the organisation of the big raves into the structure of the street party. Instead of finishing with one stage at a huge party in the centre of Paris, they decided to hold the finale at a park with 30 trucks featuring different soundsystems. It was an event that proved to be the last for UWe and friends, who felt that the event had already been taken over by ego and commercialisation.

"It was more like a Teknival in Paris," said Frisch. "There were thirty soundsystems and people were going from one to the other. It was a really good thing but we ended our involvement with it after that one. Even after only two, the Technoparade became a huge production, it became something that had to happen every year, which was less interesting. The first one was very interesting because techno was demonised. The media only talked about drugs, but after The Technoparade, we won recognition through people working together.

"But the second one was already like people trying to get something for themselves and not the event. It was not such a good spirit. Also, we spent so much time trying to find money to finance the Technoparade that we didn't spend enough time gathering together the scene. I think now many people think that the Technoparade shouldn't happen anymore because the main artists aren't in the Technoparade any longer. So I think many people think it doesn't bring anything to techno anymore."

300,000 people at the Technoparade that year felt differently, and the event found itself becoming a tradition in Paris. One of France's most respected techno DJs, Manu Le Malin, was one of the biggest attractions at the event.

MANU LE MALIN – THE TECHNO TERRORIST

"I am a raver. I insist on that term. A lot of people use terms like free party or techno party now, but I insist on rave. I am proud to be a raver because it saved me from a lot of bad things."

Manu Le Malin, 2002

Manu Le Malin was considered one of the elder statesmen of the French free party scene. Back in 2002, when we met for this interview, he was 32 years old. His work in the hardcore arena, both as a DJ and a producer, had marked him out as a rare and unusual talent. Beyond the rave, he'd already provided uncompromising soundtracks to the 'y a un os' cartoon series on French cable channel Canal Plus. In 2002 he also collaborated with composer Rene Koering to create a stunning piece of neo-classical hardcore. Manu's sonic manifesto was to take his vision into unchartered territories wherever and whenever he could.

Sitting in the kitchen of France's Uncivilised World Entertainment (UWe) collective headquarters, Manu was every inch the old school free party raver. His dark lank hair framed the tribal tattoo that curled from the nape of his neck down his arms. His grin belied his passion while his eyes shone with a look of unbridled intensity like a man possessed. His conversation was continually punctuated by fidgeting, tapping fingers and darting looks. He was a ball of energy. A bomb that could have been detonated by crime at an early age but instead found a focus through the rave movement.

Chatting with Manu on that cold December afternoon, it was easy to get a sense of the man behind the hardcore DJ myth. His passion was rarely below the surface, whether through his continuous proclamations of his love for the music he was involved with or through the out and out dismay he felt at the government's attitudes towards his people, the ravers. One had a continual sense that the Joker-esque grin could quickly turn on you if you were to insult his family or friends. He had a street fighter's gaze.

At that time, his passion was fuelled by the presence of hardcore legend and long-time friend Lenny Dee who was in Paris to talk business with the UWe crew. If Lenny was a godfather of the global rave family, then Manu Le Malin was his natural right-hand man.

"I first started DJing maybe ten years ago," said Manu as his hands swept through his hair before returning to their tabletop tapping. "My first rave was in 1992 and I bought turntables and records right after. Before this, I was kind of a rude boy. I had my scooter, got all my Trojan tattoos. So I was more into rocksteady and ska than anything, then I heard this rave music and the atmosphere just blew me away."

Arriving on the scene in 1992 meant that Manu had missed the early days of acid house. However, he immediately felt in tune with the hardcore sound that was emanating from the UK and the techno coming from Holland and Germany at the time. He also felt an affinity with the early Goa trance sounds of labels like Hardhouse.

"I was into hardcore right away but I also got into Goa trance," he confirmed. "Every week, I would go to one or the other style of rave. I liked Goa because it was not quite so cliched like it is now. The music was a little bit harder than it is now. In Paris, we didn't have any separation between the different sounds. Hardcore people would go partying with Goa people. Everybody was just having fun. That was the perfect thing about the raves; it was house to hardcore."

This open-minded attitude amongst Manu and his peers revealed an aesthetic that was to help the country become such a leading force in the late-90s. Far from the gaze of the rest of the world, the early French ravers had a very militant, underground stance. It was as if they were isolated by their geography and culture from the rest of the world and the weekly shifts on the dance culture elsewhere had less impact. Here among the French rave scene, there was still that true underground self-belief and togetherness that marked out the original house parties in the UK before they became quickly dissipated by media obsession with the latest thing.

Soon after going to his first rave, Manu Le Malin secured his first DJ break. It was typical of the man's energy that he immersed himself so deeply in the culture that within weeks he'd put together a set that could challenge even the biggest names in the world of techno.

"I started to DJ real quick," he confirmed. "My first party was a big party in this big location in Paris called Tribal Music. It was an all-night party on a Friday night and we had 4,000 people. I was the last DJ and I remember the guys coming up to me and telling me to stop, and I was like 'no' I'm playing on'."

The look in his eyes made it clear he wouldn't have stopped playing for anyone. It was a hyperactive or obsessive behaviour pattern that was to bring him major trouble with the police later in his career. Inevitably when it came to the government clampdown on raving, Manu was still in the thick of it, fighting for his cause.

"We started to get trouble with the government really quick," he exclaims. "In '94, it was like a witch hunt. I got arrested several times just at the entry of the rave or even at the airport. The government wrote a dossier on the rave parties and sent it to every mayor and prefect in the country. They were told that if they had any suspicion that a little party was attracting people from outside locations, whether it was a birthday party, or whatever, just don't trust them because it will definitely be a techno party which means a drug addicts party. So everywhere in the country, people were given the power to shut down any party they wanted shut.

"Laurent Garnier was organising the biggest party in France ever, it was in the style of Tribal Gathering, big tents, different rooms. And the party got cancelled just before by the local authorities. Laurent lost a lot of money. After this, it was just a nightmare. It just pushed everyone under-ground. Everybody started organising free parties. There was a free party info line to call. You had to drive for hours to get to the party because cops were always chasing us. And it was like this for three years, then suddenly police pressure just stopped. This lasted for five years until now [2002], when it's worse than ever. I don't know why.

"The thing is young people don't accept that club dictatorship any-more," he continued. "They don't want to stand around and get drunk. They want to go to raves and have a good time with a big soundsystem, and see DJs from all over the world. But this worries the authorities that want to control people more. So they starting the same fucking argument against raves again."

With the continued struggle for the rave generation to hold their parties, it was almost inevitable that some events became legendary. The parties underneath Pont de Tolbiac were talked about continuously, however.

"A big party for me," he exclaimed. "One which was underneath the Tolbiac Bridge in Paris in 1997. These parties really pushed me upfront because I was the one who organised it. Well, not exactly organised, but I was the one who brought the energy and purpose to it. I would play every weekend. Even if I was booked to play somewhere else, I'd get the first flight back to play under the bridge.

"We used to organise the most freak dog acid parties under there. Almost every weekend with the guys from Technotrance. We didn't get permission, just brought a soundsystem in. So we started with 50 people and then all of the sudden it went too far, you know the score, it goes to 400 people. Then the last one we had, there were all these cops everywhere. I was playing and I got told to stop the music but people went crazy shouting 'Manu one more, one more!' So I played another one and I got beaten by the cops."

When Manu's people call, he is compelled to deliver. It's been the same since his earliest days behind the decks. Through this attitude, he and his closest friends had a mission to bring the best parties to the strangest venues. A trademark of the free party movement. One such series of parties took place in Paris' numerous mushroom farms. Quite literally, they went underground!

"My friend did a rave in '92 called 'Zombie Rave No Limit' in a mushroom farm; it's like a place under fields where they grow mushrooms. We have a lot of places like this in Paris and at the time there were a lot of parties in these places. It was crazy. Totally from hardcore to house to Goa."

In 1993 Manu left France for Holland. He had grown dejected with his home scene, feeling that it had become very safe and to use his term, 'cliched'. With the extreme sound of gabba soundtracking the Dutch raves it was perhaps the obvious destination for him.

"For me, everything went really quick," he said. "I was more into the trance-core things, so I was playing faster than normal DJs and I was a little bit of melody. This was '93–'94, so it definitely was not the trance-core years in England. Then it all went harder and darker and I thought it was getting a little too cliched, so I went to Holland and discovered the big, big, huge sound of hardcore and gabba. Again, at that time, it was different than it is now.

"As a raver, I was in this big party in Utrecht. At this time, I was doing records with Lenny Dee and he was playing this really hardcore techno, no clichés, no pop song, just hard, ruff, slow but so big. I got a big crush on this kind of music, so I went back to France with this music and totally changed my direction. I don't know if I was bringing a new sound, but the way I was mixing was different. I really touch the records all of the time, touch the EQ – I just can't stay behind the decks and play records. I have to play the decks as well."

Soon after returning to France, he was booked to play an aftershow party in Switzerland. It was to prove to be his first real break.

"In '94, I was booked to play the after party of NRG in Zurich, Switzerland. The organiser was running around the party and he saw me and said 'Manu are you ready to play?' It was 3am, and there were 15,000 people. But the main DJ had missed his flight, or his records hadn't turned up. I think it was the Belgian guy, Robert Leiner. So he said, have you got your records with you?' I did and five minutes later, I was playing in front of a huge crowd. It was so cool, 'cos I was only supposed to be playing the aftershow party! So here I was by accident playing in the main hall at 3am and it worked. After this, I was booked to play in Switzerland every weekend after that."

It was inevitable that Manu would start to create his own productions. He had developed a unique DJ style, but he had yet to translate this to vinyl. This all changed when, in 1995, he delivered his first single on I.S.T., the experimental trance sub-division of Lenny Dee's Industrial Strength imprint. The single was rumoured to have been engineered by Daft Punk's Thomas Bangalter.

"I did something with Daft Punk in the old days," he said enigmatically. "We were friends. There is a rumour that Thomas Bangalter worked on my first record, but that was just a rumour. Some rumours become legend because... can you imagine a meeting between Daft Punk and Le Malin? It's inconceivable for many people. But I know Thomas, I like him and respect him."

The debut single was called 'Memory' and it perfectly summed up Manu's DJ sound of the time. Pounding but fluid, with a lot of noise – from frequency snatches to strafing distortion.

"At this point, I was listening to a lot of the early Industrial Strength stuff and early Underground Resistance," he explained. "Because for me, the roots of hardcore are in Underground Resistance. It was the atmosphere. I also liked some of the Belgian stuff, but they lost it real quick. I also really like PCP, Caustic Vision. I also started to discover Aphex Twin. All these people really influenced me to discover older records to create my own vision of the culture. For me, I'm from the second generation of rave because it had been in France for two years before I went to a rave. In '91 there were big parties with LFO and I missed that one. Things go really quick in this scene and I'd already missed so much, so I had to discover what had gone before."

Manu released numerous singles both for major labels like BMG France ('Da Trojan Mob' with El Doctor) and Sony Germany ('Let it Grow'), while also delivering vinyl through the underground network of labels like Industrial Strength ('War Dancer' under the pseudonym Manga Corps, 'Three Bad Brothers' with regular collaborators Torgull and El Doctor etc), Omnisonus France ('No Justice') and, of course, his own label Bloc 46 which he launched in 1997 with Torgull. The Bloc 46 lorry was subsequently a huge presence at the first Techno Parade in Paris in '98. Laurent Garnier, Carl Cox and Fréon were the guests.

The Techno Parade came to be something of a disappointment to Manu. Over the years, he and his friends had fought so hard to have their kind of music and lifestyle recognised. It's a fight that has brought many producers global acceptance while on a local level, it created a business infrastructure that is effective, extensive and interactive. The free-party people of old have organised into a fighting force of globally distributed labels, large events promoters, media orchestrators and political pioneers. Manu himself extended his role to include the programming of the hardcore tents at the largest raves in France, Astroplis (for which he released a mix album 'Il Etait Une Fois 1995-2000') and Boréalis in Montpelier.

Naturally, Manu had hoped that the first Technoparade would be the beginning of a new understanding between ravers and the authorities. As with his associates at UWe, and many other techno artists, the reality represented a hollow victory. The draconian outlawing of raves elsewhere in France, coupled with the increased commercialisation of the Techno Parade, meant that he and his people had become sidelined once again.

"Now we have the Techno Parade. It looks like techno has been accepted by everyone, but suddenly there are some fucking very bad ghosts. We received a paper for organising parties in the east of France. The mayor of one city just said 'we don't like these kind of parties, they're for dealers and fucked up people', same fucking words that they used six or seven years ago, and I mean, yeah there fucking drugs in raves, no doubt about it, but they're everywhere. You want me to take you out on the street? I'll get you anything you want.

Towards the end of 2002, Manu Le Malin finally released his debut album, *Fighting Spirit*. A 22 song strong double CD set, it features collaborations with Lenny Dee, DJ Producer, Torgull and Dee Nasty, and it's as uncompromising a piece of work as you're likely to hear.

Fighting Spirit found Manu moving away from the hardcore beats of his 12"s into dark ambient territories. An album of discordant layers, white noise distortion and machine drones, it pulled on the influence of industrial techno acts like Skinny Puppy and Greater Than One (aka GTO) as much as it hinted at the perverse sonic wanderings of Aphex Twin. Furthermore, the album displayed structures that owed more to the music of Stockhausen than the hardcore uproar. Thus displaying Manu Le Malin as owning a production talent that stretches way beyond the dancefloor's needs.

He introduces a freeform jazz aesthetic to the techno landscape on 'Conversations'. The result was a bruising onslaught of fractured symphonic drum & bass. 'Green Bison', the Lenny Dee collaboration, offers the sound of footsteps beating out a rhythm on concrete, echoing in the darkness. 'Swamp' found depth charges dropping into the murky waters of techno noir where spiralling strings adopt the calculations of system music over the sound of knives sharpening. 'Share My Wings' is far more direct, coming on like a rave cut and going out like metal fatigue, while 'Break Syndrome' delivers a horror soundtrack to the accompaniment of beats that fly like bullets. Ironically it represents the most obviously structured track on this collection of uncomfortably obtuse sounds.

The classical elements of *Fighting Spirit* were first hinted at in 2000 when Manu collaborated with one of Europe's most respected classical composers Rene Koering. The concept was to create a symphonic piece that combined philharmonic elements with electronic music. The work would then be performed in public.

Manu was barely able to contain his excitement at the memory of the event:

"The orchestral thing was a fucking huge experience," he exclaimed. "We had a major festival called Boréalis in the south of France and I was the only hardcore DJ there, but I was the only resident because I've played every time. Each time I try to make it special but in 2000 they asked me to programme a full lineup. So I got one of my favourite people, DJ Producer from England, but still wanted something special.

"Those guys from Boréalis knew Rene Koering, who is this very important classical composer. They knew he was looking for someone to do something with him for an orchestra. But he wasn't looking for a house musician; he wanted something less polished. So he wanted something intense, so they suggested me. I met the guy and he wanted to do a DJ set with an orchestra. So I had to explain to him that I couldn't do the same DJ set every time. Even if I try my hardest, I just can't do it, so I suggested doing my own music with my man Torgull. Who has been there with me from the beginning."

The process involved Manu and Torgull stepping out of their studios onto the live stage for the first time in their careers. Furthermore, in order to work within the strict confines of the classical medium, they had to score the entire piece. A far cry from DJing at an illegal rave with Spiral Tribe.

"We'd never done a live act, so we brought our machines out of the studio and composed a track at the opera," confirmed Manu. "Then he asked us to bring some music to him and he liked it. So he asked for all of the discs and a score of every note. We were like, 'whoa OK.' So we had to transcribe it all onto paper, which took time. Then we went to Opera Berlioz in Montpellier where we practised with l'Orchestre National de Montpellier Languedoc-Roussillon every day for a week, which was hard as well because this was so different from DJing. We had 92 guys on stage playing strings, horns, and percussion. It was quite an experiment.

"I'd like to do it again, Rene Koering too, but it can take a long time. We don't wanna do exactly the same again. We wanna do the same parts but longer and reworked. Because it was the first time we'd done this, I think we missed some points."

With a DVD of the performance, it is clear to see why Manu is keen to explore the concept further. The piece is a brilliant exercise in tension and space, with the symphonic elements of the orchestra winding around the electronic parts and taking an ever-tighter grip until collapse seems inevitable. On the point of no return, the ambience loosens and air rushes in, only amplifying the underlying friction that has been slowly at work throughout.

"This was the biggest orchestra ever to work with an electronic music DJ," he concluded. "I'd never before stepped into an opera and here I was bringing some hard beats to them. I just thought this isn't happening. But it was."

He may not have been one of the darlings of the dance media, but Manu Le Malin had been there all along, staking his claim on the electronic music landscape.

RAVE'S LAST STAND...
SPIRAL TRIBE VS THE MINISTER OF THE INTERIOR

As the millennium came to a close, techno parties seemed to have taken an irreversible step into France's greater culture. However, with the new year came a new government and things quickly turned sour with new laws being introduced to close down raves for good.

"In summer 2001, the Deputy banned legal raves and large size soundsystems completely," says Frisch. "We had a festival that summer called Astropolis, it was the biggest festival of electronic music and arts. But the Mayor of Avignon banned the festival. We went to court to fight the decision and they decided that it was OK to happen. But this was just one week before, so it was impossible to organise it."

A year later, the government took the most extreme measures yet in their attempts to outlaw rave culture for good. They created blockades on the roads to stop traffic getting to the party site for Teknival. Strangely the event was being held on the Italian side of the border!

"It gathered many people together and the media didn't understand why it was possible to have a rave in Italy, which is not very open, so they said that the government was too tough with rave parties," says Frisch. "What they did in Italy was get all of the media involved, so the government couldn't ban it, But they took the decision to block the roads, and the television showed images of policemen hitting the cars with batons. This shocked many people. They wanted to know why this was happening. They had no right to block the border. We have rights, you know."

Skirmishes between the ravers and the French police erupted high in the Alps, on the Alpine pass east of Gap. Central to the government stand was the newly appointed Minister for the Interior, Nicolas Sarkozy, who was determined to go down in history as the man to restore law and order to France.

Throughout the summer of 2002, he introduced draconian policies, including a circular ordering an unbending enforcement of a new law introduced by the previous government, which banned unauthorised raves. The Mariani Law was actually brought in as an environmental act – to protect the countryside!

Of the opposition, one of the most vocal was Spiral Tribe DJ Allan Blinkhorn, who had moved to France from England to escape the Criminal Justice Bill and Thatcherism a decade earlier. Talking to The Independent in August 2002, he said:

"I have been to the Elysee. I have been to Matignon (the seats of the French President and Prime Minister respectively). I have been involved in negotiations for months now with various parts of the French State.

"Sometimes, the last government would talk to us reasonably. Sometimes they wouldn't but this new government will not talk to us sensibly at all. Their attitude is against youth, against liberty. They want to commit genocide on the rave movement."

One of the major bones of contention between Blinkhorn et al., and Sarkozy had been the suggestion that parties could only go ahead if chairs were provided for everyone!

"We are not against the principles of advanced permission for raves and guarantees of security or whatever, but they have to talk sense to us," continued Blinkhorn, who only a few weeks earlier had been placed under criminal investigation for 'furthering the use of illegal drugs'. The only evidence against him being the fact that he was a known party organiser. "We are now told that, if 20,000 people are expected on a site, we have to provide 20,000 chairs. Chairs at a rave? Be serious."

Among Blinkhorn's tactics for defying the government was the organisation of "500 kilometres of *bouchons*" (traffic jams), an idea borrowed from the farmers. In the event, only a few cars turned up to help create the jams.

Despite Blinkhorn's failures in talks with the government, a committee was set up to discuss possible ways forward. The intention of this committee was to create a dialogue between organisers and government; however, this may well be Sarkozy's greatest victory. In creating a forum for discussion, the main promoters and organisers have been placated. With the illusion that things are in the process of change, they are scared of going against the government and putting on parties for fear of these talks collapsing.

"The group includes Technopol, members of the underground scene and politicians," says Frisch. "We have a dialogue but nothing has come of it yet. Often these things are just put into place to keep people happy. Let them think things are changing, so they don't talk to the press. Basically, the government doesn't like people coming together and dancing till 8am; they don't like alternative culture."

A major reason used by the government for the need to crack down on raves is the fear of terrorist attacks in the post-September 11 era. The first victim in Paris was that years Technoparade which was to have been held a week after the World Trade Centre tragedy. However, everything was cancelled in the French capital. Following this, they cancelled anything that went against their cultural ideals. In effect, they used September 11 as a smokescreen

"For the moment, after September 11, everything is tough," explains Frisch. "It's not only techno that's restricted here; the French government are very tough on squats, alternative culture, prostitutes, anything that is considered to not be a good way. And techno is seen as a part of that."

However, the Mariani Law wasn't seen as a bad thing by everyone involved in the dance scene. Some welcomed it, as, in truth, the raves had become playgrounds for kids who had little respect for either the land they were partying on or the people organising the events. Their sole intention was to get stoned.

"There was a really bad attitude from the young ravers in France, not caring about things," says Frisch. "People organising parties found that the public didn't care about things. The media interest brought people in that didn't even like the music. The thing is, you'd get the free parties being talked about on television all through the summer. They'd be saying, there's going to be a free party in South of France, we don't know where yet, but we'll let you know."

"I think that a part of the electronic scene in France doesn't want things to change," adds Laurent Garnier. "I am critical of the techno scene because they are very happy with the way things are. When you see these things, after a while, you have to say, I'm just part of the scene, not all of the scene. I just bring my own vision. That's true for both of us."

Olivier Pillet of leading Lyon house label Superhuit takes the anti-rave debate even further by suggesting that the huge party aesthetic has no place in today's society because it is no longer an underground force but a commercial product.

"Free parties are prohibited and it's a good thing because there are a lot of rules in respect to others. The most important thing in a musical movement is expression, so you have to listen. But now, raves are specially made for fun. Today raves have no relevance because this music takes place in society."

The Teknoparade in 2002 drew only a fraction of the previous year's crowds. Many of the original ravers felt that it had outgrown its use, while others had simply lost interest. In the face of such legal opposition, it may be true that the rave scene had been forced underground, but the truth may also be that the ravers no longer have a powerful voice in today's society. They are out of touch with the youth. So rave parties may have collapsed without government intervention, simply the natural cycle of pop culture.

If the rave era provided the techno and free party scenes with anything, it was the creation of a strong and self-sufficient infrastructure. Every aspect of the culture from conception to production was achieved by a scene that developed at its own pace, in the face of government and public opposition. It is true that Eric Morand and Laurent Garnier created the foundations, but it was with other labels that the free party aesthetic grew.

Perhaps the finest example of this self-sufficiency came with the creation of Uncivilised World Entertainment (UWe) in 2000. UWe was a collective that brought together artist and label management and underground party promotion under one banner. The collective was put together by Antoine Kraft, Laurent Ho and Arnaud Frisch following their involvement with the first two Techno Parades in Paris. After the second Techno Parade, they resigned from the organisational committee, while Kraft stood down from his considerable involvement with Technopol.

The UWe umbrella covered a wide range of styles, from the dark techno of Laurent Ho's Epiteth to the industrial noise of the UW imprint. Other labels represented included jungle imprint Woody Stuff, techno labels ANLX and Gazole, downtempo division Opulsion and house label Bossley Records. Also included in the collective was the mix CD imprint Human and Manu Le Malin, Torgull and El Doctor's Bloc 46 label, which specialised in hardcore and hard techno.

Although the resilience of the French techno scene was echoed in other parts of Europe and America, it is arguable that, despite the global coverage gained by French Touch in the late 90s, the true sound of the French dance underground was represented by UWe. Through many of the individuals represented by this collective, the underground party scene was able to flourish to the extent that they could boast the biggest rave parties in Europe.

MEANWHILE... SOMETHING WAS BREWING IN PARIS' BACKROOMS

As the rave wars raged, a small revolution was starting to take shape in Paris. In the backrooms and house parties, groups of people were offering their own version of house music. A group of producers and DJs who would become known collectively as The French Touch. And the catalysts in this movement? Two events. The release of 'The New Wave', Daft Punk's first single in April 1994. And the opening of the Eurostar in November of the same year.

4. A QUIET STORM – SOWING THE SEEDS OF THE FRENCH TOUCH

"The movement with Laurent Garnier and F Communications is not the same music at all as the movement we created after. Our movement was from rap and hip hop culture. With Serge Gainsbourg as well."

Philippe Ascoli (Managing Director, Source/ Virgin), 2002

"We were a bit surprised because we didn't see it arriving. It just wasn't from the same generation as us."

Eric Morand, 2002

If the dance media in the UK were to be believed in 1996, one night that year, Paris finally discovered house music and delivered its own version the very next day with morning coffee and croissants. Such was the sudden rush to cover all things Parisian.

The truth, of course, was a very different thing. As we have seen, Paris already had a long history within dance music. However, what occurred in the second half of the 90s represented the coming together of three separate stories, each running concurrently. Collectively they offered enough momentum to create a massive hype that would see Paris turned into the coolest music capital in the world for the remaining years of the twentieth century.

The first of these stories emerged from the hip hop and funk scenes of Paris and beyond. The second story came from the affluent Parisian suburb of Versailles – or, to be more exact, from two of the area's indie bands. While the third tale was represented by one-time indie kids turned clubbers who hung around the shops and cafes of the Bastille district of Paris.

Inevitably the three stories overlapped. At times they literally snaked each other, events wrapped up in one another's coils. However, by the time they reached the ears of the British media, these stories had become simplified by a single term – The French Touch. A name that I first used to describe the music in the British press and which quickly became a collective term for this new school of dance music artists emanating primarily from Paris. French Touch, a throwaway comment in a review, became the name to send disparate groups with unique sounds to a global audience under the same flag of convenience.

At the turn of the 90s French hip hop found a voice that was to turn into one of the most powerful musical forces in France. The music had become embraced by the second generation African immigrants, providing them with a means of expression in what had become an extremely racially divided country. Nowhere was this more evident than in Paris, where the city's urban projects were quickly turned into ghettos that seemed a million miles removed from the bourgeois affluence of Versailles.

Surprisingly a government directive also aided the growth of hip hop in France. In a move aimed at slowing down the cultural homogenisation created by the spread of US concerns like McDonald's, the French government imposed a limit on the amount of non-French language music allowed to be played on the radio. Although French pop quickly fit into this, airplay was also accessible to hip hop artists rapping in French.

As a result, the words of artists like MC Solaar, NTM and Iam were quickly spread throughout the country. Philippe Zdar, who worked extensively with MC Solaar at this time, considers this to be the most important turning point for French music culture.

"Hip hop was the key thing in French Touch because when NTM, Solaar, Iam, the other first bands who were successful, came up, it changed everything," he explained. "In England, you were OK because you'd always had a lot of bands, but in France there was nothing. Just pop music for years and years. A few good ones, OK, but a lot of shit. So with hip hop, it was the first time that music was done by kids in France.

"Hip hop was a great emancipation in music. It was the first time that people were able to make music in small studios and put it out on small labels. Suddenly kids were getting samplers and they could do it for themselves. And at the same time, the kids from the suburbs could speak about their lives with the rapping."

The success of hip hop in France was unparalleled in any other country in the world. With other territories unable to find their own voices in the face of American domination, the French rappers went beyond simply rhyming in their own language; they invented dialects and words which remain unique to the French scene.

"In the UK, you had the weight of American hip hop to live up to," explains Zdar. "But here, people didn't speak English, so naturally they rapped in French. If you go to a kid here who's into hip hop, he'll listen to 85% of French stuff. They have their own style, own language, everything."

The French hip hop scene may have introduced the cheap production methods which would fuel the French dance artists, but the direct link comes with three people who all worked at the same studios together – Philippe Zdar, Hubert 'Boombass' Blanc-Farancard and Etienne de Crecy. A trio who, in various combinations, would produce some of the most influential records. Pioneering releases that heralded the arrival of French Touch – La Funk Mob and Motorbass. The common figure in both outfits was Philippe Zdar.

PHILIPPE ZDAR – THE LINK BETWEEN HIP HOP AND TECHNO

Montmartre District, Paris, December 2002

Philippe Zdar is not well. Sitting in the offices of Pedro Winter, his long time friend and manager, the man behind some of the greatest records to emerge from Paris, is suffering from food poisoning after eating some out of date chicken. He's been up all night. His girlfriend, too, is stricken with the illness. The only person in the family unscathed by the bad chicken is their 18-month old daughter, who is with Philippe.

I've interviewed Philippe several times over the years. With one notable exception (when one Motorbass interview was conducted in the back of his Mercedes), each meeting has seemingly revolved around food. Today our conversation is punctuated by Philippe feeding his daughter. Ironically it's a reassuringly endearing situation. In a dance music world full of bullshit, Philippe Zdar is that rare thing, a sincere person. In fact, in the parlance of hip hop, he keeps it real.

Hubert Boombass, his partner in La Funk Mob and Cassius, was to have also been present, but he too was busy with family thanks to the premature birth of his first child.

"When I was 14, I first started recording music," says Philippe as he spoons a dollop of baby food into his daughter's mouth. "I was still young but a good friend of mine put a band together. He asked me if I wanted to sing but the day I came to a rehearsal, the drummer was ill, so I went behind the drums and loved it. Somebody in the family bought me a set of drums the next Christmas. After this, I joined a few bands."

Philippe Zdar grew up in a small town in the Alps. It was, he says, a very boring life, especially for the youngster whose heart was already set on the world of music. Albeit music which was miles removed from the sound he would become known for.

"As a kid, I was really into punk, heavy metal and hardcore. I was in two

Philippe Zdar (Mark Stringer)

heavy metal bands, which was how I started with music, really."

Indeed his love of heavy metal and punk remains. When the subject moves to talk of The Clash, his eyes light up with excitement. They are his favourite band of all time.

Philippe moved to Paris following his national service, becoming an expert skydiver. Soon after, he took up a position in the renowned Studio Plus XXX. Here he cut out a name for himself as a talented sound engineer, working with French pop and rock artists and at one time Serge Gainsbourg. Philippe's introduction to the world of hip hop came when MC Solaar was in the studio working on his debut single. Hubert 'Boombass' took up the production duties. A one time A&R man at Polydor (where he worked alongside Philippe Ascoli, who was by this time Solaar's A&R man), Boombass was a regular at Studio Plus XXX and had already struck up a friendship with Philippe. He subsequently asked the sound engineer to do a mix for the single.

"I did a few mixes and because I used a lot of bass, the guys from hip hop started to call me to do mixes for them," recalls Zdar. "But I wasn't really into hip hop at this time. I worked on hip hop, but more because I was asked to do stuff."

Following this session, Boombass and Philippe Zdar worked together on MC Solaar's debut album. Their production alias was La Funk Mob, and quickly they became the most in-demand team in Paris.

"I remember bands like De La Soul started coming through and I really started getting into hip hop then," he says. "But I was not into the production. Hubert was, but not me. I was more into doing mixes, really. I never really wanted to do hip hop songs. In fact, before I went to a rave and discovered techno, I wasn't interested in doing songs at all. I just wanted to do mixes. La Funk Mob was Hubert doing the music and me doing the mixes. I didn't make the songs themselves at all until La Funk Mob became a band much later."

People would drip into the studio throughout this period, talking about the raves happening around Paris. Philippe resisted the invitations because he hated the techno that he had heard. However, while working with a female artist called Rousseau, he finally succumbed.

"One night, I went to this rave with my studio assistant [Etienne de Crecy]. It was on a boat over the Christmas of 1990 or 1991 and the music was this crazy Goa trance. We dropped an E. I'd taken E before, but only in the countryside, you now, but never with music. The next day we talked on the phone for hours. It was a revolution to me. We decided to do some techno tracks the next day. So I went out and bought some turntables and a sampler and Hubert taught me how to use it. And that was really when Motorbass came along."

Dimitri From Paris recalls the time when Philippe discovered dance music. Talking in the suave sophistication of his apartment about his early days as a radio DJ and house remixer, Dimitri confirmed: "I first met Philippe when I was doing a remix for a French act which had been produced by Arthur Baker. On the day I was there, it was also Philippe's first day in the studio. He saw me editing a lot of tapes and he was really interested in what I was doing. I was doing a lot of work in the studio with my remixes at the time and Philippe was a tape op. But we became friends and eventually, I asked him to engineer for me. He didn't really have any knowledge or experience of house music, so I had to play him a lot of records to give him an idea of what I liked. At this time, he was still listening to Led Zeppelin in his car. He never said he didn't like house, but he was doubtful about it.

"Then he'd be finishing these sessions really late and he started going to raves. I was never into drugs or raves, so he would go there without me. But thanks to the raves, he started to like the music I was playing him. Then he started buying records. I blame the raves for getting him into the music rather than me, but after the raves he understood what these records were for. We did make an attempt to produce a house track together but it never really worked!"

Philippe actually cited Dimitri as being the person who got him into house. Although he specifically recalls this epiphany happening when Dimitri took him to New York's Paradise Garage. However, Philippe's main thing was still techno and for a while absorbed the rave scene like a kid in a sweet shop.

Interestingly Boombass still refused to go to a rave until years later, when he and Zdar had formed Cassius.

"Hubert just wasn't into all of this techno thing," laughs Philippe. "He didn't want to come to a rave. We were all trying to get him to a rave, but he didn't want to. But now he really regrets it. Now he's the one who is getting high and saying, 'I want to go to a rave'. Last year when we played at Pacha, inside they were playing techno and I said Hubert, you should take an E and go to listen. He had to understand what happened to us ten years ago. After he was different, he was so sad to have missed out."

Philippe Zdar and Etienne de Crecy released their first Motorbass EP '001' in 1992. A selection of rough cut techno tunes, the debut single barely hinted at what was to come. A further EP '002' in 1994 saw the duo shape the sound for which they would become known. A raw marriage between Detroit techno and the sonic stylings of hip hop.

"Motorbass was always something we did for pleasure," says Philippe of the slow pace the duo seemed to work at. "My main ambition was still to remain a sound engineer and Etienne was fighting to become a sound engineer because he was still an assistant at this time. We were both cmpletely into this."

In 1994 Philippe's attention was once again focused on La Funk Mob. He had continued to work on mixes for Boombass' productions throughout this period but they had never been a proper band. This all changed when James Lavelle approached Boombass to supply some instrumental hip hop for his Mo' Wax imprint.

"For me, my main band was Motorbass," explains Zdar. "But by 1994, we did some stuff for Mo' Wax. James Lavelle said he loved the instrumentals of MC Solaar, so he asked for an instrumental EP. Hubert just thought, 'Who should I ask to help me with this?'. I was making these six-minute-long tracks. So he asked me to do a Motorbass track with no four on the floor kick. Just a six-minute track that we could do together in the studio. So we did a track, 'Motor Bass gets Phunked Up', and that's how La Funk Mob became a band and not just a production team.

"This was also the first time that Hubert had seen the possibilities with instrumental music. He was an ex-artistic director for a record company and he thought entirely in terms of formatting for singles with singers, chorus and everything. And then he discovered this."

La Funk Mob released two EPs for Mo' Wax. The first was a six-track affair featuring the original version of downtempo favourite 'Ravers Suck Our Sound and Fuck'. The second instalment was the remix package 'Casse Les Frontiers Fou Les Tetes En L'Air' ('Breaking Boundaries Messing Up Heads'). 'Ravers Suck Our Sound' was the lead track, along with mixes by Leeds outfit Nightmares on Wax (who were just losing their bleepy hip house sound in favour of downtempo trip hop) and two others by La Funk Mob. A new 'Electrofunk Remix' of 'Motor Bass Gets Phunked Up' completed the package by Ritchie Hawtin.

La Funk Mob would go on to be considered godfathers of the trip hop scene. Their mellow beats and film-esque samples informed a generation of producers that followed. However, throughout 1995 Philippe and Ettiene were working on what was to become the debut Motorbass album *Pansoul*.

By this stage, the duo shared a flat together in Paris. Together they talked for hours about ideas for the music, spinning records on the decks and going out to every party, rave or club that was happening (Mozinor was a favourite of theirs). Surprisingly, however, they created their own tracks for Motorbass separately. It was a testament to the extent to which they'd defined their sound through their many conversations that the finished results fit together so perfectly.

Pansoul initially came out in October 1995 and it immediately sold out of its 6,000 print run. The buzz was almost immediate, thanks to the quality of the music. Eight deep house tracks with a hip hop attitude; subterranean jack tracking with rough cut exotica samples and stealth defying programming. The album presented a unique sound where comparisons fell sadly short.

From the opening beats of 'Ezio', the Motorbass manifesto was made clear. This was a funk thing that could ignite even the frostiest of dancefloors. It is a journey deep in sexual urgency where b-lines slip and slide through percussive salsa action while distant voices call for the break to kick in. 'Flying Fingers' could have been Larry Heard, or Mr Fingers himself thanks to its liquid keys, which snaked around a shuffling hi-hat until the sixteens kicked in with a solid Mantronix bassline. It would become a huge influence on Daft Punk and could be described as a defining moment in the French Touch emergence. With 'Les Ondes', Motorbass took the funk ingredients and threw in a vocal refrain that could have come courtesy of Lalo Schiffrin. It was pure exotica seduced by harp flourishes and a low level, swinging groove. Thanks to its offbeat percussion, 'Neptune' brought more than a dash of 70s Superfly action into the proceedings, which pushed the groove to the very edge. Percussion was also to the fore on the manic Afro-jam 'Wandence', while 'Genius' pushed the vibe towards a Latino celebration. 'Pariscyde' and 'Bad Vibes (D-Mix)' finished the album in a similar style drawing on the by now expected multifarious styles and sounds sourced from a trainspotter's paradise of samples.

A thing of indescribable beauty, *Pansoul* represented the sound of Paris delving headfirst into deep-fried funk, throwing a fresh colour onto the paintwork of techno and licking the lips of nineties electro-soul.

Pansoul also represented the moment when the new generation of dance producers gained a foothold on the global market. It was an album that heralded a new school of producers. A school that was creating a more defined French sound, which would eventually become known as French Touch. For such an important album, *Pansoul* did surprisingly badly in commercial terms. The main reason was that Philippe was taking care of the business side.

"It was impossible," he admits. "We started putting it into the shops in October '95 and we sold out very fast. But then I couldn't get any new records for about six months. During this time, the album started to get good reviews but I couldn't get any new stock, so it was very bad. In the end, we only sold about 20,000 copies which was ridiculous because of the amount of reviews we were getting."

Not that Philippe was short of offers from companies willing to sign *Pansoul*. James Lavelle was keen to release the album on Mo' Wax, and Philippe Ascoli was interested in putting the album out through his newly launched Virgin subsidiary Source.

"Philippe came to my office with the Motorbass album and played it to me really quickly," recalled Ascoli in his London offices in November 2002. "I said I would really like to release it, but he never got back to me. To me, this album was fantastic. It was one of the best albums from this time. But there was no commercial sense with Philippe. He didn't realise the impact the Motorbass album could have had. So it didn't sell very well. Which was a shame."

Eventually, Philippe and Etienne signed the album to Carli Kopff at PIAS, who reissued it in 1996 with an extra track, the ambient echo drop intro 'Fabulous'. However, by signing to a bigger label, Motorbass's working methods were instantly impacted. They weren't allowed to release a remix of 'Ezio', which had been huge in Philippe's DJ sets. The issue was a glaring uncleared sample of a Prince track that simply would not have bothered Philippe before this. The remix is also interesting because it saw the beginnings of Philippe and Boombass' Cassius guise.

"This was the first time we did a techno track together," says Philippe. "It was the first Cassius mix. Before this time, Motorbass had done things alone, bringing our records to London, Amsterdam everywhere. I used to put the records in my car and drive thousands of kilometres to London, Gent in Belgium, even in Germany. We did our own distribution totally and then we signed to PIAS. We did this 'Ezio' remix and PIAS said we couldn't put it out because of the Prince sample. If it had still been only us, we would have put it out."

The remix may have been the first time that Boombass had created a techno track, but he had already discovered house soon after La Funk Mob's EPs. Among his own house productions was 'Sexy Lady' under the Six Million Dollar Man pseudonym – a track that would become one of the blueprints for the filtered house sound that typified Parisian production in the late 90s.

Pansoul is regarded as one of the finest albums of the decade. Surprisingly, however, Etienne and Philippe failed to deliver either a follow-up single or album. Furthermore, they moved into separate apartments and started working on their own individual projects – Philippe with Cassius, who would quickly sign to Virgin and Etienne with his Super Discount project on the Solid imprint he'd formed with long time friends Pierre Michel Levellois and Alex Gopher.

In February 1996, I brought Philippe and Etienne together for *Muzik* magazine in a rare Motorbass interview. Fittingly it took place in the back of Philippe's car, as outside the streets were lashed by torrential rain. A transcript of the interview reveals the humorous bond between the two friends. A humour that also informs their music.

Etienne: "We were very surprised about the reaction to *Pansoul* in England but in France, there wasn't too much response at all.

Philippe: "We knew we were doing good music but we never expected such a good response. We didn't make very many promos and we fucked up everything about the output of the album. We put it out a year after we'd made it, so it lost a lot of impact. But it's all right because we like it like this. I was also surprised because there are a lot of influences in Motorbass and I thought that it might be too much for people. Both Etienne and me listen to a lot of different music, so the influences are going to be wide. Lots of the tracks are from the time that we were living together, so we were playing a lot of records to each other. We'd be listening to jazz, soul, funk and hip hop, so this came naturally in our music. We also love some kinds of music that the other hates. He loves rock 'n' roll, which I hate but I love heavy metal, which he hates!

Etienne: "No, I love Metallica!"

Philippe: "Ah yes, we listened to a lot of Metallica in our apartment. I'd love to remix them, especially a track called 'The Four Horsemen' from their first album. That track is timeless, which is something we aim for with Motorbass. Some people think that house music has to have a short life but I think it's good that a track still sounds good after a few years. I have friends who still listen to *Beggars Banquet* by the Rolling Stones, years and years after it was first released. This is how it should be with Motorbass."

Etienne: "The next Motorbass album is going to be more commercial, with vocals."

Philippe: "And there's going to be a lot of live stuff on it as well because Etienne used to play bass and I played drums, so we're forming a real band."

Etienne: "Rock and roll music!"

Philippe: "With a bit of country. We've got about fifty per cent of the record already but we haven't worked together on any of the stuff yet. It'll be deep country house, or deep house in the country. It'll have loads of animals on it like cows and lambs. In fact, this is going to be on the next Motorbass cover (points to a knitted toy lamb in his car). More French hype!"

Etienne: "No more French hype please!"

Philippe: "You see a lot of the French scene getting really big heads now just because they've had one twelve-inch reviewed in your magnificent magazine [*Muzik*]. It's all your fault. You say, 'this is a great record' and the guys are like so big-headed about it. We can't do that because we're too involved in making music to worry about what people think. So it doesn't matter how much you tell us we're brilliant, you can't affect us... So how good did you say we were again? Did you say 'genius'? No. Why not? Ha, ha, ha."

Etienne: "We hear our influence everywhere now. When people just take the recipes from Motorbass, it's going to be shit."

Philippe: "Guy-Manuel from Daft Punk has been working with some guys in the studio and he comes up to me and says, 'man, they're doing Motorbass'. Afterwards, I'm going to BPM and a friend of mine says to me 'each track I do sounds too much like Motorbass' but I'm OK about it because I know that these people aren't stealing from us. They love the music and they are just adapting it for their own needs. The others are definitely stealing. Like they want to be Philippe and Etienne. They want to be Motorbass.

"Actually, we're just the people who do the publicity for Motorbass. Etienne's brother is doing his tracks and one of my best friends is doing mine. But they're very timid and shy. Just now, my friend is in the closet at home. I open the closet maybe two or three times a week, just to make him samples. I only feed him once a month to keep him keen. If I feed much more, he would start thinking he was too important."

"That interview was a great laugh," exclaims Philippe when I remind him of it in Pedro Winter's office. "It was the first time that we talked to each other for months and months because we'd been so busy. We were like really happy to see each other and we talked about Metallica. You know, the biggest drag about dance people is that they only want to talk about dance. Etienne and me we love to talk about rock music as well.

"You know, I really had no problem with people copying *Pansoul*," he continues when we talk once again of the influence of Motorbass. "People were coming to me and saying, 'listen, this sounds just like Motorbass' and I wasn't bothered. I'm not the kind of person who gets angry about this because I was already copying other people. Motorbass was copying Carl Craig's '69'. We were trying to do our version of the first '69' single. So how could I say that they were copying me?"

Some seven years after *Pansoul* was released, Motorbass had failed to come up with any kind of follow-up despite claims during that Muzik interview. Ironically, however, only 24 hours earlier, Philippe and Etienne had agreed to work on a new Motorbass album.

"We've talked about the new Motorbass album for five or six years," says Philippe. "We're working on the new album now. Yesterday I talked to Etienne on the phone and the time is right for us both. We have had a lot of songs over the years but we never finished them. Now we're starting from scratch. It's a good thing for us to work together."

When I question Etienne about it a couple of days later, he admits that he wants to record an album really quickly, using analogue synths and old drum machines.

"It'll be a trance album," he laughs.

Perhaps one of the main reasons why Philippe and Etienne had avoided doing a follow-up is the amount that the album represents to them both creatively and personally. It would have been hard to equal the acclaim of such a highly regarded record as that debut album. Furthermore, people would have had too many preconceived ideas of what the follow-up would sound like, thus stifling the duo's creativity.

Pansoul also represented something of a milestone for both artists. It was an experience that proved to be an epiphany, sending both of them hurtling in different musical directions and turning their backs on previous ambitions.

"After doing *Pansoul*, I really discovered my life," explains Philippe. "I wanted to do albums and concentrate on the music production. When we finished Pansoul, I thought it was cool but no more than this. But I played it to my friends and they were really into it. I realised then that I wanted to do this full time, so I quit my job. I decided to only engineer maybe three times a year for friends."

There is little doubt that *Pansoul* took on monumental proportions for the duo. This personal perspective represents a far greater barrier than the critical acclaim for the album.

"I don't ever think of Motorbass as pioneers," concludes Philippe as his little girl starts to explore Pedro Winter's collection of skateboards. "Geographically, perhaps yes, but to me, the pioneers were in Detroit. I was really into Detroit. All we did with Motorbass was copy Detroit. But because I was working with hip hop still, there was some hip hop influence in Motorbass. For example, I remember on one or two tracks I was in the studio and Jimmy J was there. So I asked him to scratch for me. So it became like a mixture between our version of Detroit done through the eyes of what we were doing with hip hop! But I never ever thought of us as pioneers."

Philippe Zdar's humility may be typical of the Motorbass philosophy. They create music for the love of it and not to be a part of the hype. It is certain that many others would have used the situation that surrounded *Pansoul* to their best advantage and pursued a full and fruitful Motorbass career throughout the French Touch era. But not these two.

Since *Pansoul,* Philippe enjoyed great success with Cassius, while Etienne de Crecy enjoyed similar reactions to the *Super Discount* collection and his *Tempovision* album. It is perhaps fitting that then the duo waited until the French Touch hype died down before deciding to record that second Motorbass album… even if that record ultimately failed to materialise. Etienne and Phillipe did, however, record a track together for *Super Discount 2* in 2004. 'Poisoned', the album's opening track, offered a blistering funky acid take on disco. A delicious appetiser, sadly the main course would never materialise.

'Poisoned' had represented the first opportunity either had to work together despite plans to record that second album. For Zdar, the main thing during that time had been Cassius. In the beginning, Cassius was a remix nom de plume for Zdar and Boombass' house guise. However, late in 1998, they emerged on white label as a unit in their own right. That promo was the insidiously funky 'Cassius 1999' and it marked the beginning of the duo's claim on the Paris house crown. Naturally, the single came through Virgin, who, more than any other major label, had a strong understanding of the prime movers of French Touch.

Early in 1999, Cassius delivered their debut album, the appropriately titled *1999.* Anyone who had expected a slight return to their La Funk Mob output was in for a shock. This selection was informed by the forces of Chicago house, electro, techno and, like everyone else in Paris, it would seem, 80s electro-funk. However, the glue that stuck the while thing together came from a much more contemporary source; Basement Jaxx. Indeed *1999* was filled to the last groove with Jaxx's punk house approach to melodic groove, rhythmic cut-up and hands-in-the-air joi de vivre.

This was especially present on the second single, 'Feeling For You' that combined classic Chicago techniques alongside diva-esque vocals, delivered with a definite south London accent. The reworking of Boombass' 'Foxxy Lady' (now called 'Foxxy') brought the funk bass and guitars to the fore, while also emphasising the Blaxploitation soundtrack horn stabs, while its keyboard refrain fused the 60s soul Hammond groove with 80s acid house sounds. Elsewhere 'Mister Eveready' displayed the duo's love of 80s funk with a groove that fused the sound of hip hop crew The Neptunes, who were just coming through at this time, with the disco flavour of DJ Sneak. While 'Club Soixante Quinze' updated those ever-present influences of Cameo and Parliament with a deep house flavour.

Even though the album came from a duo who had been at the very forefront of the major developments on the beats scene in Paris for nearly a decade, there were still suggestions that *1999* was a bandwagon jumping album. Indeed, by this stage, so huge was the onslaught of people all after that Parisian sound that Zdar and Boombass' pedigree got lost amid the anti-hype. This was, according to some, their attempt to get some of the glory, and money, that had come to people who came after La Funk Mob and Motorbass.

Philippe Zdar's answer to the criticism? "No, I've never thought this way at all. I'm just happy to make music. I don't feel jealousy about other people. Of course, I have my opinions about their music, but Cassius wasn't for us to make money. This music is made from love. And we weren't following people. In actual fact, we were signed to Virgin a long time before Air. So Cassius were one of the first to get a major label in actual fact!"

Despite the criticism, no one could deny the quality of the album's dancefloor-friendly tracks and, over the course of the year, as the duo continued to DJ all over the world, the album grew in stature. By mid-1999 they were being hailed as the true Kings of the Parisian underground house sound.

That said, the release of their second album *Au Reve*, was met with a huge amount of criticism, especially from the UK dance press.

"I don't know what it is about this album," complains Zdar. "I'm really proud of it, but people said such hurtful things about it. I just couldn't understand why."

Au Reve actually met the full force of the backlash against Parisian house music. The truth was that, as a collection, it was far more assured and cohesive than its predecessor. With *1999* there was a sense of polite reverence about it, however with *Au Reve*, Zdar and Boombass were back to doing what they did best, breaking the rules. As a result, they fused the influences of the first album with Jamaican bashment dancehall, epic rock, old school video games, classic electro, the rhythm clusters of Missy Elliot producer Timbaland and heavy-duty funk.

Standouts included the funk-rock meets acid house epic of 'The Sound of Violence' (featuring the vocals of Steve Edwards), which saw the duo receiving some success in the US, 'I'm a Woman' with Jocelyn Brown on vocals found heavy rock guitars meshed with frenetic house, Basement Jaxx style and 80s electro-funk sequence basslines. Sadly the fusion of sounds was too much for many people and the album sold poorly. Furthermore, many of the Parisian musicians who had been fans of the duo's work in all of their guises felt betrayed by comments they made in the media.

"They [Cassius] were in magazines saying that sampling was dead," complains Guillaume Atlan, who runs the Lafesse imprint, and records as The Supermen Lovers. "I thought this was terrible. They were saying that sampling was bullshit and the only people still using samplers were idiots. I just thought that it was so wrong. A lot of kids look up to them and respect what they say. Now they've written off the whole basis of house music."

"No, we meant that for us sampling was a thing of the past," argues Zdar when I put Atlan's claims to him. "We love house music. Why would we say that sampling was bad? But for us, it was more creative to not just use samplers. Also, so many people in Paris now are making tunes from samples without much thought. We're against that."

In 2003 the *Au Reve* album continued to find new fans around the world. Its presence grew in the US and, despite the press criticism, it slowly gained respect in the UK. However, Zdar was already onto his next project. The first of which was a reissue of the Motorbass album on Virgin, complete with a second disc of new tracks.

Philippe Zdar may have been an accidental convert to hip hop who found his true voice in the world of techno, but his La Funk Mob releases on Mo' Wax represented just the tip of the iceberg among the Parisian downtempo scene. Partly due to the affinity already felt with hip hop and the strong position held by jazz in French culture, the abstract hip hop instrumentals which would become the trademark sound of DJ Shadow in the US and DJ Krush in Japan found a healthy, if small, stronghold among Parisian DJs and producers.

In the early 90s, two labels launched that picked up on the abstract hip hop vibe that would become known as trip hop. Both labels were important in the foundation of the creative bed that would evolve into French Touch. The second of these imprints was Yellow Productions, masterminded by DJ Yellow (aka Alain Ho) and Chris Le Friant (aka Chris the French Kiss), in 1994. The first abstract beats label, however, was Street Jazz. Launched by DJ Cam, primarily to release his own music, Street Jazz arrived in late 1993.

DJ CAM – THE ABSTRACT SOUL SURVIVOR

"In the beginning, I really wanted to make hip hop but I didn't know any rappers. So I had to make abstract hip hop, putting samples in place of the MC."

When DJ Cam talked music, his eyes seemed to take on a clear gaze. It was the look of a man who was utterly wrapped up in the sounds he created. A naturally stoned image of someone lost on a journey into the smoky vibed world of the loose-limbed break and freeform samples. When coupled with the slim lipped smile framed by a downy goatee, he seemed every inch the thinker. A man who was happiest working through his ideas and formulating his music than justifying them in words.

DJ Cam (Mark Stringer)

"When I started, there were a few like-minded people in Paris, like Chris with his Mighty Bop and La Funk Mob, but it was very difficult to get noticed," he told me in 1995. "Even in other countries, there was only one DJ Shadow, one DJ Krush, the sound wasn't big. So I was obliged to set up my own label, especially in France, because it was impossible to get that kind of music signed to a major label in 1993. There was only Yellow who were doing a similar thing, but we were inspired by independent labels in the UK and the US who were doing the same kind of thing as us. But setting up your own label was also a part of the culture, I think. It meant we could keep control."

Parisian Laurence Daumail was born into a jazz loving house. His father introduced him to the delights of Miles Davis and John Coltrane before he was eight years old. He subsequently studied piano until he was 12 and then took up drums. By the age of 17, he had discovered hip hop culture, started organising "barbarian" evenings, took to spraying graffiti on the walls of Paris and dropped his drums in favour of a pair of decks. He was a b-boy through and through.

With the huge growth and influence of French hip hop among many of Cam's contemporaries, it is somewhat surprising that he had little time for the local talent. His references were from the US old skool, plain and simple. It was a grounding that would inform his production s over the years that followed, thus enabling him to gain strong support in the US.

"I came from the hip hop scene but I'm not into the French sound at all," he said with a smile. "I'm really into American and English hip hop, but not French. When I first heard Eric B and Rakim, I was blown away. France is very rock orientated, so when this stuff started to come over here, loads of people hated it, but I loved it straight away. Later on, I loved the production of DJ Premier. He's just untouchable. Jeru the Damaja's album *Wrath of the Math* is so bad. I love the way he uses samples. Really raw, not like live musicians but definitely samplers. But I didn't like the production of French stuff. I'm not even interested in knowing about what's happening now with French hip hop."

Cam's earliest work belied a love of the abstract grooves of DJ Krush, with 1994's *Dieux Reconnaitra Les Siens* displaying a strong understanding of the power of a well-considered sample over languid breaks and stoner ambience.

"For me, the biggest inspiration is DJ Krush," Cam told me on another trip to Paris in 1996. "I love his beats; they're so far ahead of what other people are doing."

At the tail end of 1994, DJ Cam delivered his debut album *Underground Vibes*. A collection that positively ached with that smoky jazz ambience fused with stoned beats, it had an immediate impact on the post-club chill-out bars of the UK, Japan and US. It was an important album in that it painted another picture of Paris to the one being portrayed by the techno fraternity. Furthermore, its heavy use of easy listening and jazz samples offered a blueprint to the sound that people would soon associate with the city. As with just about every other musical pioneer in France, DJ Cam was all but ignored in his home country.

"When my first LP came out, nothing happened in France at all, but I sold a lot of records in the US and Japan. I only got noticed here about a year later but the LP did sell a lot very fast elsewhere. In fact, it all happened very quickly."

France's resistance to his music not only occurred in the usual mainstream areas but also in the hip hop arena. Indeed, despite his love of hip hop, the abstract beats he was creating were despised by the hip hop kids. The feeling was mutual. Indeed, it was an attitude that very quickly unearthed the racial divide in Paris. Back in 1996, I met DJ Cam in Paris for a *Melody Maker* feature. The parka clad DJ arrived at our interview location on his Vespa. His short hair was flattened forward into a French crop by his half-face crash helmet and as he spoke, his conversation was interspersed with long periods of silence as he searched for the right words. Not simply a language problem for him, but a need to find the right way of putting over his feelings.

"The Paris scene just doesn't consider my music to be hip hop," he explained. "It's very strange in France. I think it's the only country in the world where the hip hop scene doesn't even consider abstract beats to be worth listening to."

Indeed this resilience to change and integration among the French hip hop fraternity would eventually lead to a near collapse of the hip hop underground. By 2002 NTM had little relevance, their beats sounding tired, MC Solaar had turned to pop music and Iam's output was negligible. Indeed, French hip hop's dogmatic approach to abstract beat production hinted at a fundamental problem that sat at the very core of the city itself. Perhaps the least racially integrated city in Europe (check out the film *La Haine* for a frighteningly accurate portrayal of life in the Afro-Parisian neighbourhoods), hip hop was predominantly the preserve of the black working class in Paris. As such, the crews were obsessively protective about their music.

In 1995 Yellow Productions' Chris the French Kiss explained to me that the trip hop scene in Paris had been stunted by problems with the hip hop crews.

"When we put on clubs, they come down and try to take them over," he explained. "Hip hop is very gang-related, so whenever they take over, there's always trouble. It's a big problem over here."

This gang minded attitude quickly spilt over into forms of racism. Cam himself had been at the blunt end of it, not only through making a form of hip hop that the gangs couldn't relate to but also because his girlfriend of the time was black. As a result, the couple received racist attention from both white and black communities. However, he was philosophical about the situation: "I think maybe things will change eventually. It's a historical problem and only time can take care of that."

Unperturbed by the lack of support from the very people with whom he should have had an allegiance with, Cam continued working with free-flowing beats. In 1996 he backed up his debut album with a live set called *Underground Live*. With a strictly limited print run of 5,000 copies, the set showed the DJ's deck skills to stunning effect. A year later, Shadow Records in the US reissued *Underground Vibe* as a double set with *Underground Live*. Together the albums told a complete story of DJ Cam's musical ideals at that stage in his development.

A soundclash EP on Yellow Productions in 1996 found Cam displaying strength in unity with the other main players on the abstract beats scene. *Mighty Bop meets DJ Cam and La Funk Mob*, although strictly speaking a Mighty Bop set, had unmistakable input from Cam with his deep understanding of jazz coming to the fore throughout his contributions to the set. He also provided stand out cuts for Yellow's *La Yellow 357* imaginary soundtrack album of the same year.

Cam developed his label as a stable for other artists throughout this period. Among them was Swiss drum & bass artist Minus 8, who immediately benefited from a licensing deal Cam inked with Columbia Records. To coincide with this deal, he re-christened the label Inflammable Records.

1996 saw the release of DJ Cam's third album *Substances*. Not as you might suspect a reference to drugs, but a comment on the very "substance" of his music. *Substances* found Cam's field of vision going into wide-angle. A collage of disparate influences, the album took in everything from old Don Cherry and John Coltrane samples to Indian vocals while retaining that all-important hip hop focus.

"This album was meant to be open-minded," he explained. "There's a little bit of hip hop, jungle, electro and even a little bit of house. I've always been eclectic in my music. I like to make original music with very different mixes, which is why I tried to use Indian vocals with hip hop beats. But it's very impulsive; I don't do these things as a deliberate concept. I get influence from everywhere; nothing is deliberate."

With the added weight of Columbia behind *Substances*, DJ Cam was able to reach a wider audience than ever before. Indeed his fusion approach matched perfectly with the mood of the times, where eclecticism was the dominant musical ideology. Just as the single 'Meera', with its Indian vocals, stoned beats and remixes by Parisian outfit Zend Avesta, was finding favour among DJs the world over, Cam had already moved on, however. *Substances* was already a year old by the time it was released and by this time, the producer had rediscovered his love of hip hop.

"I finished this album last February, so it's very old to me now," he told me. "*Substances* is a transitional album. When I made it, I was disillusioned with hip hop, especially with the Paris scene. I'm back into hip hop these days. I still think it's cool to make tracks with jungle and house in them but there's already so much good original stuff from these styles that I don't need to borrow from them anymore. I don't want to make second-hand jungle or house. Which is why these days, I don't want to mix things up anymore. I came from the hip hop scene and it's there I want to stay."

Of course, as the French dance music scene took hold in the months that followed *Substances* the smart money would have been on DJ Cam retaining the downtempo meltdown for another album at least. His immediate move was to release an album of jazz and world music powered tunes on the largely ignored *Abstract Manifesto* in 1996. It's an album that has gained notoriety in the intervening years and is now considered by many critics to be one of the finest examples of the abstract beats genre. It was his last foray into that area for some time, however. In 1998 Cam's *The Beat Assassinated* found him true to his word during that interview around *Substances* and deep in hip hop territory.

"People were really surprised by *The Beat Assassinated* because it is a very strong and hard LP," he admitted. "But it sold very well in the US and Japan. But it was a response to people thinking that I came from the techno and house scenes, so it was an attempt to show people that I came from a hip hop culture. I was young at the time, though."

The Beat Assassinated was a far less satisfying collection than *Substances*, thanks partly to Cam's choice of rappers and also the limitations that vocals placed on his arrangements. Furthermore, Cam's declared intent to be less eclectic found him sampling from a narrower sound pool than previously; the overall productions subsequently sounded stifled.

'Raise Up' featuring New York rappers Channel Live represented one of the strongest moments with their energetic delivery playing counter-point to Cam's mellow vibes. However, UK MC Silvah Bullet's clumsy delivery on the static groove of 'Renegade' proved to be surprisingly dull, given the individual pedigrees of both MC and producer.

However, the Beat Assassinated did succeed in bringing Cam wider acclaim from the hip hop scene in the US, and the abstract beats scene also took a greater interest in him. When US label Shadow Records licensed a Cam mixed compilation from Parisian label Artefact, they marketed it as a DJ Cam album called *DJ Cam presents the French Connection* – much to the disgust of both Artefact and Cam.

"I'm very ashamed of this project because it wasn't really me at all," he said. "At the time, there was a French label called Artefact and the guy from the label is a friend of mine. He asked me to mix a CD of their tracks. It was supposed to be called *Artefact – The Collection*. But Shadow licensed it for the US and they aren't very cool and they put *DJ Cam presents The French Connection*. I was really ashamed and I refused to work with the label again. A lot of people thought that this was my album but it wasn't. I was very upset and so was my friend from Artefact. Shadow also re-released my first LP with a different sleeve. People think that it was a new album."

Nonetheless, *Cam Presents The French Connection* was a stunning mix set featuring the finest releases on the Artefact imprint cut up to fine effect by Cam. Ironically it was also the only album that tied Cam directly to French Touch. Artefact was very much at the heart of the movement thanks to owner Jérôme Mestre's day job at Rough Trade Record Shop in Bastille. A shop that would have a huge significance with the scene. Despite Cam's influence through his releases laying the foundations for others to follow, he always appeared to be separate from the hype. Ironically, however, he did see himself as being a part of the French Touch. And was very aware of how he'd benefited from it.

"Yes, I think I was a part of the French Touch, but we were all different," he suggested when we met again in 2000. "Over the years, journalists created a package and said what artists should sound like. But I was a part of the original energy definitely. And I'm proud of this. And it did me a lot of good, you know. I get recognised wherever I go. I never have to pay for a drink. I go everywhere free, I get discounts in shops without asking but I'm not arrogant about it. I know that the French Touch made me recognisable. But for the last three years or so I haven't been so aware of what's gone on in France. I do my own thing now."

In 2000 Cam returned to the abstract beats arena with the extremely accomplished album *Loa Project*. Once again painting from a wider palette, this album found him exploring live instrumentation alongside his usual sampladelia. His main source of influence was voodoo culture.

"Every time I make an LP, I try to have at least one major idea to start the album on," he explained at the time. "With this album, I was interested in the voodoo culture. For me, the beat is very important in music and this is the same with voodoo. I tried to be inspired by voodoo, it was the main idea but I didn't want it to be a concept album. I also didn't want to be seen as the white guy who uses voodoo sounds for his own music. I wanted to be more like an investigative journalist trying to make an exposé on voodoo. I wanted to be very pure, to put some very strange ideas across which were good. So I did a lot of research, travelled a lot to create the basis for the album. What I felt was that a lot of people talk about voodoo but don't actually realise what voodoo is. So I made a CD-ROM to go with the album, which explained everything. But Columbia in France is a little bit stupid and they didn't want the CD-ROM. Then when they asked for it, it was too late."

Loa Project represented the end of a production cycle for DJ Cam. The use of live instruments had opened up the possibility of doing a pure music album with no turntables or samples. This notion came to fruition in 2002 when he released *Soulshine*.

"*Soulshine* is the LP I've really wanted to do since the very beginning but I didn't have the means to do this kind of record," he explained when we met just after the album's release. "Also, I'm really into soul these days and have been for about three years, so *Soulshine* reflects this. In fact, I was very inspired by the last album by Erykah Badu, the new Philly sound, so I tried to make an album like that but from the perspective of my culture. And I used a lot of good musicians to play my songs which gave the album a different perspective."

Certainly, *Soulshine* represented the least expected album from Cam's career. Here he embraced the difficult area of US soul and delivered an album of sublime beauty. In fact, all of the old skool DJ Cam trademarks were present, the languid refrains, the feline melodies, the smoky ambience, the simple and precise grooves – however, these interludes were no longer as a result of his ability behind the decks and on the sampler. He successfully transposed all of the key themes of Cam the DJ into the live instrument set up. The result was new Philly soul, Cam style. And, as if to underline his new status sans decks, he dropped the DJ from his moniker.

"I am still DJ Cam though. It's just for this project that I am only known as Cam."

Despite seeming like something of a curve-ball album, *Soulshine* felt like it could have provided Cam's passport to mainstream US recognition. Not only due to the strength of Cam's songs and arrangements but also through his choice of collaborators. Among them was the legendary Cameo, whose influence cast a long shadow over French dance music. Cameo featured on the low-slung jazz funk standout 'Love Junkee' came complete with handclaps, muted twilight horns, and wandering Fender Rhodes. It was the sound of a 6am jazz dive after an injection of electro-funk.

"I've loved Cameo since I was about ten. My music is bigger in the US because I think I'm more in tune with the US culture. That's the music I like. In the UK, I've got a lot of fans but last time I was there DJing, I met a lot of people and they were asking when my new LP was coming out, and *Soulshine* had already been out for maybe a month. Columbia fucked it up, really."

In the years since his first release on Street Jazz, DJ Cam had continued to push at the boundaries of his own chosen path. It's an individual journey that had become increasingly at odds with his fellow Parisians, for just as they embraced house culture, he delved deeper into the American R&B arena. However, at the time this book was originally published, he had already left a legacy of six albums; five of them classics, and a brace of brilliant remixes for the likes of Michael Jackson (Cam turns 'You Rock My World' inside out), Miles Davis ('In a Silent Way') and Serge Gainsbourg ('Ford Mustang').

He also continued to develop Inflammable Records with collaborations with DJ Gregory ("It's kind of ragga, hip hop and house," he says). More work with Cameo and an album with Filet of Soul, who featured on *Soulshine*.

"I've never had a set plan. I've just followed my heart, really. Every album has been a reflection of where I was at that time. Right now, though, I'm still so happy with *Soulshine*. I'm very proud of it."

Since the golden era of French Touch, DJ Cam continued to explore the fringes of hip hop, abstract beats and soul to varying degrees of success. *Liquid Hip Hop* (2003) felt stuck in a rut with few great surprises. *Seven* (2011) found him moving into soulful acoustic rock. It featured 'Swim', one of his most successful tracks to date that combined a skipping jazz beat fused with aching strings, countrified acoustic guitar and the liquid voice of Chris James.

An album of tracks inspired by *Miami Vice* (2015) attempted to add his abstract magic to the 1980s pop of the TV series soundtrack. Although an interesting idea, it was ultimately quite weak, unable to dislodge the iconic sounds of the originals. Phil Collins' 'In the Air Tonight' felt like a huge improvement from the original, however. 2022 collection *Tropical Gypsy* recaptured some of his early magic. However, it felt like it was exploring the disco, house and Latin territories already unpicked by Chris the French Kiss back in the 1990s with Yellow Productions.

As the DJ Cam story unfolded, so did the tale of fellow Parisian abstract beat travellers Yellow Productions. However, their history starts less in hip hop than in the early 90s world of acid jazz before becoming the single most important independent label in the early years of French Touch.

YELLOW PRODUCTIONS – WHERE ACID JAZZ, HIP HOP AND LALO SCHIFFRIN MET

Yellow Productions was born from a chance encounter in a record shop between Chris le Friant and Alain Ho in 1993. Le Friant was looking for a particular record and, after a conversation struck up between the pair, Ho exclaimed that he had a copy of the record at home. It was the beginning of a friendship that would find the duo forging one of the most influential labels to emerge from early 90s Paris.

The duo's working methods were simple to start with. Ho would rifle his record collection for samples while le Friant would then mix them in the studio. It was a basic setup that echoed the duo's love of hip hop production techniques. An early remix of Dave Pike's classic sitar 'n' beats track 'Mathur' quickly brought Yellow Productions' talents to global attention.

With le Friant now working under the pseudonym Chris the French Kiss, and Ho becoming known as DJ Yellow, the duo then delivered the tack 'Indian Vibes', which proved to be a huge club track thanks to the remix by Brendan Lynch and a licensing deal with Virgin, France.

"I worked with them on this track," recalls Philippe Ascoli. "They were coming from the hip hop thing and that funky-Arabic sound which was popular in Paris. 'Indian Vibes' was huge at the time."

The funky-Arabic sound that Ascoli refers to was a fusion between the 80s jazz-funk sound and the influences of music from the one-time French colonies of northern Africa. It was a sound that bore a huge resemblance to acid jazz, which had been popular in the early 90s in the UK and US.

In 1994 Yellow Productions released their first albums in the shape of the jazz-tinged *Quelque Chose de Jazz Volumes 1 & 2*. It was a series that would continue a couple of years later with the *Bossa Tres... Jazz* collection.

Their third album was the hip hop collection *Fusion of Black Tempo*, which featured numerous French MCs. This album was notable because it represented the first time French hip hop DJ/producer Cutee B would record with Chris. He also worked extensively with DJ Cam.

The next album from the label *French Connection* followed later that year and found Chris extending his production remit to incorporate acid jazz and funk. It also offered an insight into Chris' next venture Reminiscence Quartet.

Reminiscence Quartet was a collaboration between Chris and a live band featuring horns, percussion and Fender Rhodes. The subsequent 1995 album *Psycodelico* offered a fusion of Brazilian batucada, acid jazz and hip hop. It was also the first introduction to Brazilian chanteuse Salome de Bahia who would record for Yellow in her own right years later.

Psycodelico gained a certain amount of interest in the rarefied circles of the London acid jazz scene and received positive coverage from acid jazz magazine *Straight No Chaser*. However, like all of the releases thus far on Yellow, it failed to make any great impact on the wider dance culture. Furthermore, the label had yet to find its true identity. Instead, it was happy to align itself with the styles that Chris and Alain were in awe of.

The true beginning of the label identity was to happen with Chris and Alain's abstract beats venture Mighty Bop which they began working on at the same time as Reminiscence Quartet.

"We can talk about plans, but really we just focussed on what we liked," he said in the offices of Yellow Productions in 2001. "We were interested in being like Mo' Wax and Talkin' Loud with that clever choice of image and thoughtful artists on the label. So Alain and I had this attitude where the image was important, the quality of the sleeves, weight of card, all important things in the overall impression of the label. And then we wanted it, so the label itself was a stamp of quality."

At that time, Chris le Friant was the epitome of smooth. With shoulder-length hair and classic Gallic looks, he had the air of a movie star about him. His energy for creating music was matched only by his self-assured manner. Some would call him arrogant. True, it takes some kind of arrogance to call yourself Chris the French Kiss. But his kind of arrogance came from total absorption in the desire to be successful. Little surprise then that Chris' own musical output had appeared under approximately eight guises, devoted to as many different styles. It's for this reason that he had been called an opportunist by some of his fellow Parisians.

Chris grew up and still lives in Le Marais, the happening gay quarter of Paris. "It's the centre of Paris," he once said. "A bit like Notting Hill in London. It's got The Force."

The very fact of growing up in such a flamboyantly cool area gave Chris his self-assured poise. It also gave him a certain wry humour that played with the stereotyped ideas of the Parisian male. I'd interview Chris on numerous occasions over the years, but I will never forget the first time we met. As Chris posed for photographer Mark Stringer, a stunningly beautiful girl strolled up to him, planted a full-mouthed kiss on his lips, and then walked away as if it was an everyday occurrence. Chris returned to the photo session, totally unfazed by the event. No wonder they called him the French Kiss.

Despite such events, Chris was unknown in his hometown by everyone but the close-knit abstract beats community. By 2002 however, he was a star in France. Thanks mainly to the house music persona he launched in 1996, Bob Sinclar. A persona that delivered one of the definitive French Touch records and revived the career of Ceronne.

In the early 2000s, Yellow Productions' offices were next door to the Picas Museum. The shop style interior was stylish but functional as numerous people worked on further developing the company's global profile. One wall was covered by a huge work of art that landed the space an air of creativity. Beyond this area was a cluster of glass-walled offices, while the basement below housed the Yellow Productions studio. It was all a far cry from the single chaotic room that doubled up as an office and warehouse back in the company's early days when Yellow was almost totally alone, with the obvious exception of Cam's Street Jazz, of course.

"At the beginning, there was nobody doing what we did," exclaimed Chris when reminded of the struggle he, Ho and Cam had in the beginning. "There was FNAC doing techno, but nothing like what we were doing. So we had no influence or roots other than the UK and US imports. When acid jazz came from the UK, it gave us the opportunity to produce this music that used the beats from hip hop, which we loved, and some of the jazz sounds we also loved. So that opened things up for us. But there were no other labels or anyone else doing what we were doing in the beginning. We all felt quite alone."

Those earliest forays into acid jazz and hip hop may have failed to set the world alight for Yellow Productions. However, when Chris arrived with his Mighty Bop project, not for the last time, he was in exactly the right musical place and exactly the right time. Mighty Bop trod a similar path to DJ Cam. Beats were culled from downtempo breaks, melodies lifted from smoky jazz tunes and ambience a few degrees below chilled.

Contemporaries at the time included the aforementioned DJ Shadow and DJ Krush, but Mighty Bop was far more aligned with UK producers like Howie B and the Viennese duo Kruder & Dorfmeister. The Mighty Bop records were far less the work of a DJ than the creations of a producer.

1995's debut Mighty Bop album remains a classic among the abstract beats fraternity. Called *La Vague Sensoriell*, it drew on African influences as much as it lifted cues from hip hop and jazz. The albums and EPs that followed developed Mighty Bop as a collaborative unit. *Mighty Bop Meet DJ Cam et La Funk Mob* delved deeper into the experimental breakbeat arena, while 1996 album *Autre Voix Autres Blues* found Chris employing the sultry tones of vocalist Louise Vertigo over a melange of beats which drew from the usual palette but also added flourishes of drum & bass and house.

The 1996 EP 'Ultraviolet Sounds' found Chris the French Kiss puckering up to a selection of low down and delicious slo-mo breaks brought to life, once again, by the vocals of Louise Vertigo. Standout tracks coming in the shape of 'Je N'ai Pas Les Choix' and 'Peau D'Ane'.

Over a period of two years, Mighty Bop became one of the most sought after Paris outfits, with their records becoming snapped up by DJs and punters alike in the US and the UK. Suddenly Yellow Productions seemed to have a defined style, somewhere between the impromptus they were first inspired by; Mo' Wax and Talkin' Loud.

During the early days of Mighty Bop, a couple of singles by new artists had further enhanced the label profile. One came in the shape of the downtempo jazz-house grooves of Fresh Lab, while the second was a four-track slice of easy listening, cocktail house fusion called 'Esquisse'. The artist in question was Dimitri from Paris and the album he would release late in 1996 would completely revolutionise the label.

In the meantime, however, the artists affiliated with Yellow Productions came together to create a superb concept album under the creative guidance of Chris the French Kiss. Called *La Yellow 357*, it was intended to be a soundtrack to an imaginary film. This collection represented a true coming of age for the label. It found Mighty Bop, Fresh Lab, Dimitri from Paris, DJ Cam and Magnetic delivering a collected sound that was so unified that it was hard to tell where one artist was finished and the next started. Furthermore, the album presented an identity that would become synonymous with the label. It was a picture of cocktail chic, 60s spy films and suave sophistication. Gritty glamour and sleazy adventure with pimps, hustlers, sports cars, guns, spies in ill-fitting tuxedos and girls in cheap leather mini-skirts, *La Yellow 357* had the lot.

"We'd always had this dream to do a soundtrack but the chance never came up," explained Chris. "In the end, we just wrote a script and a storyline and got different people to do the music. It was our ultimate film".

La Yellow 357 paid homage to the great thriller soundtracks. Those scores underpinned the action, theme tunes that captured all of the adventure and the romance with their sordid melodrama and kitsch sophistication. It was all about the themes to Bond, the 'Get Carter' soundtrack, the title music to The Persuaders. Classics of their time. However, just as the mid-90s easy listening revival attempted to breathe new life into the corpse, it was with the slo-mo beats, brassy flourishes, sleazy grooves and pining strings of ...*357* that the spirit seemed resurrected with a 90s attitude.

This is how I described the album in a review for Muzik magazine at the time:

"Imagine... A high speed chase. Tabatha Channel sits in the passenger seat, hair flowing in the wind, leather mini riding up to reveal the gun holster strapped to her thigh. In the rearview mirror, you catch a glimpse of the black Citroen as it swerves across the road to give the gorilla with the matching black moustache and pistol a better view. His aim is bad. The bullet skims past your head and scratches the car's otherwise pristine paintwork. But still you drive. You drive because the sun is bright and the skies are bluer than nostalgia. You drive with a smooth abandonment because you've got the girl, the car, the looks, the roll-neck sweater and the money. The vibes are wild and the music is cool as the Parisian purveyors of downtempo seduction lick the air like Miss Channel's scent. Dimitri from Paris smothers smouldering house beats with lush wet-dream scapes as The Mighty Bop skim pebbles across the Seine with their slow motion grooves. Meanwhile, DJ Cam twists through the film-noir score with low-down and subversive breaks, so you turn the radio up and drive even faster. You've left the Citreon behind and life has never been better... You're starring in the greatest movie never made – *La Yellow 357*."

"We were influenced by people like Lalo Schiffrin who composed the *Mission Impossible* theme and stuff like *Dirty Harry* and the Bond films," enthused Chris. "Ultimately though, the album is dedicated to the kung-fu films of John Woo, Jacky Chan and the great Bruce Lee – he's the man.

"The way to think of the visuals to this record would probably be 'David Lynch directing *Dirty Harry*'. Kind of a surreal thriller," was Dimitri's take on the album. Indeed all of the LP's influences come to the fore in the opening cut and paste epic, Dimitri's 'Sequel'.

Just as the rest of the world was catching up with le Friant's trip hop vision, he had already started flirting with house music. In 1996 he released the debut 'Space Funk EP' by Bob Sinclar. Not only did it represent the beginnings of a musical venture that was to bring him global notoriety, but it also represented the very first release by a French label in the style most associated with the term French Touch. Namely house beats, disco loops and heavy filtering.

"People came to us from a certain style because we were associated with that original acid jazz wave," he explained. "The turn into the house scene was definitely a big thing for us. We were a part of the scene, you know. And in the scene, people started to get into house. James Lavelle started getting techno projects on Mo'Wax, and Gilles Peterson was getting some house projects – the scene started to open up a bit. So we started to work with a few French house musicians. It wasn't opportunism. But it was a way to keep up to date with what was happening. Also, I'm a DJ first, so

I was a little bit frustrated with lounge stuff. In '96, hip hop was getting bad; there wasn't much happening. So I created a club project to satisfy my needs as a DJ."

Perhaps the most obvious sign of Yellow Production's newly discovered commitment to house music came with the arrival of Dimitri from Paris. Already a legend in France thanks to a high profile dance music radio show on national station NRG and remixes for artists including Bjork, Dimitri brought the history and knowledge of the house music obsessive. Even if this wasn't immediately clear on his hugely successful debut album *Sacrebleu*.

SACREBLEU – VIVA LA FRANCE, VIVA MONSIEUR DIMITRI!

Few artists of the French Touch golden age truly lived up to the image they portrayed to the public quite like Dimitri Yerasimos. As Dimitri from Paris, we knew him as the cocktail swigging, smooth-talking professional bachelor whose every smooth move was soundtracked by shaken but not stirred lounge house. Why else would he be the chosen DJ at the Playboy Mansion?

The person behind that persona, it transpired, was not so different. Except for the fact that beyond the tongue in cheek character was a DJ with unparalleled passion and encyclopaedic knowledge of house music. However, everything else about him seemed to have stepped straight from the inside cover of his acclaimed *Sacrebleu* album.

Dimitri, at that time, was the model of studied sophistication. From the black slacks and roll-neck sweater to the greased back hair and pencil moustache, he had the aura of parody. He exuded the kind of cool that belonged to a former age, rather like a 50s lounge lizard. His apartment on Paris' Boulevard de Nation depicted an equally nostalgic air. From the 50s plastic chairs to the radiogram, his space was dedicated to clean lines and retro chic. The only colours were red, black and white. On one wall hung a poster of cult Brigitte Bardot movie *She*. Stripped floorboards were covered by a single rug depicting a Manga character. It was an image that belied one of Dimitri's famed passions – collecting robots.

Dimitri from Paris (Mark Stringer)

In his previous much smaller apartment, the collection of some 3,000 robots dwarfed the entire space. Here though, they were set into the walls on either side of the fireplace in sealed glass units and were merely a feature, balanced out by the room's size and sophistication. It was an impressive collection that hosted everything from the earliest tin robots to the latest Manga figures. In fact, Dimitri was a serious collector who was as happy travelling around the world to toy fairs as he was globetrotting on his quest as one of the finest deep house and house DJs on the planet.

As a testament to his DJing trade, the hallway of his apartment was lined with records. Elsewhere he had a collection that was carefully organised and filed, but those in the hall were the records that provided him with a constant source for his sets. There were literally thousands of them, all stacked in piles that threatened to spill into his living room to mess up those clean lines and open spaces.

It was all a far cry from that first apartment where his records (and the boxes to his robots!) were kept in a loft space that could only be accessed via a very narrow spiral staircase.

"I wasn't as popular back then," he laughed when I pointed out how much more luxurious his new home was. "Only people like you liked me then. But now I actually sell records!"

Dimitri first came to prominence as a DJ not in the clubs but on the renowned French radio station Skyrock. He'd developed his DJ technique at home using spliced tapes and loops of his favourite tracks. However, his first break in radio found him speaking in between tracks. To all intents and purposes, he was a jock, a brand of personality peculiar to radio. However, his choice of music gave an early clue as to the man's future.

"The first radio station that I had my own show on was called Skyrock. It's only hip hop now, but at the time, it was playing everything. In 1985 and 1986, I had two hours on a Sunday night, which became four hours on a Sunday night. I played a lot of funk, early electronic music, electro-funk, some hip hop and so on.

"The first kind of music I really got into was the stuff which came directly after disco. That funk sound. It was slower than disco, and it was really big here because of all of the black communities. It was artists like Slave, Leon Burgess, not really P-Funk. James Brown was huge. So was Barry White and Cameo were gods here. A lot of the French house focus was from this funk music rather than the disco sound. Funk was the culture of the young people as opposed to disco, which was the music of the mums and dads. Funk fuelled hip hop and house in France.

"For a lot of people, if you say you play disco, they think you mean ABBA and Boney M! Before '86, I hated disco because of this. But when I discovered the stuff that the black gay community in the US were dancing to, I started to understand the other side of disco. This is the music they were listening to in the ghettos of Chicago and that's what inspired house. They were trying to recreate these huge orchestras with cheap machines. So they ended up with the house sound. When the first house record came out, for me, it was all a part of the evolution from funk, then electro-funk with 'Planet Rock' and then it became house with JM Silk. This was the first house record that I heard and I loved it. It was a step on from D:Train, and I was a big fan of the D:Train sound, you know, funky basslines and electronic beats."

In 1986 Dimitri went to the New York New Musical Seminar and discovered house music. It was a discovery that revolutionised his career, as he eventually chose the house sound over his other musical loves.

"When I went to the New Musical Seminar, it was the year of the house explosion there," he said. "There were house showcases everywhere by people like DJ International, Traxx Records. Farley Jackmaster and all those guys were there and it was huge. So I brought back a lot of records and started mixing house with the rest of the stuff. And that was the start for me.

"My music of choice was the Frankie Knuckles style deep house. The early days of really nicely produced stuff. So I focussed on this kind of thing on my shows and mixed it in with funk. When I went to NRJ in '87, which was the biggest station in France and still is, my hours were cut to two. I'd had four hours at Skyrock. For NRJ, I was on between 8-10 on a Saturday evening and was presenting with this other guy. At first, no one took much notice to what I was playing, which is why they allowed me so much time. Then when they started taking notice, they were like, 'what is this music he's playing?'. Then I was cut to one hour in 1991, so I had to focus on one thing. And that was deep house."

Dimitri remained with NRJ for eight years, during which time he made a name for himself as an expert jingles producer and even, for a while, an accomplished programmer. However, it was his weekly show that people really knew him for. When fans of deep house were still few and far between in France (techno was still the main music until the late 90s), Dimitri's show offered a rare peek into the musical developments that other parts of Europe took for granted.

"A lot of people have cited me as an influence because of the shows. But house didn't really get popular in France until after I was taken off the air, I think. There were always a small group of people who were into the music, but it wasn't popular with a large group. It was very underground. I mean, there was a house music boom when Bomb the Bass came out with 'Beat 'Dis'. I remember at this time, the boss of NRJ said they were going to be a house station and they started to play S Express and so on, but it was just a fad that lasted six months. But that wasn't the kind of house that I played. What I was into wasn't played anywhere else.

"When Radio Nova started opening up to deep house with people like DJ Deep, a lot of new people got introduced to house. Nova was more of a world music station at the time. So the people who listened to this were more serious about their music than the people listening to NRJ. But my listeners were like the hardcore following. People from out of Paris because NRJ was a national station. Nova was just Paris. Which is why I got a cult following in France."

While still at NRJ, Dimitri was approached by fashion giants Jean Paul Gaultier and Yves Saint Laurent to create some music for their fashion shows. Chanel even asked him to produce some music for an advert. He'd already delivered numerous acclaimed remixes and had worked on a few house cuts, but the fashion and perfume markets asked for a much less dancefloor friendly approach. Dimitri's only direction for the fashion shows was that the music had to be stylish. So he set about working on tracks that eventually catapulted him to global notoriety.

Dimitri's first four tracks for Jean Paul Gaultier appeared on the 'Esquisses EP'. A delicious combination of cocktail melodrama and lazy deep house, the EP received instant acclaim from the UK's house DJ elite. However, had it not been for one Philippe Zdar, the tracks may never have been released.

"When I played the 'Esquisses EP' to Philippe Zdar – he was the first person to hear the tracks – he said 'wow this is something that the girls would like!' I was like, 'that's a good idea'. I realised that a lot of DJs were playing their music for their brothers, you know it was all very much about men. He made me realise that the tracks that I had didn't fit into that macho environment. They had a wider appeal. Then, because that first EP was only in vinyl, I was thinking that the only people who would get to hear it would be the guys with their turntables, so I wanted Yellow to put out a CD of it for the girls. Yellow said they could only do this if it was a full-length album. So I never intentionally put together an album."

For an unintentional album *Sacrebleu*, which appeared four months later, was a work of inspired brilliance where easy listening met deep house in a high camp meltdown – like Serge Gainsbourg at a Paradise Garage after-show party. Not the kind of thing people had come to expect from techno-orientated France! Furthermore, the whole project came with a tongue in cheek attitude that seemed to poke fun at Frenchness – or, to be more accurate, the stereotypical view of the French man. For starters, there was the name Dimitri from Paris.

On the face of things, Dimitri was tapping into what was becoming a tradition among DJs named Dimitri. Dimitri from New York (aka DJ Dimitri from Deee-Lite) and Dimitri from Holland were already renowned figures in the dance world. The addition of a Dimitri from Paris seemed like a natural thing. At the time, Dimitri pointed out that part of his reason for choosing that moniker was a response to Deee-Lite Dimitri taking credit for one of his remixes.

"The Deee-Lite Dimitri claimed my remix of Bjork's "Human Behaviour" as his own," he told me in 1996, as we sat in the restaurant of the British Museum. "So I decided to become Dimitri from Paris, which makes me sound like a cheap Parisian hairdresser. But it also distinguishes me from the others".

However, there was another motivation for employing the name. On the one hand, he was keen not to hide the fact that he was French as many others had done in the past but also aimed to create a persona that played on the image of French people as portrayed by Peter Sellers in his Pink Panther films. Dimitri aimed to take the cartoon image of Inspector Clouseau and reveal true depth, a substance beneath the surface.

This wasn't the first time Dimitri used a name that seemingly mocked the French stereotype. In early 1996 he released the excellent 'Jazzin' the House' twelve under the guise of Da Mothafunkin' Phrog on Nitegrooves Records. However, the artists who gave him the courage to use French-sounding names came from the unlikely source of techno imprint F Communications.

"If I did take a very French name and concept for my first album, it was because of St Germain. I wasn't into the Laurent Garnier stuff because it was too techno. In fact, I was never into acid house and that Detroit techno thing. That was a far cry from what I was inspired by. The only French producer who did stuff that I liked at the time was probably St Germain. I think he really paved the way for people like me and DJ Cam – the very first wave of French producers – because he was the first house producer from here who had a French-sounding name. He was the first one to make a point of saying that he was French and doing house music. It was really thanks to him that I started thinking we should stop feeling guilty about being French people making house music. Because anytime we did any kind of music, people were dissing us for real. So we all thought, let's take the piss with our names. St Germain was the inspiration to us to accept the fact that we were French."

Sacrebleu took this concept to an extreme, however. Titles were a combination of French and English (Franglais). The sleeve had 50s style typography over a silhouette of the Eiffel Tower, while the images of Dimitri depict him as the ultimate bachelor. Sleeve notes for the album were written by the imaginary US Marines Sergant (sic) Bill T. Hawthorne whose words reminisced about an affair with a Parisian girl named Monique immediately after the WW2 liberation. They only added to the sense that this was a pastiche of the international image of French cool. More kitsch than stylish.

Dimitri explained the thought process behind the album: "Most of the songs had been created for fashion shows where the only thing I was told was that the tracks had to fit within the collection and be stylish. So I was starting to make music that would make people think that what they were seeing was stylish. So it had a lot of camp elements. When the whole thing was put together, I thought of the name and how I could present it on a record. So I came up with this French-sounding album title and the image of the Eiffel Tower. One thing led to another and the songs were given these names, which were half English and half French. I think this is what people liked, the way it was what they thought French was. It was presented in a very touristy way, which is how people perceived the French.

"I meant it all as a joke but people took it at face value," he continued. "That French thing was a way of saying that I was French, but as a joke. It was supposed to be like Monty Python and Peter Sellers because I really liked those guys. I was being French but with that fake accent. I gave this sting image and concept without really thinking about it and people just bought into it. It was accepted first by English speaking people thanks to the power of the English music magazines, which were talking about music then – unlike today, the album started to touch the rest of the world. It only really came back to France about a year and a half later."

If the record buying public now had Dimitri pinned down as a lounge artist, then his radio shows continued to display a DJ with a love of deep house and funk. However, *Sacrebleu* had created a stylised straightjacket that threatened to suffocate Dimitri. His only response was to return to the music he loved and develop his DJ career. However, despite his high profile presence at NRJ, Dimitri had found problems getting bookings.

"The radio work has caused me a few problems with the house underground," he told me back in 1996. "They think that I just play what I'm told. The thing is, I'm probably the only radio DJ left in France who can play what I like. And what I like is good quality deep house."

Dimitri did find one supporter for his DJing talents in the shape of Pedro Winter. As it tuned out, he could not have found a better ally as Winter's Hype nights pretty much shaped the French Touch scene in the same way that Garnier's 'Wake Up! Paris' had the early 90s techno scene.

The day after this 2002 meeting with Dimitri, Pedro showed me flyers from those Hype parties. Sure enough, they represented a coming together of all of the premier names of the scene. Dimitri was, to all intents and purposes, the resident.

"I think Hype was important because it gave everyone a focus," recalled Pedro. "Thomas [Bangalter of Daft Punk] used to have parties at his place which were important too, everyone was there, but Hype kind of gave an outside place, a front to these people who were coming through. And we gave Dimitri his first regular gigs, which I'm very proud of."

Dimitri took up the story: "You know, despite DJing on the radio, I couldn't get a DJ gig in a club until maybe a year before the album came out. The first serious gigs I got was at Pedro's Hype parties. Because of the kind of people who were going to these parties, they started to take notice of who I was and thought I was a good DJ. But they didn't know that I'd been DJing for ten years. But it was Pedro who got me back into it and since then, I've been working as a club DJ rather than a radio DJ. This helped me travel around the world as a club DJ, so Pedro was essential in bringing me to the club DJ scene."

Despite Pedro Winter's Hype parties maintaining a key role in the emergence of French Touch, another club night, Respect, was often cited as the focus of the scene. However, Respect opened its doors on 2 October 1996 at Paris' premier gay club, the Queen on Champs-Elysees, sometime after Hype started.

"Everybody thinks of Respect being the first parties who booked these French DJs," confirmed Dimitri. "In fact, they were the first in the bigger clubs, but they actually went to Pedro to get his help. But he'd just done the deal with Daft Punk and couldn't do it.

"Respect is really good because it provides us all with a place to play and a rare chance to meet because most of us spend our lives in the studio recording." Yellow Productions artist Kid Loco explained in August 1998. "Personally, I'd rather roll a giant spliff, get stoned and record some music, but if I do go out, Respect is the place."

Respect continued its weekly Wednesday night residency until July 1999, when their Paris is Burning promotions team took the Parisian sound on a global tour starring Dimitri. The tour ended up at Hugh Hefner's famed Playboy Mansion, which heralded the next stage in Dimitri's DJing and found him releasing a series of compilation albums that drew on this finale. The collections *A Night at the Playboy Mansion* and *After the Playboy Mansion* found him delivering sets that were far more representative of his musical tastes – fusions of Latin, deep house, 80s funk and black disco.

"After doing the lounge album, I started to push all of my dance stuff again. That's why I did all of these compilations. I wanted to say to people that I like to make people dance – that's what I'm about. And the compilations put people straight."

The compilation put Dimitri on the world stage as a renowned DJ. However, in 2002, seven years after completing his own artist album, he was still yet to release a follow-up. He had recorded that elusive second album, but it was unreleased.

"The new album comes with a different perspective because now I have some popularity," he said. "I have made a lot of tracks over the years but I like to approach making music as my hobby. It's what I do for pleasure. I never want it to be my job because then I would have to worry about it beginning commercial or whether the A&R likes it or not. My job is as a DJ. When I did the first album, my job was at the radio station. But now my job is as a DJ. If I do a remix for someone, it's my job. If I do music under my own name, it's a hobby."

One of the proposed guest vocalists for the album was Ashley Slater. However, his contributions weren't used in the end. Talking to Ashley during the summer of 2002, he told me that he felt Dimitri's problem was an inability to find a style that worked. He was, it seemed, creatively unfocused due to a need to get away from the gimmicky aspects of the previous album and produce something which could stand up to the artists he was so enamoured by.

"Yes, I wanted to get away from the gimmicky aspect of the first album," Dimitri confirmed. "So I took all of the samples and recreated them in the studio with live musicians. I really like to be where people do not expect me to be and I'm not interested in doing the same thing twice. So I've had this more acoustic approach, which is less tongue in cheek than the first album. It's as diverse as before, and it doesn't really fit into a format. But I'm in the same position as before in that I've no idea how it will be received.

"I'm sure that some people would expect me to come out with another *Sacrebleu* but it's taken me six or seven years to come up with a second album, so obviously, I haven't paid too much attention to what they were saying. Also, when I did this album, it only really came out because I was commissioned to do the tracks for someone else. This new album will be the first one where I've done it all for myself, with no directions from other people at all."

That album *Cruising Attitude* would remain unreleased until 2003 and was met with barely a ripple of recognition from a media that demanded *Sacrebleu* part 2. After all, *Sacrebleu* sold 300,000 copies worldwide and was named Album of the Year in 1996 by UK dance music magazine *Mixmag*.

Dimitri from Paris may never release another album that captures people's imaginations as much as *Sacrebleu*. That album came at the perfect time. Interest was growing in France and it delivered a vision of Paris that was fun but deep enough to not be a joke. However, any more of that particular style would be more like a remake of a classic. And as we all know, there is only one Inspector Clouseau. Just as there can only be one *Sacrebleu*. In that one album, Dimitri made his point with clarity.

As Dimitri's star rose, another Yellow Productions artist received long-overdue acclaim; Kid Loco. Born Jean Yves Prieur, Kid Loco had actually released his 'Blues Project EP' some time before Dimitri's debut.

However, the EP's combination of slo-mo breaks and abstract ambience ("I'd been listening to DJ Shadow a lot at the time," he says) came too soon to pick up on the early media attention placed upon Yellow. Indeed 'Blues Project' was one of the first abstract hip hop releases in France. This hasn't stopped him from being written out of much of the magazine coverage of French Touch.

"In the bible, it says that the first will be last," he told me in 1996. "That's how it is with me. I may have been one of the first, but I will keep going on producing things in my own way. Which is why I last."

Jean Yves Prieur's introduction to the music industry came in the 1980s through his involvement with indie rock pioneers such as Les Beruniers Noirs and Les Satellites. At the turn of the 1990s, he formed the rap, soul, funk and reggae crossover act Mega Reefer Scratch whose first album *Honky Soultimes* was signed to Squatt/Sony. By 1993 he had returned to his rock roots with the band Catch My Soul, whose *People Ya Gotta Love 'Em* came out on Vogue/BMG.

'Blues Project', a collaboration between the newly named Kid Loco and Yellow mentors, Chris the French Kiss and DJ Yellow, appeared in 1995. However, it was with his 'Real Popcorn Blue Sound' 10" EPs that he started to receive some attention from the media. 'Real Popcorn Blue Sound' found Kid Loco exploring the space age pop moods of Jean-Jacques Perrey and combining them with abstract hip hop.

In 1997 the debut Kid Loco album *A Grand Love Affair* was released to huge critical acclaim going on to sell over 50,000 copies. *A Grand Love Affair* picked up where the previous 10" singles left off, swimming in space-age pop waters, but with the added influence of psychedelia.

"I'm mainly into hip hop, like Public Enemy and Beastie Boys. I like psychedelic music and some indie," he said of the album's influences, "but I wasn't really inspired by the electronic scene for this album."

Among the album's highlights were 'Relaxin' With Cherry', with its gorgeous snaking jazz guitar licks, and 'She's My Lover (A Song For R)', which found Indian vibes melted over a salubrious break and dream-scaped melodies. A single version of this track followed with Katrina

Mitchell from The Pastels on vocals a year later. "I was really happy with this single," said Kid Loco. "Katrina sang as a part of a deal which saw me do a remix for them."

The Kid Loco remix of The Pastel's 'The Viaduct' turned up in 1999 on the enigmatically titled remix collection *Kid Loco Presents Jesus Life For Children Under 12 Inches*. A twelve-track selection of Kid Loco remixes for other artists housed in a cover that aped Jimi Hendrix's *Electric Ladyland*. This stopgap album from Jean Yves Prieur displayed just how much his natural space was among the indie world. His Moog sounds and slo-mo breaks sat perfectly next to the works of St Etienne, The High Llamas, The Pastels and Pulp, while reworkings of more electronic based artists like Uriel, Tommy Hools and Badmarsh & Shri fell short of the original versions.

His remix of Pulp's 'A Little Soul' was especially interesting. His version replaced the pompous indie overtones of the original with a svelte, undulating blues ambience. No doubt it would have pleased Pulp's main man Jarvis Cocker, a very public supporter of Kid Loco, having included the man's music in a show for BBC Radio 1 in 1998.

"I had been told that he was playing some of my tracks on the radio. Which I was really pleased about. Then he asked me to remix something from the Pulp album and to support them in London. To be honest, I'm not really into their stuff that much – I hadn't really listened to their music before then. But I love his lyrics, and I thought it was brilliant when he got on stage in front of Michael Jackson and danced like an idiot [at the Brits Awards Show in 1996]."

2002 saw Kid Loco consolidating his position as a songwriter with a leaning towards indie, as opposed to dance music. His second full album, *Kill Your Darlings*, found the Parisian slow beat merchant giving into his indie, folk and blues roots while keeping a firm grasp on the downtempo film-noir oeuvre that ran through his debut. Ironically, he developed his most experimental sound by returning to such strictly formulaic styles. In the tradition of the greatest left of centre pop albums, *Kill Your Darlings* was the sound of pop music consumed and subverted.

The opening cut, 'Cocaine Diana', set the tone for the entire album. Strummed twelve-string, distorted ambience, naive keyboard motifs, chocolate box strings and atonal folksy vocals. Not the most inspiring combination, but Loco succeeded in bringing a perfectly honed perverted pop classic to the fore. The same was true of 'A Little Bit of Soul' with its honky-tonk piano and Motown groove, the 60s beat movie soundtrack of 'I Can't Let it Happen to You' and the joyous, happy clapper 'I Want You'. 'Horsetown In Vain', on the other hand, was a close cousin to Rob Dougan's timeless 'Clubbed to Death', with its ghostly ambience, stuttering beats and soundtrack strings, while 'Going Round in Circles' used epic Pink Floyd-style Hammond and synth discordance to surprising cool effect.

The disparate elements of the album's sound were glued together by melodies lifted straight from the Leonard Cohen school of bleakness. However, the lyrics seemed more inspired by Cheech and Chong, with the main themes being getting stoned, getting the munchies and getting laid.

Kill Your Darlings was met with far less acclaim than the previous albums, and instead of propelling him to global prominence, it found him turning into a cult artist. The irony is that this was probably his most commercially viable set. Indeed, it is possible that, had his name not been associated with Parisian dance music, he would have been approached totally differently.

BACK TO THE HOUSE WITH BOB SINCLAR... AND CERRONE'S RETURN

Yellow Productions may have had a strong roster, but thanks to a distribution deal with East West Records in 1996, they managed to market their product so effectively. The first artists to benefit from this alliance were Dimitri from Paris and Kid Loco, with Xavier Jameaux's Bang Bang project also attracting a lot of attention. However, the biggest results came from Chris le Friant's house *nom de plume* Bob Sinclar. Thanks mainly to his collaboration with Thomas Bangalter on the club track 'Gym Tonic', which featured a sample from the infamous 'Jane Fonda Workout' exercise video.

"When I did that first twelve-inch, I couldn't imagine the power of the club hit," said Chris in 1999. "Then I did 'Gym Tonic' and it was amazing. A club hit like that means that you're like an icon immediately, especially with English people. They can make it seem like at one moment you are a genius and in the next, you're worth nothing. So you have to work hard to impress and stay longer on the scene. So, at the beginning, I had 'Gym Tonic' with Thomas Bangalter, but after that, I had to prove that I was really a producer on my own."

To prove himself as a producer in his own right, Chris had developed an assumed character that he has described as "like a porn star or a disco hero or a spy – a James Bond parody, but cool, like the Fonzie". The name Bob Sinclar actually came from the main protagonist of 60s French spy film *Le Magnifique*.

"When I started all the music, all I wanted to do was some productions and not really put a face to anything," he explained. "So I did Reminiscence Quartet, Mighty Bop etc. And then the label started to get known and I became the face of the label. Then in 1997, I wanted to do a club project, and I didn't put my face on it at all. I just imagined a style, an image to put to it. That was Bob Sinclar."

So, according to legend Monsieur Sinclar was an international man of mystery. A spy, a jewel thief, arms smuggler, Riviera playboy, mercenary, Studio 54 bellboy, gigolo, model and hardcore porn star. The ultimate fantasy role model for Chris le Friant, in fact.

The huge Ibiza reaction to the second Bob Sinclar release 'Gym Tonic' in 1998 brought a mass of unwanted controversy. First of all, Thomas Bangalter, who had co-produced the track, claimed that he never thought that it would be released. Furthermore, he insisted that the single should never receive an official release. He even went on record as suggesting that le Friant was using the success of Daft Punk to raise the profile of Bob Sinclar. However, it is possible that Bangalter didn't want 'Gym Tonic' to compete with his own filtered disco anthem

'Music Sounds Better With You' as Stardust, which was also getting a massive reaction in Ibiza at this time.

Next, Jane Fonda refused permission for clearance of the sample of her, which resulted in the track being withdrawn. Indeed promo copies featured the original version of the track, while the finished version had a new mix of 'Gym Tonic' with a different actress delivering Fonda's words. Finally, as the furore continued around the track, Bob Sinclar's licensees in the UK, East West, put out a new version of the track to meet the massive demand. This new version was created under Spacedust and was called 'Gym and Tonic'. The connection was hardly veiled and offered an ironic echo of Cerrone's experience with his first single, which was re-recorded and released in the US by a major label.

But it was the situation with Thomas Bangalter that upset Chris the most.

"I don't want to talk about this story, really," confesses an obviously still bemused Chris in 2002. "All I can say is that I'm not interested in this guy at all. He took a very bad attitude. He was very successful at the time and he tried to claim things in magazines, but I didn't know why. I was really hurt. He tried to keep everyone behind him, on his side and he said I was hiding behind his name. But now my name is as big as he is in France, so I'm over it now. It was really an education for me. You know what? Friends shouldn't work together if they don't want to fall out. We were together in the studio. He asked me what I wanted because it was an exchange of ideas, so the collaboration was there."

Paradise, the album that followed early in 1999, not only introduced le Friant as a house producer of some talent ('Gym Tonic' proving to be the worst track in the set), but the album title also introduced the beginning of his links to Ceronne. This connection was taken to deeper levels on the second Bob Sinclar album *Champs Elysees* in which le Friant took Ceronne's Angels, sampled his songs and borrowed his suits! Now Bob Sinclar was presented as a disco-fied gigolo amid a bevvy of circus freaks – albeit beautiful circus freaks!

Musically *Champs Elysees* found le Friant moving away from the Chicago jack trax, which informed "Paradise", and delving deeper into the styles of disco and jazz-funk, with liberal amounts of filtering along the way. The main reference points apart from Ceronne being D:Train (whose James Williams is the featured vocalist on two tracks).

"The first album was just a set of DJ tracks which I really hurried to get out," he said of Paradise three years later. "But with *Champs Elysees*, I wanted to tell a story from beginning to end. So I approached it as an album from the very start. What I wanted to do was create a collection of classics that stay in DJs' sets for months, years even. These days everybody's buying a sampler and doing a track. There's so much of shit around. What I wanted was to bring back that classic feel. So I to refer to the 70s and 80s but not just with samples, I used live musicians as well".

In many ways, this collection represented the definitive French Touch album thanks to its mixture of throwaway pop hooks, disco strings and melodic house. However, in le Friant's attempts to create an album of classic tracks, he forfeited the depth that marked out his other releases and concentrated on the hooks and fills. Ultimately the set failed artistically because, quite unlike anything else he had created, *Champs Elysees* sounded like a man chasing hits rather than shaping dancefloors.

There were strong tracks on the album, however. The filtered disco classic 'I Feel For You' is just cheeky enough to get away with its heavy reliance on Cerrone, 'Striptease' echoed the electro-funk rush of 1980s TV Themes like 'Knight Rider' while 'Darlin' (featuring James 'D-Train' Williams) sounded like Cameo in collision with Chic at an 80s electro-disco revival party. Surprisingly, despite its retro action, it works beautifully.

In 2001 those Cerrone links were further explored in the compilation mix set *Cerrone by Bob Sinclar*. As previously mentioned, following this le Friant even went as far as to team up with Cerrone's main songwriting team of Alan Wizniak and Lene Lovich to create the third Bob Sinclar album *Bob Sinclar III* (the numbered album being another reference to Cerrone). If Bob Sinclar wasn't the millennium Cerrone, as he claims, then he was doing his best to fill the godfather of disco's shoes.

The first fruits of the Sinclar, Wizniak and Lovich partnership came at the end of 2002 with the single 'The Beat Goes On'. Once again using

80s electro-disco as its reference, the track combined analogue synths with throwaway melody to create a cut that was every inch what Cerrone's 2002 material should have sounded like – modern retro disco.

"I took the team from Cerrone from the 70s, Lena Lovic on lyrics, Alain Wizniak who produced Cerrone," boasted Chris. "I decided I should use them because they did such good work on tracks like 'Supernature'. So Wizniak brought me a tune that was excellent, but the production was shit. So I used an acapella of it and created an entirely new tune. And that's how I created 'The Beat Goes On'. So it started like this and then I decided to do a full album with him. I think it's a dream team for me."

The impact of the Bob Sinclar project resulted in a new market opening up to Yellow Productions. Suddenly they were able to aim records directly at the dancefloor. Surprisingly, however, the first non-Bob Sinclar dancefloor orientated releases actually hinted back to the label's earliest records, but with a contemporary club update. The *Bossa Tres… Jazz – When Japan Meets Europe* album featured collaborations between French and Japanese artists focussing on the Bossa Nova style.

A hugely ambitious project found Yellow Productions in the position of being teachers, employing the jazz aesthetic to draw direct a line between the attitudes and cultures of Paris and Tokyo. The cement for the argument comes through the techniques of contemporary dance production.

It was their suggestion that both Tokyo and Paris had long been the capital cities of jazz in their respective continents. Tokyo had embraced bossa nova in the 60s and forged a sound that would have a huge influence on Detroit techno originator Carl Craig. In the following two decades, Japan developed its own take on jazz and became a global force. Collaborations between Japanese and European artists became commonplace and universally respected.

Paris, on the other hand, had been a sanctuary for jazz since World War II, with the discotheques employing this music of black America as their chosen soundtrack. By the 50s, many jazz musicians sought refuge in Paris. The US still had laws that segregated black people and this music was seen as being inferior in their homeland. In Paris, however, it was celebrated.

The black American musicians that flocked to Paris discovered an open-minded and tolerant city. This was a period in which France desperately sought to forget the destruction of WWII and the celebratory aspect of jazz fit perfectly with the city's needs. The musicians subsequently became revered for their talent rather than the rejection they received in their homeland.

From here, Paris became the central hub of jazz in Europe with the St Germain district ringing out to the sound nightly, while everyone who was anyone in the world of jazz, at some time found solace in the city. The influx of new technology through the 80s and 90s found these jazz roots bearing fruit in a contemporary setting. In Japan, artists such as Mighty Force and UFO were evolving at the same time as Yellow Productions and links were gradually forged between the prime movers of the abstract jazz scenes in both cities. Chris le Friant and Alain Ho were invited to play at Tokyo's appropriately named Club Yellow. Within a week, they had met all of the most important producers and artists in the Japanese abstract jazz underground scene.

Bossa Tres... Jazz – When Japan Meet Europe was met with a hugely positive reaction. Most specifically from Internationally renowned DJs like Masters at Work and seminal figure Francois Kervorkian. Indeed so enamoured was Kervorkian with the Tom & Joyce track 'Vai Minha Tristeza' that he licensed it for his Wave imprint.

A remix selection *More Bossa... Remix Album* appeared a year later and featured a Francois K reworking of the Tom & Joyce track alongside Little Big Bee's 'Searchin', which was remixed by At Jazz (aka Martin Iverson, the man behind the soundtracks to the Tomb Raider Playstation games!) among others. The 2002 instalment of the series *Bossa Tres Jazz II – Step Into the Gallery* was equally good as its predecessor, this time featuring Francois K's 'Awakening' alongside French artists Gotan Project, who took the bossa nova style even deeper into the dancefloor with their outstanding *La Ravencha del Tango* album in 2001.

Meanwhile, Yellow artists Tom & Joyce also delivered an understated eponymous album for the label. Despite the electronic music leanings of the *More Bossa...* albums, Tom & Joyce's own effort was entirely acoustic. Despite the warmth of the Tom & Joyce album, it failed to translate to the dance market, so far was it removed from the aesthetic of house music.

In terms of Yellow Productions' output, the Tom & Joyce album was also overshadowed by the latest series that the label had embarked upon – The Africanism series under the name Africanism Allstars. The Allstars comprised of Bob Sinclar, Condor, DJ Gregory, Eddie Amador, and Martin Solveig. Matt'Samo, Julien Jabre, Lego, Liquid People, Salome de Bahia and Soha. Together they compiled tracks for a number of twelves that combined the melodies of African music with the production techniques of house.

"On Yellow, we can't do one-off singles like on dance label," explained Chris le Friant. "We have to do projects that become albums. So we were working with DJ Gregory and we wanted to create something that wasn't overproduced and clean. We didn't want to sample disco but instead different kinds of exotic music. So we took loops of African rhythms and if they were working on the dance floor for the DJ, we did the tracks. The only thing I asked of the producers was to do club tracks with exotic influence."

Thanks to France's huge Afro-Caribbean communities, Yellow were able to source a wealth of musicians for the project while also finding instant recognition in their home country.

"We had the opportunity to work with different kinds of bassists and guitarists from the African and West Indies community," he said. "I had a band called Exile from the Dominican Republic who did five or six Afro-Disco albums. We had their records in our collections, so we started to sample them. We cleared everything we used."

Apart from launching DJ Gregory on a worldwide market thanks to his input on the series, *Africanism* also heralded a breakthrough in the African market for the label.

"It was really surprising," exclaimed Chris. "We had a gold record in South Africa. We've sold 40,000 now. But there is no real influence on this project. It wasn't us trying to do African music. We explained to them that we weren't pretending to have African influence. It's just a European project with African flavours. It's nothing at all like appropriation. We didn't want to do something African."

The *Africanism* series was marked out by a few notable tracks. DJ Gregory's 'Tourment d'Amour' and 'Block Party' became staples in the sets of Ashley Beedle, among others. Bob Sinclar's 'Bisou Sucre' was picked up by Little Louie Vega, who played it at the start of all of his sets after being blown away by it at the Miami Winter Music Conference in 2000. While the stunning 'Do It' found Bob Sinclar reaching the deep house crowd through this collaboration with Los Angeles based producer Eddie Amador.

If there was one criticism that could and had been levelled at both Yellow Productions and Chris le Friant, it was that they were opportunists. On the face of things, each development had coincided with major developments elsewhere. It could be argued that Kid Loco emerged on the back of Air's success, Bang Bang was a part of the Air family tree, Bob Sinclar arrived at the same time as the filtered disco sound of Stardust, Africanism appeared in the wake of the Afro-beat revival and so on. The only constant, it would seem, is Chris and Alain's love of hip hop, jazz and acid jazz.

However, closer inspection would reveal that the label had forged ahead with new styles alongside the big names of musical breakthroughs. Essentially both Chris and Alain were brilliantly intuitive A&R people who had a sense of the coming developments before they happened. This was naturally translated into their musical output both as label owners and artists.

As a result, Yellow Productions has been able to deliver consistently strong albums over the years. Similarly, Chris produced a number of excellent records. He had a populist touch that resulted in his music having a commercial and unchallenging identity. Yet his ability to move from style to style with confidence revealed a strong understanding of the common links between disparate music.

The only time Chris has failed to create a worthwhile, long-lasting sound has been when his output has either smacked of a lack of integrity or direction. Ironically it's with the former that he found his greatest commercial success – Bob Sinclar. Despite the artistic intentions of the earliest Sinclar material, the project very quickly appeared to be little more than a cash cow for le Friant's more rewarding ventures.

"I like Bob Sinclar. I honestly do. I'm not against him at all," he complained before revealing his ambitions with the Sinclar moniker. "I hope different collaborations are going to come with bigger artists like David Bowie or George Michael. Just to be a producer."

Quite simply, Bob Sinclar was his fame project. It enabled him to traverse the underground and the mainstream worlds with a sense of integrity intact. This may have been the case at first. By 2002 a more negative reaction to Chris' apparent creative schizophrenia emerged. His previous sense of integrity had become damaged by the loss of respect for the music of Bob Sinclar in the underground.

"My favourite project? I have to say I have a special affection for Mighty Bop because it was the beginning, and it got Yellow started in other countries. But I can't do any promotion for the new Mighty Bop album. Alain has to do it because now I am Bob Sinclar. This is who I am. I've been taken over, but it's not unpleasant. It's very good."

Ironically the third Mighty Bop album *Mighty Bop featuring Duncan Roy* represented the worst album yet put out by label or band. Released in 2002, it found Chris and Alain pursuing their jazz roots over the instrumental hip hop of old. On the other hand, melodies were lifted from soul and R&B. Musically, there were a few strong ideas – 'Too Deep' was a superb rolling jazz-in-the-house cut. However, they were dragged down by too many cheesy 80s jazz-funk inflexions and Duncan Roy's limited vocal delivery. For example, 'Tell Me' was a sickly ballad and 'Lady' was a sexless soul smooch that thought it was pure seduction! The end result was an album that found Mighty Bop out of touch with the developments on jazz, hip hop and R&B scenes but attempting to fashion a new sound of their own. They were out of touch and out on their own. And it's at this point they tripped up. As A&R men Yellow are second to none. As artists relating to the flows of popular culture, they were exceptional. But as a groundbreaking unit, Chris and Alain didn't quite cut it.

The contribution of Yellow Productions to both the French and the international dance scene is all too often overlooked. However, their finest releases have been a little short of inspirational. From Dimitri's cocktail hour to Africanism's booty call; early Mighty Bop's languid smoking grooves, to More Bossa's joyous jazz celebrations, Yellow have been a constant source of excellence, if not always innovation since their inception.

SOURCELAB – THREE COMPILATIONS, ONE SCENE: THE FRENCH TOUCH CONCEIVED

"To me, it was the UK who made this happen. The feedback from France was not very good but the UK were very receptive to the compilations."

Philippe Ascoli – Managing Director, Virgin UK.

In May 1995, Virgin subsidiary Source Records were approached to put together a promotional covermount CD for a magazine. The seeds of a concept were subsequently placed in the minds of Philippe Ascoli and his team. What happened next was a series of compilations that were to change the music world's view of France. No longer would it be seen as a country where a few good producers were creating the odd good record. Following these compilations, France was shown as a hotbed of talent with a focussed and vibrant scene. Even if the truth was that this scene was actually a Parisien phenomenon.

Initially, the compilation was to have been a six-track hip hop affair. Ascoli had himself come from a hip hop background. He'd been A&R for MC Solaar at Polydor and hip hop was the music he'd been into. However, soon after starting out compiling the collection, he realised that the wealth of new music produced by many of his friends from the hip hop scene would make a more interesting set. Thanks to his association with Solaar and his time working with Hubert Boombass, he was already aware of La Funk Mob, but as he started to explore things, he discovered a huge burgeoning scene of producers emerging from the hip hop arena.

"At first, a magazine wanted the soundtrack of Source, under the marketing name 'Ecoutez Foume', or 'Listen, Smoke'," explained Ascoli. "We didn't have artists on the label, so we asked a few friends to do some tracks. We started with hip hop because that's what people thought we were about because I was more into hip hop music. We asked a couple of hip hop people to give us tracks and then we got Etienne [de Crecy] on board. I knew Philippe Zdar from Motorbass because he also worked with MC Solaar with me. The same with Hubert [Boombass], who was involved with me as an A&R when I started in Polydor. So it was easy to start this compilation."

Other names from the world of hip hop came along in the shape of Raggasonic, Bazbaz, Lamumba and Gilb'R. The latter of whom had a background as a hip hop DJ before he graduated to a more eclectic range of genres for his radio shows on Nova. Gilb'R then brought DJ Manu from Nova, while old school house DJ Eric Rug arrived with his Daphreephunkateerz project. Abstract beats were represented by DJ Cam and Mighty Bop, while Motorbass, La Chatte Rouge and La Funk Mob represented Philippe Zdar, Hubert Boombass and Etienne de Crecy in their various guises. To complete the package, Etienne brought old friends Alex Latrobe (aka Gopher) and finally Air. The final double set *Source Lab 1* presented a picture of France defined by a new sound. One which was far removed from the techno world of F Communications.

"Techno for real was the music of white people who were into drugs," argued Ascoli. "This culture was more a hedonists culture than a serious culture. *Source Lab 1* was, I think, the seminal compilation, though. I can say that now because it was the first compilation and we set up the scene with it. We did it as a good business card for Source, not as a way of making money because these compilations never sell. The French don't like it when something works outside. But we defined the movement with that compilation because everyone was on it.

"It was a posh scene," continued Ascoli. "All these people who had time to have fun with the music as opposed to the hip hop movement who had to make money from the beginning. But this movement had time to develop because they were people who had money. The compilation gave them all a start but the success of Daft Punk and Air made everyone realise that it was possible to be successful everywhere."

Perhaps one of the most notable inclusions on the album came with 'Modular Mix' by Air. Although Air's Nicolas Godin had been an old friend of both Etienne de Crecy and Alex Gopher, Air's involvement came through Marc Teissier du Cros, a young assistant at the company at the time and another old friend of Godin's. However, 'Modular Mix' was only a last minute inclusion.

"My friend Nicolas Godin was doing music at this time but he wasn't very confident," explained du Cros. "So I had a tape he had done of 'Modular Mix' in my bag, but no one was really interested in listening to me about the song because I was just the trainee. Then at the last minute, one of the tracks Philippe had ordered dropped out, so I said I had this track. Philippe really liked it and just asked Nicolas to shorten it. And that was how Air began."

If *Source Lab 1* presented the illusion of a movement, then *Source Lab 2*, which followed a year later, brought together a selection that more closely represented the scene that had started to focus itself around BPM, Rough Trade and the cafés of the Bastille district of Paris. The press reaction to this second instalment propelled this nascent scene onto the public consciousness at an alarming rate. With major features in *Mixmag*, an album of the month in *Muzik* and coverage in all of the other music magazines in the UK, a hype suddenly emerged. Aided and abetted by a concerted marketing push from the team at Virgin Records UK, who were completely supportive of the project, Ascoli was all too aware of how the original dance frontline of Paris might have had their noses pushed out of joint.

"I understand if people were pissed off with us when we came along," he laughed. "I don't know if that was the case, but if it was, I understand. Because we were really a bunch of wankers against all these people who were really serious on the scene. We came with this funky fresh attitude and humour, more from Parliament style funk culture. We weren't involved in the rave culture. Before Masters at Work, I had never even listened to house music."

Source Lab 2 once again included Etienne de Crecy but in his Main Basse (Sur La Ville) guise. It also included tracks by Air and Alex Gopher. However, this is where the similarities between the first and second compilations end. Here the Versailles connection was supported by Ollano, while Rough Trade employee Arnaud Rebotini was present in his Zend Avesta and Krell guises. Rough Trade colleague (and Artefact Records boss) Jerome Meste was also present as Extra Lucid, while the final selection came from Dimitri from Paris (whose album *Sacrebleu* was released on the same day as *Source Lab 2*. Doctor L married drum & bass, turntablism and Afro-funk and Le Tome, whose music was a homage to Jean Jacques Perrey. Perhaps the most important inclusion on the collection came from Daft Punk with their stunning 'Musique'.

"We were the first major label to sign Daft Punk for a compilation," explained Ascoli. "I really wanted to sign them but we were told that the boss of Virgin wanted them, so we had to leave off."

"We were the first major label to approach Daft Punk but didn't succeed," confirmed Marc Teissier du Cros. "I think it's the biggest disappointment of my career not signing them."

Ascoli took this sense of disappointment a bit further, suggesting that he wished he'd had the foresight to sign more of the artists from the first two compilations.

"I was really surprised with the success of some of these artists," he said. "I knew that it wasn't working in the French market but I wasn't really aware of the British market at the time, so I couldn't forecast it. To tell you the truth, the biggest mistake I made was that I didn't sign everybody on the label after the compilations. I wasn't opportunistic enough. I knew that it was a cool thing to do to set up the label, but I didn't realise that the artists were going to be as big as they became."

Source Lab 3 was released in 1997 but it failed to have the same impact as its predecessors. Not only did it prove to be a sprawling double set, but it also came across as an unfocussed selection. By this stage, the

French scene had exploded in all directions and *Source Lab* was no longer needed to support it. There were a few notable inclusions, however. Air's collaboration with Jean Jacques Perrey, 'Cosmic Bird' was interesting, if not exactly essential. Tele Pop Musik's 'Sonic75' suggested great things to come. Sadly their own album that followed was a huge disappointment. Gilb'R's Chateau Flight project with I:Cube brought a moment of class with the stunning 'Mondorama', as did I:Cube's own electro house classic 'Power Sandwich'. Other stand out cuts included Black Strobe's breathtaking 'Paris Acid City' and DJ Gregory's gorgeous 'No Pain without Your Love'.

Source Lab 3 would have been better served as a single album, such was the lack of impact of the rest of the album's tracks. However, by the time of this third instalment, Ascoli and his team had already produced the definitive compilation. Anything after this was bound to be a disappointment.

What Source managed to do with the first two *Source Lab* compilations was tell all three of the stories that created the French Touch, as if they were all from the same source. That the most important aspect of the scene for Ascoli was the hip hop connection was inescapable. With the second instalment, he covered the new Parisian clubbers. However, the thread that tied both together was the story of a group of indie kids from Paris' posh suburb of Versailles. And without the third part of the story, the French Touch story would have been a very different tale indeed.

5. THE VERSAILLES CONNECTION

Back in the mid-1980s, as many of France's dance movers and shakers soaked up the US electro-funk sounds crackling over the radio and the Kervorkian remixes on import at record stores, two bands did their best to keep their own versions of the rock flag flying.

Their names were Orange and Louba. Orange played music reminiscent of David Bowie in his Berlin and Scary Monsters periods. Louba, on the other hand, attempted to create their version of The Violent Femmes. Both bands played gigs with each other in their native Versailles. Neither looked likely to set the world alight. Except the ranks of both bands featured people who would literally rewrite the dance and electronic music rule books in their own inimitable ways.

Orange comprised of Nicolas Godin and Jean-Benoit, Alex Latrobe and Xavier Jameaux. Louba consisted of the trio of Etienne de Crecy, Pierre-Michel Levallois and Mr. Learn.

When the turn of the 90s saw these bands collapse from a lack of interest from anyone but their own friends, the various members would go on to play their own significant part in the growth of the Paris scene, under the aliases of (among others), Air, Super Discount, Bang Bang and Alex Gopher. Their stories would be intertwined with bands like Cosmo Vitelli, Mellow and Motorbass, while their presence would occasionally seem to be as powerful as a secret lodge. This was the Versailles connection, where the old school tie network ran as deeply as the region's aristocratic roots.

"The Versailles side is just one side," argued Pierre-Michel Levallois, then label manager of Solid Records. "It's not the biggest side of the French Touch, but I think because of the first *Source Lab* compilation. The artistic director was from Versailles, so on this compilation were a lot of people he knew from home. Now though, we're just a small part of French Touch."

A small part in Levallois' mind, but in reality an integral aspect of French Touch.

DISQUES SOLID – DE CRECY, GOPHER AND THE HYPE DISCOUNTED

"When I hear music that has come out of France, it makes me proud. In fact, I am proud of the shit as well because for so long we had nothing, but now French producers are everywhere."

Summer 2000. Etienne de Crecy sat by the man-made lake in the surreal surroundings of Parcs des Buttes Chaumont, a little bit of 18th-century paradise in the middle of Paris. Dressed down in his blue jeans, white T-shirt and black v-neck sweater, he had more the air of a chemistry student rather than an internationally respected producer. As he posed for the camera, he looked more like he was being put through a form of torture rather than being pictured for yet another magazine cover. His apparently quiet demeanour hid an anxiousness that was ever-present. Indeed there was little to suggest that this balding Parisian had been a central player on the Paris house sound for almost a decade.

"I think the first La Funk Mob record was the most important," said a typically self-effacing Etienne when I brought up the subject of his own records. "Maybe Motorbass could have been more successful if we had been more organised. But we just put the records out ourselves. We didn't expect them to sell. Even when the album started to do really well, the people who were putting it out in the UK would be on the phone saying, 'we need more copies now', and we'd be saying, 'can it wait?' we're busy right now. We just didn't understand the music industry.

"You know, all of my music is just from one sampler," he continued. "I lived in an apartment with Philippe and we just worked with one sampler, so this is how all of my music has been made since. I'm not a virtuoso of the keyboard; I am really bad with my hands, you know. Unless they're operating a mouse. I make mouse music."

Etienne de Crecy, mouse musician, was born in 1969 in Lyon and moved to Dijon as a child. When he moved to Versailles at the age of fifteen, however, he would meet the people with whom he would develop a lasting passion for music. As a teenager, he formed a band called Louba with Mr. Learn and Pierre Michel Levallois.

"I don't think it was very good music. We were just learning our instruments," recalled Etienne when pushed about his days in the band.

Soon after the demise of Louba, he moved to Paris with thoughts of becoming a studio engineer. He soon started to work as an assistant at Studio Plus XXX. Still keen to make music in his spare time, he hooked up with Stephane Luginbuhl (later of Mellow fame) to work on sounds that combined the psychedelia of early Pink Floyd with the electronic moves of Detroit. Sadly it failed, however following a chance meeting with Philippe Zdar in the studio, a couple of Es and a night of unadulterated raving to the sounds of Goa trance, he found himself working on the Motorbass project. And French Touch history was in the making.

"Before I went to a rave and took drugs, I didn't like electronic music," said Etienne. "So for me, it's simple. Before drugs, I listened to mainly hip hop. After drugs, I listened to techno. So drugs were the most important turning point for me!"

During this period, long-time friend and Orange guitarist Alex Latrobe played him some tracks he'd been recording in his bedroom. Immediately after Orange, he had collaborated with Nicolas Godin on a proposed project. But the pairing proved to be unfruitful. Alex's solo songs were far more effective, however. Downtempo, chill-out cuts using real instruments rather than samples, but put together like house music. He was already creating a template that would be used by many of the other slo-mo abstract beats artists in Paris. As soon as he played the tracks to Etienne, he was hooked.

When Etienne was called in to help with the first *Source Lab* compilation, he suggested including one of his friend's tracks. Source agreed and 'Mandrake', under the name of Alex, proved to be a standout moment from the compilation thanks to its languid breaks and dub atmospheres. In the meantime, however, Etienne and Alex called on another old friend and ex-member of Louba, Pierre-Michel Levallois, who suggested they set up a label to release Alex's material. Before the release of *Source Lab 1* in 1995, Alex adopted the surname Gopher after a somewhat sleazy character on the 1970s ultra kitsch 'Love Boat' TV show and turned his exploration of downtempo grooves into the classic 'Gopher EP' – with production from Etienne, naturally. It was a landmark single for the nascent Paris scene for many reasons. Firstly it was among the first singles to epitomise the downtempo space pop groove that Paris became renowned for through artists as diverse as Kid Loco and Air. Secondly, it represented the birth of Disques Solid (Solid Records).

The 'Gopher EP' was also notable for its stunning silver sleeve. Created from the technique known as 'heliophore', it actually cost more than the single to produce. Even though Alex's grandfather invented the 'heliophore' technique! To save money, the Solid team glued the sleeves themselves and distributed the single on an old moped that still sat in the company offices in 2002. At the time of its release, very few people in France were interested in the emerging style, so few outlets were open to them. Alex, in the meantime, took a day job at Translab as a mastering engineer.

1996 saw the release 'Est-ce Une Gopher Party?', an EP that quickly became a regular feature on the turntables of the UK's leftfield DJ elite. The success of this single was nothing compared to what was to follow, however. Later that year, Etienne de Crecy masterminded a collection of tacks under the title of *Super Discount*. The idea was to get some of the city's artists to create tracks inspired by the annual sales in the Paris supermarkets. Initially released as a series of ten-inch singles, limited quantities made it into some of London's leading record stores. All were sold out within twenty-four hours.

Super Discount was supremely conceptual from the start. Each 10-inch single was known by a different currency (Pound, Dollar, Franc and Yen), and together made up a four-piece jigsaw of the *Super Discount* logo. The only colours were the black and white writing on a yellow background, while the information was kept to an absolute minimum. Featuring cuts by Air, Alex Gopher and, of course, the production talents of one Etienne de Crecy under his La Chatte Rouge, Minos Pour Main Basse (Sur La Ville) and Mooloodjee guises (although he denied his involvement in the latter project at first), the quartet of ten inches were then collected together on one CD thanks to a deal with PIAS. Extra tracks from DJ Tall (pronounced "digital"), aka Mr. Learn, were thrown in for added enjoyment.

"The whole thing was a joke for me," Etienne confided with a wry smile that suggests that a wicked sense of humour lays at the heart of much of his work. "It was all a concept from beginning to end. We were making bargain disposable music. I would take huge samples and just add a big kick drum, and then loop the whole thing and call it my track. It was a joke. When the album had been around for about a year, it started to sell all over the world and then we started getting calls from lawyers. We just said the album hadn't been released yet."

Super Discount was also notable for the debut 10-inch single receiving the very first use of the term French Touch. It was a term used in passing in a twenty-word review, but it quickly took hold in the UK media before being transported to the global press. I have subsequently been attributed with coining the term and even received an invitation to the Frech ambassador to London's Bastille Day party as 'the man who invented French Touch'. Up to this point, the French scene was being called Paris Hype, or Paris Disco.

LE GARE DU NORD – FEBRUARY 1996

Etienne de Crecy, Pierre-Michel Levallois, Nicolas Godin and Jean Benoit Dunckel sat in a café discussing the making of *Super Discount* for Muzik. In an act of pure genius, the features editor of the time had come up with the idea of us walking around the sales in Paris' boutiques. Sadly no one had accounted for the teaming rain that had engulfed Paris in rivers of water. So we opted for the inside of a cafe, with black coffee on tap and conversation flowing. The following interview was taken from that meeting.

How did the concept for *Super Discount* come about?

Etienne: "I'd had the idea for this for a long time. Super discount means a lot of things. It has universal meanings which are similar to the music."

Pierre-Michel: "It wasn't supposed to be like a huge comment on our consumer society or anything. Etienne had this idea to do something which was very expensive. Something which would represent complete quality."

Etienne: "That's why we did the 10" format because it's a first class, expensive format. It's a beautiful object."

Pierre-Michel: "I was totally against the idea of making a high price product. I think the high cost of CDs in France (£30 each) is just bullshit. So when Etienne suggested we do this expensive idea, I said it had to be cheap enough for people like my little brother to be able to afford it. But we still wanted a first class product! What is wonderful about *Super Discount* is that you can imagine it to be what you want it to be. If you are a high-class DJ maybe you'll want it to represent champagne. And if you're not so high-class maybe it'll be about lager. It's entirely up to you. *Super Discount* is a fantastic vehicle for your own imagination."

Etienne: "It's a twenty-first century disco machine."

So who exactly is available at Super Discount?

Etienne: "Well, there's DJ Tall, who is also Mr Learn. He's a friend of ours who makes "bug" music!"

Pierre-Michel: "I think he's the only man in Paris or the world who puts "bugs" into his sampler. He takes sound from everywhere. TV shows, little pieces of music, internet, engines everything. He then records these sounds with the "bug" creating the rhythm pattern. Usually with the sampler you have loops which are always the same but with the "bug" the loops are random. They're never the same twice."

Etienne: "La Chatte Rouge is the hip hop side of Motorbass. That first track on the *Pansoul* CD ('Fabulous') is actually a La Chatte Rouge track. Alex Gopher is Alex Gopher and all the rest are me. Except for Air's 'Solidissimo', which is my remix."

Nicolas Godin (Air): "'Solidissimo' is a remix of the B-side of 'Casanova 70' [Air's second single]. It's taken from a very small part of the track, though, where the guitar comes in. We really like it. The style is very hypnotic but if we had done the remix, it would have been very different. This is very much Etienne's vision."

Pierre-Michel "We had to put out the first EP in a massive hurry and we didn't have the chance to play 'Solidissimo' to Air. Also, we forgot to put that it was a remix on the covers. Air were upset that people thought it was their new stuff and also, they were upset that they'd not been played the track first. It was all just a mistake. But everything is OK now, though."

Jean Benoit Dunckel (Air): "Do we like our music being discounted? Ah yes, we do. We have a problem with people thinking we want to be very sophisticated making something which is very precious. With the French hype, a lot of musicians have become quite big-headed, so it's important for us to say that music can be discounted. It helps us not to act like superstars."

Do you think the hype surrounding French music has been a bad thing?

Pierre-Michel: "For some, yes. The original plan for Super Discount was anti-French hype. We were going to make a lot of tracks from the Paris scene under pseudonyms. In fact, in the beginning, there wasn't going to be any credits on the sleeve at all. The music and the concept were supposed to be more important than the artists."

Etienne: "And we liked the idea of saying to some of the Parisian artists who have become a bit big-headed 'hey, we can discount your music'."

Pierre-Michel: "The hype is a little dangerous in this respect. We believe that we have to take things to the next step. We know that there is some very good stuff here but there's also some bad, so it's important that people stop looking to Paris as a whole and start concentrating on the music."

So who would be the ideal customers in the Solid supermarket?

Pierre-Michel: "I'll tell you who I'd like to have as customers in the Solid Supermarket. I'd like Stevie Wonder to come in and say, 'Oh what's going on here? Ah, that's a nice piece of music. I'll buy that.' We'd do braille sleeves for him. Maybe we could have people like Curtis Mayfield, John Coltrane for the melody, Freddie Hubbard, Miles Davis."

Etienne: "Oh no, I wouldn't say Miles Davis. In fact, I think I'm the only person in the entire universe who doesn't like Miles Davis. I'd say Joe Humberton because his music never repeats itself. It's not only the jazz musicians we'd want but all the musicians who are open-minded."

Pierre-Michel: "There are loads of people we'd like. For them, we'd have a super *Super Discount*. Who's the manager of The Solid Supermarket? Clark Kent! And on the check-out, it has to be David Soul."

Pierre-Michel: "The best deal is 'Prix Choc'. I'm going to tell you why my friend. So maybe you're a DJ; in fact, you look like you're a very fine DJ. So I tell you. When you first place your stylus on the vinyl, everybody on the dance floor will go crazy. Do you know why? It's because the track is starting at the first measure. Everything is in there straight away and it's simply a killer track. To you, my friend, I'll sell the track for… No, we're friends. I'll let you have this quality music for a super discount price of £3 and I'll throw in a couple more tracks for goodwill."

Humour was a huge ingredient in the *Super Discount* plot. From production to distribution, concept to creation, every inch of the project was laced with the sound of three friends laughing. And yet it was a highly accomplished set that was deep enough to avoid sounding like a joke album. Humour Solid style didn't necessarily mean that the music has to suffer.

Super Discount was a runaway worldwide success. From its initial inception as a series of four 10" singles, the music captured the imaginations of everyone from the dancefloor cognoscenti to the armchair clubbers. Even indie kids and hip hop heads bought into the *Super Discount*.

Solid was subsequently propelled into the frontline of the hype that they were so against. However, they continued to pursue an almost perversely single-minded path. Rather than deliver the second instalment of *Super Discount*, they put their energies into setting up the subterranean sub-label Poumtchak (named after the sound of the beats on a house record).

In 1997 Alex Gopher returned with 'Poumtchak No 2', which continued the Gopher party with its jazz-house funky vibes. Etienne also released tracks for Poumtchak under his Mooloodjee name. The following year saw Alex Gopher return with the release of the superb mini-album *Gordini Mix* in which several of Alex's friends were asked to remix a track that had originally been released on 1996's *Source Lab 2* album.

Given the track title, the record was inevitably inspired by the sound of the classic sports racing car. As ever, *Gordini Mix* found electronica fused with dubtronics and a smoking digi soul. The remixes came courtesy of Mr. Learn and Daphreephunkateers as well as old friends from Versailles, Extra Lucid, Bang Bang, Etienne de Crecy and Air – naturally.

1998 saw two more single releases from Mr. Gopher. 'Poumtchak No8' and 'You, My Baby and I'. While the former was a worthy addition to the Gopher catalogue, it was with the latter that the sound of his first full-length album could be heard. Inspired by the birth of his son and wrapped in one of those famed silver 'heliophore' covers, *You, My Baby and I* offered a syrupy groove of spring seduction in two parts. It was also notable for being the first release under Solid's distribution deal with V2. A year later, in 1999, Alex Gopher delivered his long-awaited debut album. Also called *You, My Baby and I*, the collection opened and closed with the ultra P-funk of 'Time' and 'Quiet Storm', which both featured Parliament-Funkadelic member Clip Payne. Elsewhere the album moved between the laidback house of 'Tryin'' and the lush retro-futurism of 'Ralph and Kitty', a collaboration with Jean-Benoit from Air. Indeed the two collaborators offered the simplest definition of the Gopher sound, somewhere on the road that links P-funk with Air. The key was the bass.

"I always play bass on my records as Alex Gopher," he explained. "It's something I've done since Orange because, for me, the bassline is the most important part of the track. What I usually do is record my bass part as a sample and then replay it on keyboards. There are no live musicians apart from my special guests, but I try to give life to the computers, to make them sound like playing musicians. I think you can make live music without any live musicians."

Of course, this enlightened approach to the live musician and sampling is a far cry from that first single where everything except Etienne's programming was played live with guitars courtesy of Mellow's Patrick Woodcock.

"There was no one day when I decided to be an electronic artist; it was just a gradual process," he said. "I really got into electronic music because of Etienne. He made me understand that the interesting way of using computers was to make them sound like computers, not just to reproduce past music."

This approach was one of the main strengths of the album. As already noted, 'Tryin'' found Alex slipping between the sheets of EZ house, where a luxurious four to the floor played counterpoint to orchestral melody and film theme ambience. It was equal to anything from *Super Discount*. On 'The Child', the mood was decidedly calmer with the blues-soaked vocals and dub-funk grooves. The sound of Nina Simone laying down a lullaby over sheets of deep, garage inflected beats. On 'Consolidated', Gopher brought out the punk garage attack to create a floor shaker that would go down a storm at Basement Jaxx in Brixton. The effect was echoed on 'With U' and 'Party People', where the vocals come with a down and dirty P-funk attitude that George Clinton would be proud of.

"I first met Clip Payne of Funkadelic when I was working with Nicolas Godin," recalled Alex. "They were in Paris for a while, so we got together to make some tracks, but it didn't work out. Then when I was working on the album, I got Pierre-Michel to contact him and he was into what I was doing. He did a version of the track and we were really into it, so we got him over to Paris to work on some other stuff. Actually, it was a bit strange for us. When we sent him the first track, he'd got together a team of guys and recorded a new version totally. He'd done a mix and everything."

You, My Baby and I bucked a trend among French electronic artists, as it sold better in the domestic territory than abroad. Press interest at home, too, was far greater.

"Looking back now," said Pierre-Michel three years after the album's release, "Alex had four front covers which was fantastic for an electronic artist. The Chemical Brothers only got seven. So it was a huge success with the French media. And everywhere I go now, people know him and love his work. I heard that Norman Cook is a fan. So he did get exposure around the world, and he has got a strong following, but it happened here first."

Part of the reason for this success lay in that the album relied heavily on standard song structures and vocals. Also, it had a strong P-funk and 80s disco feel, which tapped directly into the dominant dance music tastes in France while still retaining an underground aesthetic.

In 1998, as Solid was gearing up for the release of Alex's debut album, another record by a completely new artist slipped through the net. Pencilled in for a full release, *Video* by Cosmo Vitelli offered an obtuse cut-up of videotapes and dark electro.

"Originally, Cosmo Vitelli had done two EPs with us and V2 said that they wanted to issue a compilation of these EPs," said Pierre-Michel. "So we said OK. But when they put the album out, V2 in France didn't brief everyone in the label about the album and they thought it was too weird. So it got ignored. People refused to work it and nobody had the record. The girl who was doing the press in the UK [Alessandra Margarito of the Italian Job] was saying, 'what's going on? I don't have any copies of the album and it's out in two weeks'. But we didn't have any copies of it either. So we decided to remove the contract from V2. It's a question of how far the artist is developed. If he's reached a certain level, then people like V2 can work it. But if the artist is too underground, then they can't make the link. And Cosmo Vitelli was too underground for them. So the album was shelved."

The public missed out on a collision of wayward electronica and future electro. Tracks jittered between the funky breaks of 'Nazi Surfers Must Die' and the schmaltzy ambience of 'La Dernier Sorti Ferme La Porte'. On 'Science Affliction', Vitelli created a 90s update of Grandmaster Flash's 'the Message', the tack's pre-old skool affiliation further underlining the Sugarhill-style rapping from seminal Las Poet Jalal Nuriddin.

Video may not have stunned with its originality, but it showed enough sonic invention to guarantee rerun after rerun. If it had received the release it deserved, that is. The next major project for Solid came with Etienne de Crecy's first album under his own name, *Tempovision*. In the three years since *Super Discount*, he had become so caught up in promotional duties that he'd only had time for occasional remix work (Lil Louis' Clap Your Hands', Alex Gopher's 'Gordini Mix' and Air's 'Sexy Boy' among others), production work on the second album from Source recording artist Teri

Moise (he had produced her first album in 1996) and a couple of dance-floor tracks as Mooloodjee for Poumtchak. Finally, in 1999 he began work on the new album.

"I originally thought it would only take about three months to record, but it ended up taking the whole year," he explained back in the stunning surroundings of Parcs des Buttes Chaumont. "But I was trying to capture a very special sound somewhere between digital and real. I call it digital soul. Because *Super Discount* was a joke and Motorbass was so well respected – actually, I always have people asking me about it, and when the next album will come out – it was very difficult for me to record this. It is important for me not to hide behind the concept of this album. With *Super Discount*, it was all about the concept and not the music.

"It was only when I was in the US with Clip Payne and he had got this singer to do the track. Clip said to me, 'what is the song called?' I hadn't thought of anything really, except I liked the word 'vision'. So I just said Tempovision."

From here, the seeds of a concept was born.

"Really, the concept is less important than the music," he said. "I just wanted to use the cover artwork to make a point that the rhythm of life is a special thing and that it's sometimes better to waste your time just doing nothing out in the open."

Ironically Etienne was forced to create a concept around the album after it was finished. Such was the expectation for his output to be hidden behind a highly stylised image and ideology.

"The concept came after the tracks were recorded," he reiterated. "It's all about when you channel surf on TV. After a while, you stop watching single programmes, but you change channels with a rhythm. Nothing interests you. You are hypnotised by all of the information. That is 'Tempovision'. I think that it is a bad form of hypnosis – it's a bad rhythm. Television creates a blur between reality and imagination. You can have a car accident in a movie and then have it on the news, but neither has any real effect. It all seems to be fiction. I don't want to be anti-technology because it is just stupid. I don't know how it is in England but here in France the information highway has created this big thing where suddenly everyone wants to become rich with the internet. I think it's good to have all of this information from everywhere, but that means a new social life that is not so happy. It suddenly means you spend a lot more time wasting time. People say that you have all of the information there, but it's not true because you have to waste hours and hours just waiting or looking. It's just hours behind the computer, not like going to a library. The other thing is the fact that nobody knows whether the information really is free. It may be policed. I just imagined my album to be... I just wanted to speak about the time we waste. That's *Tempovision*."

From the opening 'Intronection' with its modem bleeps, *Tempovision* represented an album of pure seductive pleasure. 'Relax' took a laid back jazz chord sequence and built it over a deep house groove before erupting into a jazz-funk inspired keyboard motif that could have come directly from the remake of Shaft. 'Out of My Hands' followed the theme with its windswept bouncing bass, shattered glass intro and echo-drop beats over which a gorgeous blues-drenched soul diva dripped vocals of pure passion. On the breathtaking 'Am I Wrong?' the same voice begged 'Am I wrong to hunger?' over a disco driven house groove that twisted through filters galore before erupting in 303 acid squelches. The first single in France, 'Am I Wrong?', was supported by a computer-animated video created by Etienne's younger brother Geffroy for One Bit Pictures. It featured a cow being force-fed television images as a butcher slices prime steaks off its rump – and other such delights.

"It's not any kind of statement on vegetarianism or animal rights," laughs Etienne. "It's supposed to mean, eat the boss. That's all. The funny thing is that when I sample vocals, because my English is not so good, I'm not sure what the words are. I go for the sound. I thought she was asking, 'am I wrong to anger?'"

In fact, the video further explored the belated central theme of the album: technology as a system that turns people into passive consumers. The theme was further explored in the videos of the singles that followed, 'Scratched' and 'Tempovision'. Once again, Etienne's brother created an animated world in which the central characters were forced out of their couch-bound lethargy to get batteries for the TV remote. They found traffic jams of people in a similar predicament in the outside world. The only shop in the city with batteries available could be seen in the distance and marked out by a Super Discount logo! The message was clear; the remote had brought with it a behaviour pattern that was system dependent. Rather than queue for batteries and waste their time, the people could have turned the TV channel themselves.

The video for 'Tempovision' followed the same two characters as they watched computers turn on the stock market and cause mass panic. The resulting chaos of bankruptcy and brokers diving off buildings was eventually brought to a halt by the words 'Game Over' flashing on the screen. Once again, mankind was shown to be subservient in the face of the technology it had created.

If 'Am I Wrong?' offered a pretty substantial main course, then the trio of tunes that followed presented the most filling side dishes you're likely to encounter. 'Noname' took Chic-style funky guitar on a journey through digi dub house while 'When Jack Met Jill' sounded like an old school jazz-in-the-house tune as reworked by Timbaland. As each new bar opened, a new surprise came as strings enveloped gorgeous, downbeat vocals. A classic, in fact. As was the next track, the instantly addictive title track that opened with the sounds of a fervent channel surfer checking out the news stations before opening up onto a string-driven languid groove, which melts easy listening over hip hop g-funk style. And if that wasn't all, the multi-hued colours of dub, P-funk and soul were also thrown into the mix for a head-spinning, lysergic meltdown.

The album's next piece de resistance came in the shape of 'Scratched' that mixed deep house with hip hop turntablism as vocalist Belita Woods delivered another aching soul lament. '3 Day Weekend' fused slap bass, the Joker's laugh, Latino funk guitar and a beat made for butt shaking. A party tune for a long weekend that gave way to the early morning jazz bar ambience of 'Rhythm and Beat'.

The final track, 'Hold the Line' offered a locked groove, which slowly built through layer after layer over an amazing fourteen minutes and eight seconds. It was Etienne's answer back to call-waiting muzak.

"I put television, internet, telephone, radio into the same bracket," he explained. "This track ['Hold the Line'] is inspired by the hypnosis of the music on call-waiting. It's actually the music we use on the record company phones."

As we wandered through the park before heading back to the hubbub of Paris in the afternoon, Etienne, whose brothers and sisters include one of France's best known cartoonists, a renowned designer and a three dimensional computer animator (as seen on the video for 'Am I Wrong?'), let slip that *Tempovision* wasn't the only piece of music he'd been working at this time.

"I have just made the soundtrack for the Peugeot cars adverts. It was very soul-destroying because so many people wanted to have their say – mostly, they didn't know what they were talking about – but the money was very good. And I needed the money."

In 2002 Solid released two albums from Etienne and Alex. The first, a collection of remixes of the tracks from *Tempovision*, which added a dancefloor edge to the original. Alex Gopher's dark and heavy remix of 'Noname' standing out for its sheer power. The second album release was a collaboration between Alex Gopher and Demon under the name Wuz. This set came through the Poumtchak offshoot and represented a far more dancefloor-orientated sound than on Gopher's own work. Much of this was due to Demon, who already had a pedigree of creating dark electro-funk as featured on their 'a/Typical' single that featured the huge cut 'Lilifuck'. In 1998 Demon, aka Jeremie Mondon, delivered 'Poumtchak #6' for the Solid offshoot. In return, Etienne remixed 'Lilifuck' the following year. This storming version ushered in Demon's debut album *Midnight Funk* which came via 20,000 ST/Sony Music France. It was a brilliant album; it received huge critical acclaim in the French media but was ignored elsewhere. Had it appeared a couple of years before, there is little doubt that it would have been hailed as a classic in all of the UK's fickle dance press.

Alex Gopher with Demon Presents Wuz was the complete opposite to Alex Gopher's previous album. Its melodies were understated and the ambience dark. However, it came with a huge funk undertow, thanks to the heavy use of distorted pulsing bass. Nowhere was this more evident than on the intense groove of 'Focus' and the bitter-sweet beat rampage of 'The Shell'.

"For this album, I wanted to do pure electronic music," explained Alex. "I knew that I couldn't do it alone, which is why I asked Demon to join me. The finished album has a dark mood because we were fed up with all of this happy disco house. OK, we wanted to make a house album, but we didn't want to sound like French Touch."

Indeed *Alex Gopher with Demon Presents Wuz* couldn't have been further removed from the popular French Touch sound of filtered disco. It was a heavy affair without much humour, but repeated listens revealed it to be something of a brooding masterpiece. Although the funk-fuelled techno soul of 'Without You' and 'Long Island' stood out, *Alex Gopher with Demon Presents Wuz* was a stone-cold classic from beginning to end.

Towards the end of 2002, the trio of Etienne, Alex and Pierre-Michel decided to close down the record label. After almost eight years in the spotlight, they felt that they had achieved as much as possible. They would now concentrate on being a production house. The label's parting shot came early in 2003 in the shape of Cosmo Vitelli's second album *Clean*, licensed to Virgin Records.

An utterly different sound from his lost *Video* album, *Clean* found Cosmo Vitelli exploring 80s electro-pop with a vengeance. In fact, it was a sound that tied into the post-French Touch musical developments in France that found artists like Miss Kitten, The Hacker, Terence Fixmer and Tampopo delivering some of the classic records of the electroclash movement.

In many ways, the closure of Solid represented the end of an era. If one label epitomised the positivity and self-belief that surrounded the hype that became known as French Touch, it was Solid.

"Today, things have changed a lot," said Etienne in 2003. "In the beginning, because there weren't many of us, we got a lot of support."

"In 1997, we had to work hard, but we got support from people like the TV stations," added Pierre-Michel. "Back then, there were no dedicated shows, and there wasn't any MTV, and only a very few electronic artists did videos. Those that did got some support. But we had to work hard at convincing the suits to support it. But now, everyone makes videos, so they only support the biggest names. It's the same as this with everything now.

"Back then, if you had support on the radio from Radio FG," he continued. "Then you would get heard by most people who were into electronic music. This is because Paris is much smaller than London is, for instance. So we only needed a small interest to get noticed. This was the same in the newspapers. We had support from Liberation, only a few small articles, but everyone noticed them. Now there are loads more magazines and a lot more artists, so it's harder to get the interest.

"Also, everyone now is anti-hype," added Etienne. "The French Touch is dead and people don't want to support people who were a part of it. But we were against the French Touch hype all along. My idea was to do something really underground."

Throughout their years, they tirelessly produced innovative and genre-defining records. Any label that can claim to have released the albums by Etienne and Alex can only ever be held in a position of utmost respect. Indeed, such is the legend surrounding Super Discount that when in 2002 PIAS reissued a fifth-anniversary edition, complete with a second disc of remixes and CD-ROM application based around the original 10-inch concept, it sold out of its reprint within a month.

"I have no regrets at all about the music we've done," concluded Etienne. "I am very proud of it all."

In the proceeding years, Etienne has continued to put out quality releases, including an electro set *Beats' n' Cubes* in 2011 and an intriguing collaboration with Baxter Dury and Delilah Holliday in 2018 called *B.E.D.* in which he applies his trademark grooves to deadpan Brit vocals. He's also released two more *Super Discount* albums and also took the *Super Discount 2* brand live.

Writing for The Guardian in 2005, I argued that the sight of three balding producers bobbing their heads up and down as their fingers manipulated mixing keyboards, desk and computers to work up a breathtaking house-music storm may not have been the most enticing proposition to many people. But for anyone who followed the late-90s French dance-music scene, the *Super Discount* live experience was as exciting as it was long overdue.

The review continued:

"Why the excitement? Arguably, without the arrival of Etienne de Crecy's Super Discount concept in 1996, Air and Daft Punk might never have enjoyed the same degree of success. It was through the 1997 *Super Discount* album that the UK's dance-music media woke up to the concept of French dance music.

"That album became the must-have house collection of the year, spearheading a musical revolution among the Parisian house cognoscenti that would not only spawn numerous Top 10 hits but even alter the musical direction of Madonna. Her album *Music* was heavily reliant on the French Touch sound.

"Despite Super Discount's subsequent influence on global dance music, the second instalment arrived only last month. *Super Discount 2* was no less inspirational, but where its predecessor was all about defining new ground, this set was defined by its search for authenticity.

"It is this same search that underlines the *Super Discount 2* live show. Augmented by his fellow Parisian producers Alex Gopher and Julien Delfaud, De Crecy appears intent on reclaiming the spirit of house and techno from the cheesy sounds that masquerade as 'dance music' these days. The band offer up an obsessive brew of tweaking acid house, deep, pulsating Detroit techno and raw-edged Chicago house, all orbiting the relentless simplicity of Kraftwerk and absorbed through the rushing peaks and subliminal beats of the best club tracks.

"Playing to a capacity crowd, Super Discount 2 (the band) deliver a series of stunning overtures that range from the twisted bleeps of 'Poisoned' to the bass-driven hypnosis of 'Overnet'. The highlight of the set comes in 'Fast Track', an adrenalised Formula One soundtrack with a bassline lifted from the vaults of New Order and injected with the deepest of house grooves. While pundits everywhere are quick to write off electronic music, Super Discount 2 recaptures the essence of house culture at its rough-and-ready best. Vintage stuff, perhaps, but also a timely reminder of how potent a force this music has been for the past 20 years."

On the other hand, Alex Gopher has been considerably quieter in the intervening twenty years. In 2007 he produced an eponymous album that harked back to his days as an indie musician. The album failed to ignite largely due to its lack of unique identity. He wore all of his influences with pride on this set and lost his own voice. However, the remix set that came with the CD double pack was essential listening. All references to bands like New Order were obliterated by deep and hard acid-infused beats in this set. "Brain Leech (Bugged Mind Remix)", featured on *Grand Theft Auto IV*, is possibly Alex Gopher's most overlooked but finest moment. In 2012 he teamed up with Xavier Jamaux to produce a soundtrack to the movie *Motorway*, which was enjoyable if not particularly startling.

In 2021 Etienne announced the return of Solid Records with the limited edition reissue of *Super Discount* as four gold ten-inch singles as a boxset. It was a move pitched at the heritage dance music market, and despite retailing at almost £100, it sold out immediately.

AIR – THE SPACE AGE POP ARISTOCRACY

"The biggest difference between the approaches of Air and Daft Punk is that Daft Punk don't present themselves as a French band. They are seen as an international act. I'm sure that in the world there are people who don't know they are French. But it's different for Air. Air make it obvious. At the beginning, they put on the records Air: French Band. They are proud of being French. They like France. And their music is full of the traditions of French culture. They like things from around the world but the

Air (Mark Stringer)

tradition and the elegant side of France appeals to them." Marc Teissier du Cros (Record Makers label manager), 2002

Versailles. A haven on the edge of Paris. A place where green lawns roll like fog, golf courses stretch like cats in a carpet showroom and areas of forestation loom large and inviting. It's a suburb of endless summers, where the world outside seems distant and the chaos of life is someone else's problem. From here, it is easy to forget Paris' appalling racial divide, which has produced the worst no-go ghettos outside of New York. From here you can easily forget striking lorry drivers and the mid-summer smell of the city centre. This is the place that time forgot; a little bit of France as the rest of the world imagines it to be stuck between the future and the past.

It was in that heat hazed, green belt paradise that I met the duo of Jean-Benoit Dunckel and Nicolas Godin in 1999 for what was our sixth interview since I wrote the first piece about them a few years earlier. Nicolas and J-B created music that pulls at our very preconceptions of Frenchness. If fellow Parisian Dimitri from Paris created his image from Peter Sellers' parody of the Parisian Inspector Clouseau, then Air drew on the apparently mythological Paris as learned from textbooks, imagined via pen pals or romanticised through foreign exchanges.

Air, an acronym of *Amour, Imagination, Rêve* (Love, Imagination, Dream), explored the melancholy that seeped into the very heart of the country's sixties pop sound while also tugging at the freeform sci-fi phonics of avant-garde opera. They placed Serge Gainsbourg happily next to Jean Jacques Perrey in an exercise of future-retro melodrama. It was a sound obsessed with aristocracy, albeit the aristocracy of pop. Theirs was music that echoed the multi-hued moodiness of French cinema so beloved by British students. Films like *Betty Blue*, *Subway* and *Diva* found their beauty, passion and despair somehow transposed into Air's grooves. Like Versailles itself, Air were the epitome of France through rose-coloured spectacles.

Air's studio was an old converted barn, hidden among lush greenery. To one side, a golf course, to the other woodland. On the day of our interview, the air was filled with the 'clomp' of golf club on ball and a constant shrill of bird whistle, beyond that nothing. No traffic hum and no crackling electricity pylons, just the sound, as Simon & Garfunkel might have said, of silence.

Nicolas and J-B emerged from their studio to greet me. They were every inch the congenial hosts with warm smiles, loose handshakes and welcoming comments. Just as their music evoked the France of the schoolroom, so too their demeanour was almost laughably foreign exchange student. Both dressed in college geek chic (slacks and tucked in shirts). Nicolas, the taller of the two, sported a huge wave of Princess Dianna-esque hair while J-B opted for the grown out French crop. Both were skinny with catalogue model looks.

It was by then a full year since the release of their seminal *Moon Safari* album and four years since the debut single, 'Modular Mix'. Over the three years since we first met, we'd developed a kind of friendship defined by their release schedule. This time we'd come together to discuss the imminent re-release of their long lost album *Premiers Symptomes*, a collection of their first three EPs, which originally surfaced in late '97 but swiftly disappeared again.

It's a strange situation for Nicolas and J-B. With no new material, they felt like they had nothing fresh to say.

"The idea is for people to discover what we were doing before *Moon Safari*. We don't feel comfortable with this old stuff being released. The originals are very rare now, so we decided to reissue it for the newer fans. But we'd rather have new stuff," said Nicolas.

There was, of course, the subject of the soundtrack they've provided for Sophia Coppolla's *Virgin Suicides* movie. However, it wasn't due for release until the following January, so it was off the agenda. At that moment in time, the duo seemed strangely stuck between the future and the past. Just like their music, in fact. And Versailles, of course.

"We grew up about a mile away from here," explained Nicolas as we settled into the studio for the interview. "It's the best part of Paris, a lot of forest. It was a great place to grow up in, except it was very boring but then I think everyone says that about where they lived. It's because your home is where you know everywhere and understand the rules."

237

"The thing is, this is a very boring place to live, so artists will inevitably rebel against it," continued J-B. "It's also a very intolerant place. It's a very catholic area which isn't very cool because they judge people by strict moral standards."

"Versailles is a very strict catholic place which can seem right-wing," added Nicolas. "If you look at the election, the south of France has more fascists than here. In the south, there are maybe thirty or forty members of parliament that are fascist. Here maybe only ten."

Only ten fascists! Is this why Nicolas escaped to art school to train as an architect, I wondered?

"No," he laughed. "I was drawn to architecture because they had the best parties. If you know the big art schools in France, they give the best parties. A lot of alcohol and girls. A lot of sex."

Somehow sex and alcohol were not the motivating factors that you'd expect to find at the heart of Air's psyche. The elegiac qualities of their music had created an almost sexless image for the duo. Sure they evoked the spirit of sex gods and goddesses (Serge Gainsbourg, Beatrice Dalle) but theirs would seem to have been an almost transcendental sexuality. Not for these clean-living boys the sweaty bump and grind of skin against skin. They were more Woody Allen's Orgasmatron.

"Air are human beings after all," protested Nicolas. "We love to get drunk; we enjoy sex like anyone else. We have a very common everyday life except that we actually do something we like for a living. I don't agree that our music isn't physical. 'Moon Safari' is a bed album. 'Sexy Boy' is a very dirty song, I think. We like to think of our music as soundtracks for sex. Music to us is an extremely sensuous thing and naturally, sex is a part of this sensuality. We'd love to do the music for a sex film or maybe a sex CD-ROM.

"We have a problem with our image in that we wanted to show the perfect world where everything is cool with the stars and the sky," explained J-B "We are very nice boys, in nice clothes and we are very glad to be here. But really, we know that the world is not perfect. Things aren't cool and there are a lot of things in this world which have to change. So this is at complete opposite to our image. In future, we'll have to appear more distraught, destroyed perhaps. We're not pleased people, really. This isn't utopia but on 'Moon Safari' we tried to create a world which was."

So just as Versailles had its dark side of Catholic oppression, Air had their hitherto unseen rock 'n' roll dark side.

"Of course, there's a lot more to us," said J-B. "The press tends to ignore what they don't want to see. We played on our French image when we started. We did all of the stereotypical things that people wanted. So we took on that arty, Left Bank image. We were all about soundtracks and stuff, so we played with that a lot."

When Jean-Benoit talked, words came tumbling out his mouth like an express train. Each sentence was punctuated with an endearing smile that forced you to nod in agreement or smile along. In earlier interviews, this caused a huge problem. His accent was so strong that it was nearly impossible to decipher what he was saying. Much of the cohesive conversation fell on Nicolas' shoulders, as his English was by far the better. Which brought with it problem number two. Nicolas was far more reticent to talk in interviews. He came over as having a far more serious personality, contemplating each question with absolute care. He even refused to answer some questions when he perceived them as too 'tabloid'. He'd rather let his music do the talking.

By 1999 J-B's English had by far improved; however, they still came over as the odd couple. By then, J-B seemed to be the flighty, joking philosopher, while Nicolas was the serious, conceptual visionary.

Air hadn't always been the duo we know today. Back in the days immediately after the break up of Orange, it was Nicolas Godin who first emerged as Air. He had initially decided to study architecture while trying to create the music he had in his mind. However, he felt he needed a musical foil, so the search was on for the perfect musical accomplice.

Initially, Godin teamed up with Alex Gopher. Both had a similar musical vision; however, they failed to create anything significant. They did, however, record some demos with a full band drawn from the ranks of George Clinton's Parliament and Funkadelic. Among them was Clip Payne, who would record with both Gopher and de Crecy.

Although it's hard to imagine the mellow moods of Godin's Air output with a P-funk undertow, it is worth remembering that the Versailles musician counts funk as one of his musical loves. At this stage, it wasn't inconceivable that Godin would have embarked on a path that took him in the direction of this music. Alex Gopher decided to leave Godin to pursue a solo career in 1994. He'd already played his own tapes to Etienne de Crecy and the plans for Solid were in place. Furthermore, one of his tracks was selected for the *Source Lab 1* compilation.

"Nicolas had a few ideas that he'd been working on," said Gopher of his friend. "But he wasn't so good in the studio at this time. So Etienne helped him to produce a track."

The resulting Modular Mix was, as I described in a review for *Melody Maker*, 'a collision between mellow Moogs, downtempo electronica and the easy listening ambience of Serge Gainsbourg'. It was released as a single along with a rough cut house remix by Etienne under the Motorbass moniker in November 1995.

In his search for a musical partner, Godin also worked for a short while with fellow architecture student Patrick Woodcock (who later became a part of Mellow). Together the temporary duo penned 'Ce Matin La', which would eventually turn up on Air's debut album, *Moon Safari*.

Soon after 'Modular Mix' Godin started work on his follow up single, 'Casanova 70', without Etienne's support. Despite using Etienne's friend from Studio Plus XXX, Stephane Briat (who also worked with Dimitri from Paris on his second album), the experience of writing and producing on his own proved to be far more frustrating than he had imagined. Godin subsequently asked his old bandmate from Orange, Jean-Benoit Dunckel to become a member of Air.

"Just after writing 'Casanova 70', Nicolas went to see his old friend from Orange, Jean-Benoit," recalled Marc Tessier du Cros, who managed Air's label Record Makers in 2002. "At this time, he was a maths teacher, who played piano in his spare time. Nicolas went to see one of J-B's shows in a piano bar and, after the show, he went up and explained that he was launching the band and wanted J-B to be a part of it. It was a big risk for

Jean-Benoit though because he already had a child. But he agreed and signed to Source as well."

Jean-Benoit's path to Air hadn't been entirely devoid of musical pursuit. Apart from his gigs as a piano player in a bar, he had also recorded demos with Stephane Luginbuhl, who would later form Olano and then Mellow. These demos combined psychedelic pop with house beats, but the duo didn't carry on with the venture due to Dunckel's workload as a teacher.

The first track that featured Air as a solid duo came with 'Les Professionels', the b-side of 'Casanova 70'. Once again, Etienne was in the producer's seat. And the difference was immediately noticeable. Where Godin's track had flowed around retro ideas, the combined forces of Godin, Dunckel and de Crecy found classic easy listening melodies fused with minimalist synths, film-esque ambience and modern production. This was the last Air recording that featured input from Etienne de Crecy.

The single that fully defined Air as a duo came in July 1997. 'J'Ai Dormi Sous L'Eau' c/w 'Le Soleil et Pres de Moi' offered a combination of the space pop Moogs of Jean Jacques Perrey, walking basslines, whooshing synths and echo on overdrive. Melodies were a pure French pop melodrama, while vocals were heavily vocodered in what was to become the trademark Air touch. They were immediately embraced by a UK dance scene keen to embrace their brand of romantic chill-out electronica.

When Mo' Wax head honcho James Lavelle licensed 'Modular Mix', Air's sensuous, film-esque retro vibes became an essential inclusion in any self-respecting DJ's after-hours set. The release of 'Casanova 70' single did little to alter this. Its languid, easy listening vibe sits perfectly next to artists like Howie B and Kruder & Dorfmeister. Suddenly Air were the hottest name on the downtempo dance block. This was very strange for Nicolas and J-B as they saw themselves as an indie guitar band with synths.

With the subsequent release of their 'Brakes On' remix of Alex Gopher's *Gordini Mix*, Air's love of guitars became all the more apparent and the eventual appearance of the near funk tune 'Californie' as a b-side to the promotional flexi-disc of 1998 breakthrough single 'Sexy Boy' confirmed any alliances that the Air duo may have had to the old six-string axe.

That their music had collided with Britain's downtempo dance scene was just a happy fluke. Nobody could have predicted the crossover success of the debut album, however. Moving way beyond the self-selected elite of the dance underground, *Moon Safari* became the staple listening for broadsheet readers everywhere. Its stunning melange of prog-rock Moogs, fey psychedelia and Gallic easy-listening provided the perfect coffee table soundtrack to after club comedowns, thirty-something dinner parties and a multitude of television overdubs. In short, *Moon Safari* leapfrogged the generation divide like no other album of 1998.

Despite the popularity of their singles in the UK, they hadn't found a label to distribute the album in the territory. Indeed all of their previous releases had come via import, with the exception of Mo' Wax licensing 'Modular Mix'. Indeed James Lavelle was the first person to be offered *Moon Safari*. But he had to turn it down.

"James actually loved it," explains du Cros, "but he had done a deal with Polygram and they didn't like *Moon Safari* when they heard it. There was nothing he could do, but he really liked it."

Eventually, the album surfaced on Virgin in the UK. *Moon Safari* found Air reinventing John Barry's score to M*idnight Cowboy* through the space pop tones of Jean Jacques Perrey and melting the results into the grooves of Pierre Henry's avant-garde opera *Messe Pour Le Temps Present* with a huge side salad of The Beatles, Pink Floyd and US folk troubadour, Beck. The effect was one of carefully crafted beauty, where simple melodies, textured layers and Moog refrains offered nostalgia wrapped up in the trappings of future kitsch. Like the brave new world of 50s sci-fi, where the future had boundless possibilities and everything would be sprayed silver, 'Sexy Boy' and 'Kelly Watch the Stars' offered glimpses into future visions long gone.

'All I Need' and 'You Make it Easy' found Beth Hirsch delivering creamy folk vocals over Air's retro-space age pictures. It was a combination that added a stronger sense of classic pop to the band. While 'Remember' sampled Jean Jacques Perrey over a beat that echoed David Bowie's hand clapped 'Always Crashing in the Same Car' from *Low*. Over this, they layered their trademark synths. Moogs, Roland string ensemble, backward electric guitars (again echoing Bowie's *Low* productions and, of course, vocoders. 'Ce Matin La', the Patrick Woodcock co-composition, was perhaps most reminiscent of Barry's 'Midnight Cowboy', its muted tuba (played by Woodcock) and sombre orchestrations offering an alternative soundtrack to the movie's more salubrious moments. The closing 'Le Voyage de Penelope' fused the psychedelia of early Pink Floyd with the melodies of Serge Gainsbourg and the melodrama of a French farce. A track that seemed ready to explode on an extended epic adventure, it quietly faded into nothing.

"We wanted 'Moon Safari' to be an adventure which took the French sound somewhere different," Jean-Benoit told me at the time of the album's release. "For us, the moon is the perfect symbol for our music. It represents something that has been here for eternity and in the future everyone will want to go to the moon. The music that we do is very respectful of the past but it's there to take you on an adventure into the future. So this mix between old and new is really representative of our music. Which is why we used the moon image. When we say 'Moon Safari', it is a logical way of saying that there is life on the moon. Which we believe there must be because we grew up believing in sci-fi."

The danger of using such future-past concepts is that very often, they are perceived as being retro. This was something that Air were very strongly against. They were, if anything, an anti-retro band.

"I don't think we are at all retro," exclaimed J-B. "We have tried to update things. We take our influences but the music we make could only have come from today. Some people call us retro; some say we're kitsch. But I think they miss the point."

True Air's music isn't kitsch music as so often suggested. Kitsch implies some ironic knowing act of perversity. It's fundamentally dishonest. When The Jungle Brothers sample "I Dream of Genie", it's kitsch. When Phats & Small (or any number of fromage sampling DJs) pull out an old disco sample, it's kitsch. But when Air reimagine the theme to 'Midnight Cowboy' on 'Ce Matin La', or build textured hues from the sonic threads of nostalgia (a Moog here, a Mellotron there), there's basic integrity at work.

"We don't steal from other people; we try to transform," said J-B. "When I listen to some of our stuff, I am almost ashamed because I know what we've actually stolen and what we've transformed. I think that we are not pure creators; we are more transformers.

"There's music that people can still listen to years later and it still sounds fresh," added Nicolas. "Then there's stuff that tries to be up to the minute that sounds old a month later. We're trying to be like the first type of music. It's not about being retro, it's classic. What is important is good or bad. In the future Air will be simply seen as music from the twentieth century, nothing more."

"There is an argument that the twentieth century didn't actually start until the First World War," J-B continues. "Now we're all waiting for the big event that kicks off the twenty-first century. Maybe it will be our album."

Certainly, the duo's future-retroism foretold of the twenty-first century's greed for revivalism and, as Simon Reynold's would put it, retromania. Air's sci-fi vision was perhaps the most retro aspect of their aesthetic in 1999. The music they had released at this point was more Dr. Who than Alien. Their sonics, as I've suggested, came from a time when the future was still exciting. The late fifties, early sixties, when man hadn't yet walked on the moon but already people fantasised about a George Jetson lifestyle.

"When I was a kid, I thought that in the year 2000 we would be all in spaceships with laser guns everywhere," confirmed Nicolas in his Versailles studio a year after the album's release. "I'm disappointed that hasn't happened. But when you go to Yo! Sushi in London it's very futuristic. And I like that a lot. Not enough things are futuristic. I love the idea of aliens and spaceships."

As if to underline the point, only one record sat on the floor of Air's studio back in 1999; the soundtrack to *Close Encounters of a Third Kind* – a space adventure presented as a blockbuster with a sense of childlike wonder or excitement. Since then, such topics have taken on either the Year 2000 conspiracy theory where the US always wins out or the Cold

War continuum of the US victorious against all dark forces with Russia replaced by aliens.

This brings us back to the dark side. The band's image had created a straight jacket from which they were desperate to escape during the tour in support of *Moon Safari*. Beneath the image were two angry young men on the verge of exploding. There were many reasons for this. On the one hand, they were still rebelling against the rigid catholicism of their hometown while also finding themselves ostracised by people in their home country. Despite the band's growing army of fans worldwide, Air were still ignored in France. The cracks began to show when Jean-Benoit and Nicolas took to the road.

"When we were on the road, things started to get kind of dull," exclaimed J-B with a wicked smile that hinted at the seemingly unprintable mischief which was to follow. "One night in Lyon, we began to be dirty. We had very dirty behaviour, saying bad things and drinking a lot. We appeared on stage very drunk and were swearing into the mics. We were fed up with touring and fed up with the people. We were awful on stage, played really badly, so I think there was a subconscious reaction to our nice image. After that, we stayed up and partied for two nights, which got it out of our systems. But we pulled out of our two last shows."

"It was very funny because most of the audience that night in Lyon, most people didn't understand us or what we're about," continued Nicolas. "France is still very narrow in its music. For so many years, the bands have been horrible and the people aren't ready for Air. In France, they just call us the band who are popular in England."

"But we don't mind about this," added J-B. "Because that means we are allowed to do what we want. Nobody puts pressure on us. They don't know who we are at all. We were at the Cannes Festival for the film and people ignored us. They were saying, 'are you famous? and 'should we take pictures of you?'. When we said we were Air they just said, 'oh that band who are big in England'. People in France just don't understand us."

Which brought us back to the dark side again. There is a strong feeling of lysergically charged psychedelia at the core of Air's music. I wondered if they advocate the use of drugs as a creative muse?

"Maybe in the future, people will say that it's normal to take drugs," Nicolas explained with his usual candour. "I'm sure that all of us here have smoked herb. When you make music on drugs, it always sounds horrible when you're straight. Even music that you love when you are stoned sounds bad when you're not. Every time I've heard great music when I've been stoned and I've bought it afterwards, it's always been bad."

"When you do yoga you have very strong feelings like you're on drugs," continued J-B. "You have the feeling that you fly and that you are without weight. We are very careful with the substances that we eat or smoke, so people think we are very straight. But that is not the case because when we make our music the pressure is off and we feel weightless. Like yoga. This makes us go further with our creation which helps with the balance in our lives."

"When you are an artist, the best way to express yourself is with the record," added Nicolas "What you think about life is in your record which makes artists uncomfortable with interviews. I think the interesting parts of us are in the records or in the shows, not in the interviews."

Back in 1999, Versaille, as we set off for a walk into the woodlands for the photoshoot, heat haze shimmering across the golf course, another side to the duo's history emerged. This idyllic home in Versailles wasn't always Air's chosen base. Indeed, all of the *Premieres Symptomes* album tracks were recorded in the chaos and confusion of Paris. Previously they'd owned a studio on a cobbled street just below the Montmartre. A picture postcard of a street with a windmill (and at that time a Domino Pizza shop) at one end, it seemed to be pretty unremarkable beyond tourist attraction. Except it was in this street that both Air and Daft Punk were hatching their plans for world domination. Surprisingly, however, it was Air who upset the neighbours

"The people in the street where we were found my phone number one day and they kept on phoning me whenever we were in the studio," Nicolas said with a broad grin. "Every time the music started we'd be interrupted. We were just down the road from Daft Punk. You'd think that people would get upset with them because it's house music. But they don't disturb anybody. And with us making this sweet music, cool guys making sweet music and there's so much noise. The windows were like this (shakes hands)."

"When we played the organ, it would vibrate everything," J-B continued. "We like the live sounds, so we have to turn it up loud."

"Sometimes, you know, the guys who do thrash rock are very calm but guys like us are the opposite," Nicolas added with a smile. "Guys like Jimi Hendrix, you know, they were making this music out on the edge but in private, they were very sweet guys. For us, it's the opposite. I can get in a bad mood and break everything in the studio. We only do this music to calm down our nerves. We like pure songs. In fact, I'd like to collaborate with Jesus… Or God!"

I wondered if they weren't afraid of what the God-fearing Catholics of Versailles would have made of such claims.

"We don't care," exclaimed Nicolas. "We're moving back to Paris to record the next album. We need to be in the city because it will affect the atmosphere again. Just as moving here changed our sound for 'Moon Safari'. We need to be back in the city."

If the move to Versailles altered their sound for *Moon Safari*, then it was to have a profound effect on their soundtrack to *Virgin Suicides*. This was a full-bodied progressive rock album lifted straight from the archives of Pink Floyd and coloured any shade of black imaginable. Ironically, however, it bore little relation to the black humour of Coppola's movie.

"The soundtrack is much darker, which was relevant to the content of the movie that makes fun out of suicide," said J-B. "But it's still very depressing, so we had to sound dark."

Talking to Marc Teissier du Cros in the offices of Record Makers in November 2002, the situation became clearer.

"A part of the magic of this record I think, is the fact that they misunderstood what the film was about. They were working in their studio on videotapes that they had received from Sofia Coppola. They didn't really know anything about the movie apart from the bits they were sent. So, according to the name of the movie, they thought that it would be depressing. So they made dark music. They had to make the whole record, with each track being purposefully created for specific scenes. And the way this music appears on the CD is how they made it."

The actual score for the film, however, was very different to the music created by Air. Coppola only lifted parts of tracks and looped them for ambient effect, whereas the actual songs were far a more literal translation of what Godin and Dunckel were seeing on the rushes. When the duo saw the film, they were horrified.

"I wish that one time we can see the original film with Air's music on it as they wanted it to be," said du Cros. "Because when Sofia Coppola received the music she re-edited the whole thing. She looped bits of it and cut the parts she didn't like. So when we first heard it at Cannes Festival, Air were like, 'what has she done to the music? It's incredible'. We were naive, really, because we didn't realise that it wasn't our decision what went on the final cut. But as long as we could release the original version on CD we were happy.

"It is true that they didn't understand how she intended the movie to be cut but at the end, this record is considered by many people to be Air's best," adds du Cros. "It is incredible how this record continues to sell. Also, I think it contains the most classic Air song ever, 'Playground Lover'. When we finished the video for this, I was sure that it was going to be a huge hit. But it didn't sell at all. I think in retrospect, this was because it was out of step with the general mood for the time. It was too dark. I think if they release it again in the future, maybe in a different version, it will be very big."

Virgin Suicides was indeed a remarkable album. It revolved around a central musical theme and took the listener through various stages of anger, breakdown, depression and pure fury. Furthermore, it presented the duo as far more versatile than previous outings suggested. *Moon Safari* had it seemed, been just the tip of an unpredictable iceberg. *Virgin Suicides* was also notable for being the first release on the duo's own label, Record Maker. The label would walk a solitary path exploring opportunities in the DVD world, soundtrack licensing and developing a roster of artists who had more to do with traditional songwriting than the dance music sphere.

One of their first artists, Sebastien Tellier, explored avenues that were more instantly recognisable to fans of Air. His 2001 album *L'Incroyable Verite* was a 70s style space opera created from melodramatic piano, Moogs and analogue synths.

In 2001 Air returned with their fourth album *10,000 Hz Legend*. Again the accusations rang out that they'd embraced progressive rock. A matter of days after a one-off gig in London to launch the album, Nicolas Godin was still smarting at the reviews. It wasn't the criticisms that hurt, but the fact that the music showcased on the night was likened to such progressive rock dinosaurs as Yes and Genesis. That J-B took to the stage wearing a Rick Wakeman-style cape clearly hadn't helped matters, the irony of the attire apparently outweighed by the reported pomposity of their new songs.

"Prog rock is the most horrible music ever made. I hate that music. I can't believe that people say we're prog. I really hate that music so much," spat Godin before staring out of the window at the drizzly Parisian afternoon, lost in a disbelieving sulk. Partner in crime J-B was much less fazed by the criticism. Mystified perhaps, but still able to defend Air's position.

"I think the new album is very original. It's progressive, but not prog. Its progressive pop," he says, losing the debate with every word that tripped from his mouth. The men from Air were visibly squirming.

Since Air first emerged, their music had become the prized possession of pop culture vultures, from Madonna to David Bowie. With *10,000 Hz Legend,* however, the duo found themselves facing the sharpened knives of the backlash. It wasn't a position they were enjoying.

"*Moon Safari* was much more naive. We were naive then," argued Nicolas upon returning from his mental absence. "It was about our childhoods and trying to understand what was around us. With this album, we realised that life is ahead of us. On *Moon Safari*, it was about looking behind us. It was nostalgic and melancholic for the past. We said goodbye to this with *Moon Safari* and were much more excited about moving forward with this album. Seeing the future and not the past."

It's true that *10,000 Hz Legend* dispensed with the chocolate box sweetness of its predecessor. Images of romance were replaced by visions of sex. In terms of the space travel metaphors, the 'future is bright, spaceships are shiny and robots are cuddly' style of films like *Forbidden Planet* had been replaced by the dank and dirty reality and cold fear of *Aliens*. *10,000 Hz Legend* was an altogether more complex affair than the duo's prior releases.

"Our audience are like vampires," said Nicolas of the potential resistance to this change of atmosphere. "They want blood like they deserve something from us. They want us to do stuff for them, so when we do something different, it's like we haven't got a right. But we have to be true to ourselves. We didn't want to be prisoners of *Moon Safari* and all the clichés that went with it. All that, 'Oh I like Air, they're so romantic, so French'. We wanted to tell them nothing and just tell ourselves something."

Perhaps one of the ironies of the musical direction of this album lay in the fact that it was actually less prog-rock than *Moon Safari*. The Moogs so beloved of Rick Wakeman and the vocoders made popular by Electric Light Orchestra were nowhere to be heard. Rhythms owed more to the distorted, crackling man-machine beats of *Low* period Bowie (most notably on the single 'Radio#1' which echoed 'Sound and Vision'), melodies were either reminiscent of the pre-prog garage psychedelia of Syd Barret's Pink Floyd or the Canterbury bands like Soft Machine, the ambience hinted at the robotic distance of Kraftwerk, while the presence of Beck in the EZ meets country kitsch style of his *Mutations* album seemed to be everywhere. Indeed he even turned in a vocal performance on 'The Vagabond'.

Nicolas and J-B first mentioned the idea of working with Beck to me back in 1999 in the woods surrounding their studio in Versailles. They were, they told me, huge fans of his lo-fi album *Mutations*. Beck, it transpired, was also a fan of theirs.

"The temptation for us was to do a song from *Mutations*," admitted Nicolas. "He was thinking he would like to do an Air song. So we started working on a song for Beck, but the more it went on, the more it sounded like an Air song. But not an old Air song. The new Air. We wanted to change. If you have kids, you want them to be different. Artists are here to say 'fuck off' and to change things. I think we are artists. Aren't we? We regret that there's not enough albums like ours."

"We've tried to be as pure as we can," added J-B. "We think these songs are modern. Modernity is in the recording, not in the songs themselves. For this album, we were very conscious that we had the time to do something original, but we still have classical stuff like melodies. We also talk more about relationships in a more personal way. Like sexual love concepts. We confess a lot to people on this record."

Among these confessionals was a song about oral sex, 'Wonder Milky Bitch', a country and western lament as presented by Kraut-rockers Can. Not only was it their most overtly sexual track ever, but it was also their most aggressive.

"You mean we sound macho," laughs Nicolas. "This is true, I think. But we don't think this kind of sex is macho. For a lot of girls, it is a gift to give blowjobs. And for me, it's a pleasure to give back to a girl. We don't consider any kind of sex is dirty. If you give your girl a good orgasm before she goes to work, it's the best thing you could do for her. In France, everyone would have been proud of Bill Clinton. In the US they were ashamed of him but here, he would have been a national hero. When Francois Mitterand died, his wife was there, and so were his mistresses, his children and unofficial children. Everybody was there and it wasn't a problem. We are not hypocrites with sex."

"I think you can hear in our music that we think about love in general," added J-B, returning to a favourite theme for interviews. "Our music is very evocative, so people feel that our music is like a caress. Like sex."

"You know," interrupted Nicolas. "We get groupies who are into S&M. We are such gentle people but we attract people who are into S&M. It's amazing. They want to touch our arse and have big spanking sessions. It's strange."

Despite the sexual confessions, Air maintained that *10,000 Hz Legend* was influenced by their travels through the US. "It's so American, like two French guys meeting an American crew. Two sweet French guys falling in love with dirty Los Angeles," revealed Nicolas. However, in reality, the album may have dropped one cliché about the French for another cliché entirely. They went direct from the pulp fiction romance to being the best-lovers-in-the-world.

Or perhaps *10,000 Hz Legend* opened up a classic communication breakdown between cultures. The true meanings of what they were trying to say were lost in the translation into broken English. What Air sees as innovation or art, the British write off as prog. Where they see the US written all over their album, the British critics hear 70s excess. Similarly, in the movie *Virgin Suicides*, what the English speaking world may have viewed as a film of, at times, black humour, all Air saw was, according to Nicolas: "the melted atmospheres between death and love. I thought we'd completely fucked up. But we weren't sensitive to the dialogue because we didn't understand."

With the elements that have been described as kitsch-retro gone from their music what we had on *10,000 Hz Legend* was Air seen to be affected by the very present world around them. It may not have offered as welcoming or warm an experience, but it still provided an evocative and hugely compelling journey. And one that may prove in time to be a longer-lasting and more enriching experience.

"I don't know where it comes from. It is more intense and extreme, especially in terms of production. We aimed to do a lot of emotional songs. We still want to make people fly and make them discover some weird universe," says J-B.

So was *10,000 Hz Legend* affected by their move back to the city?

"Oh yes," J-B confirms. "This album is definitely affected by the city. The house we recorded *Moon Safari* in has been sold now. I regret it sometimes. I used to catch the train from Paris to there. The station was in the middle of nowhere in the woods. You had to walk for fifteen minutes through the woods to get to the studio. By the time I got there, I'd had plenty of oxygen and green visions... so I felt good. I miss that."

10,000 Hz Legend may have been a less immediate album than *Moon Safari* but it was the stronger collection. It displayed Air growing beyond what they describe as the previous album's "naïve" sound. However, it wasn't as well received by either critics or the record-buying public.

Perhaps in some attempt to recoup some losses, Virgin released a remix set called *Everybody Hertz* in 2002 (and rereleased in 2022 with extra tracks). The album included reworkings of three tracks by as disparate a selection of artists as On U Sound dub stalwart Adrian Sherwood, hip US hip hop producers The Neptunes (aka NERD) and fellow French types Modjo, The Hacker and Mr Oizo. Also featured were a brand new track, "The Way You Look Tonight' and a live performance of 'People in the City' in Los Angeles.

As incongruous as the album may have seemed, it actually succeeded in revealing just how strong some of the songs from *10,000 Hz Legend* actually were. The original epic choirs and electro-rock beats and guitars of the original 'Don't be Light' were transformed into a distressed lo-fi techno shadow play by Mr. Oizo, who utilised the more brittle aspects of Air's sound alongside a cleanly spoken vocal. The Neptunes' version of the same song built a free-flowing funk-rock epic around the vocal mel odies and Moogs of the original, while Malibu's version brought a garage groove to the party. Here the main focus was the spoken vocal along-side snatches of vocodered voices. The final version of the track came from The Hacker, who brought the beats of New Order's 'Blue Monday' and turned the original into 80s electro-pop. 'How Does it Make You Feel?' on the other hand, found its original Floyd-esque acoustic guitars, choirs, steady rock beat and epic chorus transformed into a Studio 1 dub sound excursion, complete with melodica refrains by Adrian Sherwood.

The final reworking 'People in the City', featured what was perhaps the most radical and successful version. Surprisingly this came cour-tesy of French Touch filtered disco merchants Modjo. Here they turned the mellow rock of the original into a jazz-rock exploration. Where the original explored psychedelic rock and fused it with Kraftwerk's com-puter world, Modjo delivered a joyous, Brazilian-esque groove that lifted the original vocal line to new realms of funkiness. More Stevie Wonder than Pink Floyd.

So successful were some of the remixes on this package that you were left wondering how original tracks such as standout 'Electronic

Performers', with its echoes of Bowie's 'Heroes' period in the beats and ambience, would have sounded through the remix process. Or how other producers would have affected the tense power of the synth modulating hymn 'Radian' or the taut melodrama of the finale 'Caramel Prisoner'.

The all-new track on the *Everybody Hertz* collection, 'The Way You Look Tonight' sounded like Air's take on Beck's *Mutations* thanks to its fey melody, strummed acoustic guitar and cheap synth refrains. Godin's lead vocals blended with Dunckel's chorus harmony in a way that suggested that the duo might be turning into the Simon & Garfunkel of the electro-acoustic world. Furthermore, the track's epic drum climax only underlined just how close Air sailed towards prog-rock territories.

The live version of 'People in the City' further underlined this point. As a live unit Air's band played on the tension of the recorded works but overplayed the dynamics. As a result, they display prog-rock tendencies that, thankfully, never quite went all of the way. The final irony is that in the live show, Air sounded at their most retro. This accepted, their gigs were spectacularly sensual affairs that deserved respect for their breadth of vision.

In 2002 Air made one more appearance on record. This time it was as remixers to long time hero David Bowie. He had asked them to rework the track 'A Better Future' from his acclaimed *Heathen* set. The results were a stunning display of discordant synth-rock opera. And far better than Bowie's original.

"When we were asked about the remix, you can imagine, it was like a dream come true," said Marc Teissier du Cros. "Nicolas and J-B have always been such big Bowie fans. He was the hero of their teenage years. But when they got the track, well, I'm not sure if I should say this, but we were so disappointed. It wasn't very good, really. Well, we didn't think so. So they thought the only way to approach it was to take it apart and turn it into an Air song. Which they did. The funny thing is that he requested from them a club mix, which was strange because they're not a club act."

Indeed, so good is the combination of Bowie's vocals and Air's music that the track represented a creative high point in both careers. Any hope of a collaboration of some sort in the future would surely have produced a timeless classic.

"The fantastic thing about that remix," continued du Cros. "Is that it proved just how far Air have come. Now they are in a position to do what they want. With Record Makers, they can record stuff without the involvement of Virgin. We did all of the deals for 'Virgin Suicides' without Virgin's involvement and that is something which makes them able to explore many ideas. Just recently, they were asked to go to Rome to soundtrack a reading by an Italian writer. They played three times and it was beautiful. People loved it, and after this, we found out that he was a big star in Italy. Now they are going to record it with him in a studio and release it. Because of setting up the label and the way they make music Air can do this kind of thing very quickly. Which they can't do in a big company. They can be artists in the true sense.

"Air's strength comes from the combination of both personalities," he continued. "It's Nicolas' understanding of pop and J-B's classical background, because he studied at the Conservatoire in Paris, you know, so he's a nice pianist. What they do is very clever. They understand each other without talking. They're not obviously cutting edge in their production, but they aren't necessarily retro. Sometimes you get associations that work. Air are like that."

Above all of the acts to emerge from the late 90s Paris hype, Air developed their own unique style. They were quite literally in a field of their own.

"One of the most rewarding things about working with them is that they have a separate inventive side," confirmed du Cros. "They don't belong to any movement. They are on their own. They don't follow anyone."

In the years that followed, the duo cut a furrow that at times saw them verging on self-parody. *Talkie Walkie* in 2004 seemed to be trying to recapture the feeling of *Moon Safari* but with a deeper investment in Beck's songwriting. The album included the track 'Alone in Kyoto', another track that owed a huge amount to Bowie's *Low* and possibly the ambient work of David Sylvian; this was actually a track written for Sofia Coppola's

Lost in Translation. One notable addition to *Talkie Walkie* was the string arrangements of Michel Colombier, who had co-written the ballet score *Messe Pour Les Temps Present* with Pierre Henry. Air were once again exploring the French tradition of sound sculpture.

Pocket Sculpture from 2007 felt like a continuation of a very clearly outlined script. There were few real surprises on show. The album *Love 2* in 2009 was much stronger due to its free-flowing analogue synths but still felt like it was treading water. During this period, only the soundtrack work pointed to a more rewarding vein of work. *Le Voyage das La Lune* in 2012 brought with it more dynamism and aggressive orchestration, albeit at the usual slow tempo. The album was inspired by the 1902 film by Georges Melies and was intended as the soundtrack to a restored version of the film that never materialised.

Almost inevitably, the duo started to explore solo ventures. Working as Darkel, J-B released his eponymous solo album in September 2006. It brought flavours from 1980s TV themes like Miami Vice alongside a more electronic rock feel. In 2011, he formed the electronica side project Tomorrow's World with Lou Hayter of New Young Pony Club. In 2015 he produced his first solo album under his own name, JB Dunkel. Called *H+*, the album offered piano drenched film-esque rock. He also produced numerous soundtracks to varying degrees of success.

Nicolas Godin was considerably slower in developing his solo catalogue. In September 2015, he released his first solo album, *Contrepoint*, which was inspired by the music of Johann Sebastian Bach. His second album, *Concrete and Glass*, appeared in 2020, while his lone Godin soundtrack output came in the shape of a French series, 'A Very Secret Service'.

When comparing the duo's solo outings, it is notable just how reliant their sound was on Dunkel's sound, which appeared to be the foundation to Air. Godin's music was the added flourishes that gave new flavours to their music. While neither artist's work has been as enjoyable as their joint venture, it is in J-B's work that the spectre of Air is most prominent.

OLLANO, MELLOW AND BANG BANG –
THE FINAL PARTS IN THE VERSAILLES JIGSAW

Throughout the Versailles story, one name kept cropping up, Mellow. A group whose progressive rock tendencies went far beyond any of Air's Pink Floyd-isms. Imagine perfectly poised vintage future-pop. A sound where surf harmonies walk hand in hand with soundtrack muzak and dreamscaped analogue ambience aches to the flow of classic west coat melodies.

Mellow formed in September 1997 around the trio of Stephane Luginbuhl, Pierre Begon-Lours and Anglo-French singer Patrick Woodcock to work on a few songs already demoed by the vocalist. Patrick had previously worked with Air's Nicolas Godin, Alex Gopher and Xavier Jameaux.

At first, the relationship between Patrick and Pierre was purely functional. Pierre, a studio engineer who had once played in a band with Patrick's brother, had suggested that he helped re-record Patrick's tracks for higher quality. However, as soon as work started, he felt a deep affinity with the nu-psychedelic sound. He quickly invited Stephane, another engineer friend, to hear the work in progress. He immediately fell in love with what he heard, the notion of a recording trio was hatched and Mellow was born.

Pierre and Stephane had previously come to the fore as abstract grooves outfit Ollano, whose work came out on Artefact subsidiary Rosebud. Their track 'La Couleur' was used on *Source Lab 2* and featured a loose-limbed jazz dub excursion. It featured Xavier Jamaux alongside turntablism from Eric Rug. Other tracks that emerged under the Ollano name had ranged in style from drum & bass to trip hop. Recording for the Mellow project reconvened at Stephane's house in Paris where the two producers helped the ideas evolve in directions that none of them had previously envisaged.

"All we aimed to do was to make records that we would like," explained Patrick. "There was no marketing policy, no stringent plans, just a notion of a sound we all liked."

That sound was reminiscent of the early psychedelia of artists like Kevin Ayers, Syd Barrett and The Beatles, the film soundtracks of Morricone and the Moog overtures of contemporary artists like Stereolab and Californian bands like The Virgins. Yet rather than using these influences to create a simple retro pastiche, the trio took the textures and ambience of those bands and updated them with an ear for contemporary post-rock shapeshifts and electronic excursions.

"We're not a retro act trying to recreate the past," said Patrick. "We've got no problem with the new. We just like to listen to old stuff and discover fresh things in it. And another thing, we don't just use old machines like Lenny Kravitz, so we can try and sound like we're from the 60s. We use new gear because we live in the 90s."

Soon after the trio's first tracks were finished, they were approached by Parisian independent label Atmospheriques, to who they signed despite competition from several labels. Much of the interest had been generated because Mellow's studio adventures had blossomed into a seven-piece live act.

Eschewing the chance to tread the boards in their native Paris, Mellow's debut gig was in Brighton at the Big Beat Boutique. Thus joining the ranks of Parisian outfits that had grown from the foundations of studio culture gigging bands but had now embraced the live gig. The Mellow approach to the live set-up produced fluidity not normally associated with the gig.

A single 'Another Mellow Winter' was released in the summer of 1998. It immediately gained huge acclaim from the French press, most notably in the major music title *Les Inrockuptibles*. They not only invited them to play alongside Air, Lo Fidelity Allstars and Sean Lennon on the music paper's own festival tour but also voted them as the number one act to watch in 1999 (somewhat strangely topping a chart that included My Bloody Valentine and Radiohead!). The single also caught the attention of one Roman Ford-Coppola (son of legendary director Francis), who offered to direct the band's first video and subsequently keep the already deep Coppola links to the Versaille French Touch alive.

With the band's debut album – also called *Another Mellow Winter* – Mellow's unique musical vision was fully explored. From the opening analogue pulses and bad trip discordance of 'Lovely Light', through the 'Lucy in the Sky with Diamonds' style Mellotron refrains of 'Mellow', and on to the swooning Midnight Cowboy-esque horn melodies of 'Overture'. From the rolling thunder of the Moog epic 'Mellow (Analogue Version)' which presented the perfect soundtrack to Dr. Timothy Leary's last voyage, to 'Violet' which offered the sound of nostalgia melting through the cracks of contemporary pop, it was an album which oozed hazy summer warmth soaked in fine wine and various chemicals.

Mellow produced a sound that had as much in common with California and Canterbury as it did Versailles. They created vintage pop overtures rooted in the original summer of love but still reaching for the stars of tomorrow. Somewhere on the crossroads between Stereolab and The Beach Boys; checking Beck's head through Pink Floyd's stethoscope; exploring the ghosts of Soft Machine through the eyes of Ennio Morricone and surfing the sine waves of Sergeant Pepper on a board made from Air's Moogs. The nu-psychedelic tones of Mellow were where the past and future fused in a mind-melting Moog drenched fantasy to create perfectly poised vintage future-pop.

1999 also saw the final member of Orange step into the spotlight with his debut album. This time it was the turn of Xavier Jamaux, whose album *Je T'Aime Je T'Aime* under the name Bang Bang was released by Yellow Productions. Bang Bang had previously appeared on *Source Lab 2* with the moody 'Neither Sing-Sing Nor Baden Baden' (which was also licensed to the Kevin Reynolds movie '187'). However, the material on his album offered a much different flavour. True, the references to film scores were still in place, but where soundscapes had revolved around a smoky dub axis, now there was a pop sensibility at work. Again the main references were David Bowie, Pink Floyd and Serge Gainsbourg, tempered throughout by flourishes of 80s soul.

The first release on Yellow came in the shape of his 'By Bye Blues' single in 1996. It offered a smooth marriage between programmed beats and real instruments but lacked any real finesse or originality to help it stand out. A year later, he created the score for the French-Japanese movie 'Tokyo Eyes'. In 1998 Bang Bang's second EP came in the shape of 'Two Fingers', an electronic soul track that featured the vocals of Swedish crooner Jay Jay Johanson. 'Two Fingers' became the opening track to the debut album released in March 1999. It also perfectly represented the overall theme of melancholic ambience supported by smooth vocals offering their own individual sombre laments.

Among the vocalists was Gary Christian, who came to fame in the 80s with UK soul-pop outfit The Christians. His offering, 'Believe', found reversed strings, picked acoustic guitars and slow funk groove creating a perfect sound bed for his tortured soul vocals. Even if the overall feel had an overriding sense of the 80s pop acts like Furniture, White and Torch and Black about it.

Elsewhere, 'The Prisoner' found a dark jazz ambience playing counterpoint with 70s Blaxploitation soundtrack flute refrains, strings arrangements and bongo grooves while vocalist Margeaux Lampley delivered her best James Bond theme style vocal. 'Without You' had similar film-esque qualities, but this time the atmosphere was more akin to the 60s scores of Lalo Schiffrin, but with that ever-present smooth 80s soul covering over the rough edges.

Je T'Aime Je T'Aime may have been a cohesive collection but it lacked an edge. Unlike the soul and funk that Jamaux so obviously admired, Bang Bang created music where all of the suspense, unpredictability and raw edges of soul were removed. It was the sound of funk bleached white.

6. GOLDEN TRIANGLE OF BASTILLE

THE FRENCH TOUCH GETS A FOCUS

"The whole thing about the French Touch was that it was a bunch of friends that knew each other, who spent their time in Bastille. We used to call Bastille the Golden Triangle. There were three shops and a few cafes around, and people just hung around there all the time. Which was great, but we were not a part of that. I didn't spend all my afternoons in Rough Trade at Bastille."

Laurent Garnier

As with any city, the focus of Paris' dance culture started to revolve around the axis of the record shops. Initially, the only shop in Paris that sold dance vinyl was BPM. However, in 1994 this was changed by the opening of Rough Trade, located nearby. The result was that all of the young DJs, producers and promoters could be found in either of these shops or the cafes in between. It became known as the Golden Triangle among F Communications and the older techno generation.

However, this geographical focus meant that people would regularly meet up with each other and discuss ideas, swap mixes and share talk of new records. It was a situation that resulted in a suddenly increased momentum among the new generation of clubbers. As with any force, the buzz around Bastille created an energy that drew on a new wave of dance fans, too young to have been one of the original techno elite but keen to be a part of this burgeoning new movement.

Behind the counter at Rough Trade could be found numerous producers. Among them was Arnaud Rebotini, whose earliest work came in the shape of Zend Avesta but is also known as Black Strobe, Krell and Aleph. Black Strobe was a collaboration with Ivan Smagghe (who also worked at Rough Trade), representing Rebotoni's more electronic output, with 'Innerstrings' and 'Me and Madonna' bringing together electro beats and dark ambience. Aleph found tight beats merged with dub effects and flourishes of house ambience. A sound that could be heard at its best on 1997's *Source Lab 3* collection. On the other hand, Krell came from a drum & bass perspective that fused time-stretched beats with lush orchestration.

However, as Zend Avesta, Robotini received massive critical acclaim for his fusion of drum & bass, jazz and avant-garde classical. This musical approach brought the producer into the limelight with his stunning 'One of these Days', which combined taught ambience with flighty beats and an elastic bass undertow.

The debut album *Organique* arrived in 1998 and sold 10,000 copies in its first month of release. *Organique* found him incorporating a fusion of pop and electronic through the use of neo-classical composition. As a result, refrains would echo throughout, with tracks linked by movements and repeated orchestration. The album also featured a collaboration with Hafdis Hud (ex-Gus Gus), Roya Arab (ex-Archive) and numerous French artists like renowned pop singers Mona Soyoc and Alain Bashung, Philippe Poirier from Kast Onoma, France's answer to the Velvet Underground. In 2002 Rebotini composed a one-hour piece for Groupe de Recherché Musicale, which he performed live in Paris in the March of that year. Thus underlining the classical stylings at the centre of all of his work.

Also behind the counter of Rough Trade was Jerome Mestre, whose Artefact Records became a source of first class underground sounds. Unlike many other labels that emerged during this period, Artefact avoided the archetypal French Touch sound but instead explored more experimental avenues. These usually focused around drum & bass. Mestre was also behind Extra Lucid, whose ambient drum & bass scapes echoed the works of UK producers like LTJ Bukem. Extra Lucid represented the leading edge of drum & bass in Paris at the time, but Mestre's ambient style was far removed from the sound being played in the clubs. At parties like Jungle Fever, Otis would deliver harder-edged jungle sounds more in tune with the early rush of Shy FX.

Despite the efforts of Mestre, DJ Gilb'R (who presented a drum & bass show on Radio Nova in 1997) and promoter-cum-label manager Catherine Piault (Jungle Fever, Selector Records), drum & bass failed to take hold in Paris in the same way that it erupted in London. However, the rest of France featured numerous drum & bass posses that existed almost entirely separately from the main force of French electronic artists and labels. Among them was Montpellier's Black Tambour Records and Interzone Records in Annecy.

One of the most notable labels to emerge in the mid-90s around the Bastille buzz was the celebrated Versatile Records, which initially worked out of Daft Punk's offices in Montmartre. Versatile was the brainchild of DJ Gilb'R, aka Gilbert Cohen.

DJ GILB'R – VERSATILE AND THE ECLECTIC EMBRACED

"I started DJing completely by accident in 1990 in the town I grew up in the south of France. Basically, when I was young, all the parties were very rock, but me and my friends were a little bit cool; we were into hip hop, funk and other black music. We had no parties playing the kind of music we wanted to hear. Then my brother went to the US and came back with loads of hip hop, things like the first De La Soul, 3rd Bass, that kind of thing. So we decided to organise a party ourselves and I DJed. It was pretty cool, so I carried on."

Gilb'R is one of Paris' cooler customers. Not in the trendy sense of the word but in his whole outlook on what he does. Where other label bosses come over as desperate for hit singles and recognition, or in some cases bitter at being left behind in the wake of the hype, Gilb'R presents the aura of someone whose only need is to be moved by the music he is involved with.

This attitude has marked out Versatile since it first emerged in 1996. Whether skirting the edges of filtered house, as with the 1997's Sunshine People Mix of 'Venus' by Cheek and the 1996 Daft Punk re-rub of I:Cube's 'Disco Cubizm', or exploring the world of electro-jazz funk as on Chateau Flight's album *Puzzle*, Gilb'R's label has always striven for a level of excellence that few ever attain.

But then again, this pursuit of excellence has marked out his career in music since day one. And in the process, forced him to make choices that have found him eschewing the relative security of high profile DJ and radio jobs to follow his instinct. Something that takes a huge quantity of the kind of cool that no amount of designer labels will provide.

The first time we met was in a café bar near Montmartre. It was 1996 and we talked for hours about drum & bass. It was his main passion at the time. Indeed he'd cut out a name for himself as one of Paris' premier drum & bass DJs. He was intensely passionate about his chosen subject and keen to tell me about his dream for Versatile.

By 2002 many of those original dreams had come to fruition. He had had great successes on both commercial and creative levels. He had a roster that was second to none regarding the artist's own talents. And he'd released a brace of classic singles and albums. Furthermore, he had been heavily involved in creating the momentum and infrastructure that forged the French Touch while retaining enough individuality for Versatile to have its own identity separate from the other prime movers of the French Touch glory days.

Sitting in his office on a stormy December evening, Gilb'R appears far more relaxed than the first time we met. But no less passionate.

"When I moved to Paris, I started playing at a trendy club twice a week," he explained. "They were playing lots of Latin stuff, but I was starting to discover electronic music and things like that, so it started to be very restrictive for me DJing there."

Not for the first time, Gilb'R quit the job. However, he'd started hanging out at Paris' Radio Nova. He'd struck up a friendship with the head of programming and soon found himself presenting a show.

"Nova was a very important radio station," he continued. "A lot of people were influenced by the station. It was a bit like an oasis among the desert of radio, because they had no adverts or talking, just a continuous flow of music and jingles. And the way they did their jingles was very personal. It was such crazy radio that as soon as you tuned in and heard the music, you knew it was Nova."

Radio Nova's style was hugely eclectic. At this time, it drew on sounds from around the globe and fused them all together.

"You'd get some new wave tracks played next to Zouk tracks, and then a jazz track, a hip hop track and so on. The only criteria was that it had quality. I think Nova really invented the concept of world music because, at the time, they used to say sonar mondial, which meant world music. They had some intellectual people working there who were really engaged in politics. At the same time, there were a lot of African and Arabic people, and that's really the culture of Paris. Like in London, you have the Jamaican culture; here, it's more African."

After a while, Gilb'R took over the role of full-time sound programmer for the station. It was, he says, a period in which his ideas about music were continuously stretched. He would set up live jams with visiting musicians from all types of music to create genre-melting fusion sessions for live broadcasts. He experienced a constant deluge of quality music of all styles, but above all, he was encouraged to develop his own passion for discovering new music.

"The owner of the station had a huge record collection. He was crazy about music by Soft Machine and Lee Perry and so on. He has this huge record library. He's a kind of freak man who lived in a castle in the suburb of Paris and the place had records everywhere and paintings. A very cool guy. He'd invite us round all the time and we'd listen to all of these different types of music, smoke spliffs and stuff. It was a cool atmosphere."

In 1996 Gilb'R approached Nova with the idea of starting a record label. They were keen on the idea and he started requesting demos. However, during this period, there was a huge change in the musical direction of the station. Suddenly the management was putting pressure on their DJs to become more commercial. Gilb'R left. Once again, the music was more important than the security.

"I decided to leave when it became more commercial in its programming. Obviously, they wanted to make some money. I'm not someone who thinks the station has to be all about my music. It wasn't Radio Gilb'R; it was for the people. But after a while, I got a little schizo, so because I was into cutting edge music, but at the same time, I had to be more commercial for the radio. So I had to make a choice."

However, he didn't leave before approaching one of the artists who'd sent a demo in to ask if he'd be interested in being released by the label he was now going to set up on his own.

"While I was at the radio, I received Nicolas Chaix's I:Cube tape; I thought it was amazing. The tape had some techno tunes, some house tunes, some more downtempo stuff and it all sounded very mature. I was really impressed, so I asked him if he would be interested in doing something on the label. He said OK. Then I took the tape to Thomas and Guy-Man – they hadn't done their album at the time – and I played them the tracks and asked if they wanted to do a remix. They were into it. So we put all of Nicolas' machines in my house and in three days we recorded the first twelve. The Daft boys came with their mix and it was so cool. Then we put out the track 'Disco Cubizm' and I think it was just the right track at the right time. It became a French Touch anthem.

I:Cube (Mark Stringer)

"Next we did 'Sunshine People', which was even bigger, and for a while, I just didn't know what was going on. When you first start and you sell ten to fifteen thousand copies of your first records, it makes you feel so high. Also, meeting someone like Nicolas, who is very talented, a true genius, seriously, it was difficult because all of the other projects had to be at the same level."

Nicolas Chaix was indeed a rare talent in the electronic music world. His debut album, 1997's *Picnic Attack*, revealed him as someone with a mastery of a range of dance styles, which allowed him to forge his own style within the medium. Talking to me at the time of the album's release in April 1997, he admitted:

"I've been influenced by the early Detroit stuff and also trance and techno. All of this stuff in the UK press seems to have ignored the fact that trance is incredibly popular over here. It's so difficult not to be affected by it. But I think that I'm not necessarily a part of any clique does mean I can really do what I want with my music."

Indeed, the only thing that seemed to have any day to day effect on Nicolas' music-making at the time was the fact that he was still living with his parents.

"I still live at home, so I have to play my music quietly," he admitted. "It's a bit of a problem because when I'm recording stuff, I have to turn it right down after 10pm. I'm sure it's affected the music; made it more melodic perhaps."

In 1997 Nicolas was still studying at college to be a theatre set designer. It was a pursuit that made total sense when listening to his astonishing music. His programming approach is like a 3D designer, built in stages around different textures, timbres and colours, each separate entity meshing to create an awe-inspiring whole.

"I suppose I've always seen music as art," he explained. "The name I:Cube comes from school where a group of friends and me used to have this art collective. We'd do loads of stuff under the name I:Cube. It doesn't mean anything really, but it just kind of stuck with me."

In the two years that followed, Chaix delivered his first collaborative project with Gilb'R as Chateau Flight. In 1999, however, he released a three-part series of irony tinged EPs under the titles 'Scratch Robotniks', 'Tropiq' and 'Poo Pah'. These were then compiled on one CD as the album *Adore*. Again the producer was revealed as a unique talent with its mix of techno, house, electro, dub and bossa.

This second instalment from I:Cube was followed by *Puzzle*, the debut album by Chateau Flight. The collaborative venture between I:Cube and Gilb'R first started as a remix project in 1997. Together they reworked

Pierre Henry's 'Too Fotiche' and Air's 'Le Soleil et Pres de Moi' to stunning effect. The experience of working on these tracks encouraged the duo to work together on original material and they quickly came up with the 'Discobole' single, which was hailed as a classic by the dance media.

By the time of their 2000 album *Puzzle*, the media had cooled on the idea of anything French. The collection went by largely unnoticed by anyone but the specialist press. People missed out on a brilliant album that melted live instrumentation with ingenious programming, a fusion of house, Detroit techno, jazz and soul. It was a pure representation of the music that the duo loved and a flight into the eclectic approaches both had taken to their own individual projects. As with the better projects to have emerged in this period of France's dance development, the combination of the two personalities was the key to the album's unique aura and energy.

"We have a big fascination for old records and what it is about them that makes us go back to them time after time," explained Gilb'R of the ideology behind Chateau Flight and all of the artists on Versatile. "I think it is because they definitely capture every human emotion, which is so difficult to capture. That's what we try to do with our records. We try to put enough emotion into the music to support longevity. And that's Versatile's aim, really. To try and make those timeless albums."

One of the most surprising aspects of Chateau Flight was that it was almost entirely devoid of the trappings of drum & bass, despite Gilb'R's love of the genre. According to Gilb'R, it was just part of natural evolution to him.

"A lot of people were shocked when I stopped playing drum & bass, but for me, my evolution in music is like a path," he said. "When you're walking somewhere, and you see something you like, you stop and take a look. If you like what you see, you stay a while, and when you're tired of what you're watching, you walk on. I wanted to be honest with people. Instead of capitalising on the image I had as a drum & bass DJ, or even the image the label had for French Touch, I felt more comfortable moving on to the next thing on my journey.

"In 1992, I went to New York, which is where I discovered house music. I went to the Sound Factory, Junior Vasquez was playing. To me, house was obscure at that time and I had a really cliched image of the music. But when I went there, I really discovered what it was all about and got more and more into it. So I started to include some house in my DJ sets, which had been funk and hip hop until then. And then drum & bass came, which was a very big shock to me. It was like, finally, there was one form of music that had all of the elements I liked. I really went into it for three or four years. But when Optical came into drum & bass, people, I think, were so shocked by what he was doing that they all started to try and sound like him and the feeling went from drum & bass. It became like too much of a ravey thing for me. And I'm just not into that. So I completely went out of it.

"I did one drum & bass track on Versatile, which got a pretty cool reaction. But when we started the Chateau Flight project, we decided to go further than one style. The thing is, just because I was DJing drum & bass didn't mean that I was only listening to drum & bass. I was still into hip hop, house, jazz and so on. Chateau Flight wasn't my personal project. It was two of us together in the studio. Actually, we tried to do a couple of drum & bass tracks but just weren't happy with the way they sounded."

Versatile moved into ever more varied territory. Most notably, with Joakim Lone Octet, whose *Tiger Sushi* album, on the short-lived experimental sub-label Future Talk, was an abstract jazz exploration that seemingly fused Charlie Parker, John Coltrane, Thelonius Monk and Charlie Mingus with Jeff Mills, Underground Resistance and Radiohead.

"I am more confident than ever for the future," says Gilb'R of the position of Versatile in 2002. "To still be here after six years and completely independent, I think we are still as strong. Obviously, it's not huge money, but as long as I have enough to live, I'm happy.'

He is less happy with the musical climate in France in the post-French Touch era, claiming that, despite receiving hundreds of demos, he can't find anything he wants to sign.

"There's no one in France that I really want to sign now. To be honest, I'm a bit sick of French stuff. People are taking themselves too seriously. They're only interested in how many records are sold and making money and all that shit, you know. They're more interested in having the right shoes or the correct make of headphones and the correct colour underwear. That's not what we're about. We're about music. The rest of it is shit. To me, there is a huge dichotomy between the attitude and the music. Producers get too self-important and pretentious here. Especially when they're doing their albums. That's why it's very rare for people to collaborate here."

This dichotomy never seemed to be a problem with Versatile and its artists. Despite critical acclaim, they remained level headed, excited by new possibilities and touched by the ability to laugh at themselves. And it's this reason why, through artists like I:Cube, Chateau Flight and Joakim Lone Octet, they created music that touches on a very emotional level.

"Before Daft Punk, the major record companies here had no culture of electronic music," concluded Gilb'R. "So they thought that each artist that they signed would sell two million. But after a few experiences, they realised it wasn't that easy. So now it's difficult for people here to get signed and get more exposure. Me, I'm more interested in longevity. That's what I'm looking for with the acts on the label. Longevity."

Versatile was, of course, closely linked with Daft Punk in their early days. Mainly to the fact that the Montmartre duo remixed the first Versatile single, I: Cube's 'Disco Cubizm', but also because they shared office space briefly.

DAFT PUNK – THE MYTHICAL MASKED HEROES OF FRENCH TECHNO

"For me, Daft Punk showed that it was possible to be a producer and keep control over everything. Before that, I didn't know it was possible. Thomas gave me hope, really. After him, it was possible to do stuff in France."

Guillaume Atlan (aka The Supermen Lovers), 2002

Paris. January 5th, 1997, 11am. Standing at the top of the Montmartre steps, beneath the opulent facade of the Sacre Coeur, Daft Punk seemed every inch the bored teenagers that their name would suggest. Aloof, sullen and generally disinterested, the duo dutifully took up positions for

Daft Punk (Mark Stringer)

photographer Mark Stringer. You could be forgiven for thinking that these Parisians were old hands at this, victims of a million and one photo sessions; such is their demeanour. In reality, however, after four years of stoking the boiler, their particular international gravy train had really only just started rolling. And with the then imminent release of their excellent electro-acid charged debut album *Homework*, Daft Punk fever looked set to increase.

Daft Punk chose to wear transparent plastic masks for the photoshoot. It was their way of keeping a sense of control over proceedings, remaining relatively anonymous. They could have been bank robbers before the big heist or kidnappers on the lookout for a passing millionaire. Their facial expressions were sufficiently hidden by fixed and sinister smiles. But their eyes gave it all away. Thomas Bangalter and Guy-Manuel de Homem Christo were playing the press game and they were bored stupid by it all. Or at least, they were *performing* boredom.

As if to underline this fact, straight after the session, when Mark Stringer attempted to make conversation with the duo, he was cut short by a deadly silence. Guy-Man simply pretended he couldn't speak English – obviously forgetting that we'd met and talked several times over the previous few years. Long before they'd ever signed to a record label, in fact. Mark and I put it down to promo fever. Slap bang in the middle of the promotional work for the album; they were just finding out what it means to be a part of a major label. Or perhaps they were busy developing a public image about the performance of myth. Or they just didn't like making small talk with photographers!

And all the while, their press officer kept an eye on proceedings. Playing the dual role of babysitter and clock-watcher. Welcome to the frenzied fever on the frontline of the Paris hype.

Thomas explained to me three years later: "Pictures can be boring. That's one of the reasons for the masks. And sometimes in the beginning, we found it hard with all of the attention."

So we could put it down to youth then. And why not? After all, they weren't long past their teenage years at that pre-Homework meeting. Very much the youngsters of the Paris dance scene, in fact, and already the veterans of three acclaimed dancefloor monsters, a record label bidding war and the kind of media buzz normally only reserved for proper pop stars. No wonder they were bored by it all.

Daft Punk first burst onto the dance arena in 1993. Guy-Man was 16, Thomas, the old man of the duo, clocked in at 17. Previously the duo had been in an instrumental indie band called Darlin'. Thomas played bass while Guy-Man took on guitar duties. Also in the band was Laurent Brinkovic on drums.

"We really weren't that good. It was just a school band," proclaimed Bangalter in their Montmartre base (Thomas grew up in this extremely affluent area of Paris).

Darlin' released one track, however, in the shape of 'Cindy So Loud' for a double 7" compilation on Stereolab's Duophonic label. Then Thomas and Guy-Man discovered raving. They left the band with the intention of creating techno tracks, bought loads of analogue kit and retired to Thomas' bedroom to do their homework. The only thing they took with them from Darlin' was a name culled from a review in *Melody Maker* by the late Dave Jennings, who described them as 'daft, punky thrash'.

"He said we were really bad like 'daft punk'. So we kept the name and left the band," laughed Thomas.

Soon after, Thomas and Guy-Man attended a rave at Euro Disney organised by legendary UK promoter Nicky Holloway. Among the DJs playing on the night was Glasgow's Slam. The origin myth of Daft Punk is that when Thomas came face to face with Slam's Stuart Macmillan, he grabbed the opportunity to press a demo tape into the Glaswegian's hand. Among the tracks on the demo was a cut called 'Alive'. An alternative version of that myth was that a journalist from a French fanzine, most likely *Eden*, passed that tape on. The third and less well-documented argument was that a journalist from the UK had passed a tape with a few artists on it, including Daft Punk's 'Alive' demo to the Soma crew. The final story of how Daft Punk came to be signed by Soma was the least useful to the mythology of either brand, so my name became eradicated from the myth.

In truth, it could have been any one of these scenarios. The most important thing was that a great label who'd been deeply involved in the techno scene of Paris had received a great demo from a Parisian act who deserved to be heard beyond the walls of Pedro Winter's parties.

"They received a phone call from Richard Brown at Soma saying they wanted to sign Daft Punk," said Pedro, who would become Daft Punk's manager in 1996. "It all happened very fast and they really didn't expect it at all."

"We went back to their studio at Thomas's house – his father is quite well-off and has this beautiful place in Montmartre, Paris," Soma's Richard Brown told Matthew Collin in 1997. "It was immediately obvious they were an exciting proposition, especially when we saw their live set, which was incredible. They were brilliant guys – very, very sussed. Thomas's dad is a really intelligent man, and I think he definitely advised them along the way."

The first Daft Punk single, 'The New Wave', appeared late in April 1994. The lead track 'Alive – The New Wave Finale' was instantly hailed as a classic in the UK press who lapped up Soma's claims that they were "French teenage techno sensations". Utilising stripped-down Chicago house beats and nausea-inducing Basic Channel style noise interference, the single failed to ignite with the record buying public. The duo looked destined to forever remain the underground dance scene's best-kept secret.

Until they dropped their second single, 'Da Funk', that is. Like a cut and paste collision between the rough and ready breaks of old skool electro and the brash arrogance of wild style acid, 'Da Funk' immediately caught the attention of the Chemical Brothers, who constantly played it during their DJ residency at London's legendary Heavenly Social. It also made that rare transition onto the dancefloors of indie clubs and became one of the chemical beat anthems of 1995.

Later that year, Chemical Brothers, Tom Rowlands and Ed Simons, tapped the pair up to remix the second single, 'Life Is Sweet', from their debut, *Exit Planet Dust*, and to open for their UK tour. Little surprise then that Daft Punk had been called the Parisian Chemical Brothers. It's a comparison that the duo was clearly tired of. Back in the band's office, Thomas exclaimed:

"Well, if people want to call is that it's their business. I don't think we are like the Chemical Brothers at all. Well, maybe we use electronics and we have a raw sound but that's all. I don't understand why Britain likes to create competition between people. As if by calling us the 'new Chemicals', we're going to start an argument with them. It's stupid."

The notion that a comparison would be made to create tension between the two parties was a prime example of Daft Punk's seemingly neurotic mistrust of the media. In their minds, journalists seemed to be second only to the snakes along the evolutionary scale. It's an attitude that isn't unusual in dance music, yet Daft Punk had apparently taken things to an extreme.

"I sometimes wonder who these people are and why they think their opinion is so important. I think maybe journalists tell us how popular we are but we don't know until the album is released," mused Thomas. "At the moment, though, we think maybe people are a little too scared to say what they really feel. There's a whole lot of interest in Daft Punk, so people are going along with it. Especially journalists who seem unable to make up their own minds."

To challenge this idea, the duo released a third single on Soma in 1996. This time under the name of Indo Silver Club. They also set about creating their own individual labels. Thomas Bangalter created Roule and released his own 'Spinal Scratch' while Guy-Man teamed up with Eric Chedeville to create Crydamoure. They also recorded as Le Knight Club and delivered their anti-summer single 'Christmas'/'Holiday On Ice', which was a minor hit.

With the interest that followed in the wake of the second single, Daft Punk took on a manager to look after the business side of things. The attention from the industry was creating too much of a time demanding diversion for Thomas and Guy-Man. They didn't have to look far for their manager, however. They approached Pedro Winter, who had been regularly promoting Daft Punk along with DJ Gregory, Dimitri and Chris Yellow at his Hype club nights.

"I got involved in 1996," recalled Pedro. "I had lunch with Thomas and he said he was thinking of setting up his own company for Daft Punk business. So he asked me if I wanted to be involved. We didn't have an office at first; we just worked out of his house, next to the studio. A month later, we found an office on Rue Durantin in the 18th district of Paris.

"Before this, I had been studying law and after three months, I started setting up the Hype parties in Follies Pigalle, then on the first floor of Le Palace."

Pedro has subsequently been described in print as the ambassador of the French Touch thanks to the parties and the fact that he managed Daft Punk, Cassius and Cosmo Vitelli. Winter was immediately thrown into the deep end of record label negotiation. Despite intense interest from numerous labels, Daft Punk eventually set up a deal with Virgin whereby they license their tracks to the major through their production company Daft Trax. Virgin had always been frontrunners for this deal as they'd already developed a relationship through the inclusion of 'Musique' on both the *Source Lab 2* compilation and the soundtrack to the *Wipeout* PlayStation game that also featured the Chemical Brothers, Prodigy, Fluke and other artists at the forefront of the breakbeat driven UK dance scene. Virgin released the accompanying compilation album.

The duo's 1997 debut album arrived in the shape of *Homework*, which brought together the best moments from their first three singles with a host of new tracks. The album was an instant success. It was a situation that brought out the duo's cynical suspicion.

"I think a few months after the album, we'll get more honesty from everybody," said Guy-Man of the considerable attention offered to the band. "Today, [1997] there's a lot of hype."

For Thomas and Guy-Manuel, hype simply represents an example of the "star system" at work. Guy-Man is unusually animated on the subject.

"We're totally against the whole idea of any star system," he exclaimed as if spitting the words from his mouth. "To us, it's the opposite to how we are. We're producers, not performers. We don't act like stars and if someone asks me for an autograph, I take time to talk about things with them. I explain that I don't feel comfortable doing this because I'm not a pop star."

"There are some people in Paris who have changed towards us since we started getting noticed," Thomas cuts in. "Maybe they looked down on us as being kids or something but generally, all the Paris club musicians know each other, so there's always a lot of respect and support among us. But we haven't started acting like we're better than them. The attitude is different here anyway. I think it's only in Britain that people get interested in the newest thing. You all seem to need change all of the time, whereas in Paris, we are much more laid back".

Homework was 1997's first contender for album of the year. A selection of tunes that picked its way through the classic sounds of house and techno culture and then lovingly paid homage to them. Indeed, it was such an in-depth study that the duo seemed to have done their homework in every sense of the word.

Thomas: "The album was called *Homework* mainly because it was recorded in a bedroom. We weren't originally going to do an album. It was supposed to be just a load of singles. But we did so many tracks over a period of five months that we realised that we had a good album."

It was a very good album, in fact, but one that had a nostalgic, reverential atmosphere. Clearly in awe of seminal house artists, while also harbouring a love of electro and disco, the self-same influences that the house innovators enjoyed, Daft Punk had faithfully extracted their favourite things and represented them in an updated fashion. And this was exactly why Homework did work. It was the product of people who had grown up with the attitudes of house music rather than lived through it.

The indie years were just a passing schoolboy phase. However, the early Daft Punk times represented the first time the boys had experienced total immersion in a lifestyle and culture. On the other hand, the older people on the dance scene had largely come to dance culture in the wake of their own teenage obsessions. As we have seen, these were largely centred on the seemingly universal love of hip hop, Cameo and the rest of the 80s funk acts. Or, of course, out and out rock music. Daft Punk were from the first generation of house natives.

Just as the people from Orange formed their band to emulate Bowie and The Beatles, and Louba aimed to copy the Violent Femmes, so Daft Punk were trying to follow in the creative footsteps of Jeff Mills, Marshall Jefferson, DJ Pierre and Underground Resistance. Essentially Daft Punk were from the third generation of ravers. They never cried "acieed" in wild abandon, never got locked into ecstasy's unquestioning acceptance, never danced 'till dawn at a summer of love rave. But they'd read about it and enjoyed their own pure version of the adventure. And they knew what it sounded like better than most of the people who were actually there. *Homework* was their version of what happened, their search for the authentic.

The irony is that their age meant that they also sidestepped the house versus techno purism debate that divided the early years of dance music. They brought a fresh perspective that embraced aspects from the entire spectrum of contemporary dance culture. The resulting sound involved the appropriation of classic techniques and sounds from the short history of dance and house, reconstituted in a genre meltdown. It was the sum of the parts that gave a new story. The parts themselves were as retro as Oasis. Like Air, Super Discount and just about everyone else from the Paris scene, Daft Punk were retromania wrapped up in a new style.

Thomas vehemently denied the accusation: "I don't think we're retro at all. We don't want to recreate old things, although old music does inspire us."

Guy Manuel: "We especially like hip hop and sixties guitar bands like The Seeds and funk music from the seventies. We listen to a lot of stuff from different styles between us but we don't try to recreate things. We're both still young, so we weren't even around for that whole house thing. We didn't buy all of the early house records and we didn't go out clubbing until about 1992, so most of our influences come from the people we heard on the radio when we were younger. But we don't copy necessarily."

The Oasis comparison, however, went deeper than the use of retro. Daft Punk brought an almost innate understanding of pop to their studied sounds. As a result, their tracks may have included the nuances of under-ground techno, as on, for example, 'Rollin' and Scratchin'', but they deliv-ered those nuances with an almost perversely populist touch that hinted at the golden days of disco. *Homework* was full-blown, hands in the air sta-dium-house created from the parts of deepest underground and processed through ecstasy rush inducing filters. This is exactly why with *Homework* they were able to appeal to hardcore clubbers, house aficionados, techno obsessives, the big beat brigade and indie kids alike.

Despite any arguments they may have had against the retro debate, this was one of the biggest aspects of their music that they themselves chal-lenged when in 1999, they came to make their second album *Discovery*, which would go on to have a huge impact on pop's landscape, inspiring as it did hip hop, R&B and pop to embrace 1980s soft rock synths. Indeed, it was an album that would also inspire dance music's most anodyne college jock sound, EDM.

In 1997, the duo's sudden rise to global notoriety resulted in their becoming the remixers of choice for A&R people desperate to give their tired old product some credibility. However, Daft Punk took the highly commendable and extremely rare route away from the remix cash-in. Unlike many producers who simply want the money, Daft Punk were extremely choosy about which artists they reinterpreted and even choosier about the agreement terms.

For their breathtaking remix of Gabrielle's 'Forget About the World', they offered the record label three different prices, preferring to let their consciences decide how much the mix was worth. Their brilliant version of I:Cube's 'Disco Cubizm' was executed for free. However, the label was forbidden to license the mix anywhere else. Similarly, their re-rub of The Micronauts' 'Get Down and Funky' was a freebie, delivered out of respect for the fellow Parisian techno heads. Despite their demand, Daft Punk remixes had only numbered a meagre four by the time of *Homework*.

"We're not interested in remixing anymore; we haven't got time," explained Thomas as if stifling a yawn. "But we also don't like the way remixes are used by record companies. Usually, the remixer will be paid a straight fee, so they don't get any royalty payments. So people don't earn so much money, yet the record company sell a lot more copies. It's a rip off for the remixer."

Given the extended list of influences that graced the album liner notes, I wonder whether they could be seduced into remixing again by the promise of working over tracks by their heroes?

"I wouldn't want to change my favourite tunes. That's why they're my favourites!" said Guy Man.

Not even for David Bowie, who had allegedly phoned Daft Punk personally to twist their arms? The duo broke into a barrage of laughter, interspersing giggles with rapid-fire comments made in their native tongue. They may have been laid back, but it was the first time they'd truly relaxed all morning and it was a welcome interlude. But I couldn't understand a word of it.

"Well, we know he likes the album but I can't say anything else about him," said Thomas closing the book firmly on that particular subject.

It has often been claimed that Daft Punk were neither daft nor punk. And to some extent, that was true. On the one hand, they upheld many of punk's dreams of autonomy, retaining control wherever they could – a control that ranged from their astute business practices to their seemingly trivial habit of wearing masks for all photo sessions. Yet they shared none of punk's frenzied political nihilism or DIY ethics.

And as for being daft? They appeared self-conscious, unusually reserved and about as serious as serious could get. Certainly not the wild children of rocking house music that their name suggested then. At the end of the day, though, the name Daft Punk sounded infinitely more exciting than 'Serious Young Businessmen on a Mission to Conquer the World'. Even though the latter was probably closer to the truth.

With the singles lifted from *Homework* they seemed to be propelled onto the front covers of every magazine in the western world. 'Around the World' became the biggest anthem of clubs everywhere, while the reissue of the hugely acclaimed 'Da Funk' saw them discovering massive TV exposure thanks to the Spike Jonze directed video, in which a dog-headed youth wanders lost through New York City. The image was both funny and threatening, but above all, it was unique.

Jonze's film would be released as a VHS and DVD in 1999. Called *D.A.F.T. A Story About Dogs, Androids, Firemen and Tomatoes* also included Michel Gondry's promo for 'Around the World', Roman Coppola's video for 'Revolution 909' and a live film of 'Rollin' and Scratchin' filmed in Los Angeles. The package also featured various behind the scenes and 'making of' sequences.

'Da Funk' itself came with a superb filtered disco 'Ten Minutes of Funk' remix by Arman Van Helden and the classic 'Musique', which surprisingly didn't make it onto *Homework*, despite its cult status.

"We didn't put it on the album because it is a b-side to 'Da Funk'," stated Thomas when we met at Respect some two years later. "It was never going to be on the album. You know what, in the first few months after the album, the single of 'Da Funk' sold more copies than 'Homework'. So more people owned 'Musique' as a single than if they'd bought it on the album."

Van Helden's remix represented the first time that another producer had reworked Daft Punk. Although they had total control over the choice of remixer, they were still filled with trepidation at the thought of their music being taken apart by someone else.

"Well yeah, we were a bit worried, you know," explained Thomas. "Because you never know how things are going to turn out. But we chose Armand and thought he would do a good job because he'd always done great stuff in the past."

Homework was also notable for its collaboration with Parisian DJ Crabbe, who featured on the track 'Oh Yeah'. After the experience, he bought some studio equipment and teamed up with long time associate Jesse to produce music. The first release came in 1999 with a dancefloor slaying, drum heavy style on their own Fiat Lux imprint.

Jess & Crabbe came to prominence in the Paris club scene in the late-90s when one-time drum & bass DJ Crabbe teamed up with Jesse to promote the Hometown parties at The Rex, which featured the cream of the Chicago house underground. It was a favourite haunt of Daft Punk's Thomas and Guy-Man when it was open from '97 to '99.

In the two years that followed the release of *Homework*, Daft Punk toured constantly. Whether as a DJ duo or as a live act, their presence was always guaranteed to tear up dancefloors. One of the most enjoyable aspects of their live set was the intensity they would create from a feeling that they were driving machines that didn't quite know how to stop. Furthermore, they never seemed to know where they would end up. This edge of chaos brinkmanship marked them out as a premiership live dance act, along with the likes of Underworld and Orbital.

"The way we'd like to tour is to show people something new. Basically, there's no DAT or pre-recorded sequences. Everything is done at that time. Which means there is a lot of room for unexpected things."

In 1998 one of Thomas' side projects would eclipse even the success of Daft Punk. Late in 1997, he'd teamed up with Roule artist Alain Braxxe and vocalist Benjamin Diamond to record the seminal filtered disco-house track 'Music Sounds Better with You' as Stardust. It was the biggest track at the 1998 Winter Music Conference in Miami and became the dominant soundtrack to that year's Ibiza season. It then became a worldwide hit that would still be a regular presence on the radio some four years later.

"At first, Thomas wasn't involved in the project," explains Diamond from the studio beneath his Diamond Traxx label. "Basically, I knew Alain because we lived on the same floor of an apartment block. We'd known each other from before and we talked about doing some music together. He did his first single on Roule, 'Vertigo', and after he asked me to rehearse a live set with him for a performance at The Rex club.

"We came up with the original hook, 'ooh baby, you know that music sounds better with you', at the rehearsal. Then we did it live and Thomas came along. About a month later, we turned it into a record."

"Thomas changed the sound because he is a very good producer. It was rough on stage but it was good for that performance. But the record had to be different. I think that it would never have happened without the live performance. Thomas brought his understanding of how a song sounds on the radio and the dancefloor. He's a very good producer, like I said.

"I am very proud of this record now but I wasn't really aware that people had started to copy it. For me, it was a side project. It wasn't very hard to do but people thought there was a recipe for it. It was a record that came about through circumstances. We made a cake without any recipe. Sometimes when you do that, it turns out horrible; sometimes, it turns out fine. But it's impossible to do it again. We realised that we'd created a good record but also knew that we couldn't repeat it as a recipe. I'm not against selling records, you know. None of us are. But we are happier doing our own thing, so we never did a follow-up."

However, the single did bring attention to Diamond's own music, and soon after the Stardust single, he signed a deal with Sony. It wasn't a very happy marriage, though, and after one very stressful album, *Strange Attitude*, in 2000, he severed contacts with the label. The main problem lay in their wanting an album of remakes of 'Music Sounds Better With You", whereas Diamond was a musician with a history of playing live and a love of 80s electro-funk. And it was this sound that poured through his own music. Which didn't stop Sony from marketing him as "the voice of Stardust", of course.

"It is true that I am the voice of Stardust," exclaimed Benjamin. "But that was the only way they tried to promote the album. I was completely against this but I found it impossible to control that. I also found it very difficult to go back to my own style of music after Stardust because people weren't listening to anything but the 'voice of Stardust'! In the end, Sony didn't do anything for me, really."

Strange Attitude may have failed to grab the imaginations of people eager for a new Stardust record, but Benjamin Diamond has to be admired because he didn't try to emulate the sound of that project. However, his brand of Bowie-esque techno-pop revealed a strong songwriter with an ear for pure production.

Towards the end of 2000, the first white labels of Daft Punk's new single started trickling into DJs' record boxes. Called 'One More Time', it represented a quantum leap for the duo. Any allegiances to the Underground Resistance noise aesthetic had been replaced by the filtered disco loops of Stardust. Furthermore, the vocals of house legend Romanthony had been processed through a vocoder effect to produce a sound employed by pop artists like Cher. It was pop-house, pure and simple. This is not to say that it wasn't a fantastic dancefloor track. Indeed its elongated drop, in which Romanthony's vocals repeat the hook over descending chords until the drum loop fades back in towards the track's climax was a work of pure dancefloor genius. The critics of the time were divided, though.

"We don't care for what the critics say these days," said Bangalter at the time. "We used to worry about what critics say about our music, but now we don't care. Basically, we liked the track and also Romanthony liked it and that was the main thing. It's only music, you know, entertainment."

Weren't they worried about the vocoder being an overused piece of kit in the lexicon of commercial dance music?

"I've said this loads of times but criticising the vocoder is like asking bands in the 60s, 'Why do you use the electric guitar?'. We wanted to use a vocoder because we like it. And it is important for us that people react to our music with love or hate. The worst thing is when your music or art and people aren't even moved by it. Love and hate are strong reactions which are good."

Two years later, 'One More Time' would find them at the centre of more than one controversy. On the one hand, there was the attempted appropriation of the track as the French Presidential election theme for both of the main parties. And on the other hand, there were cries of sell-out when the track was used in an advert for US lingerie outlet Victoria's Secret. This came soon after the band appeared in an advert for Gap.

The political situation was quickly dealt with, despite Jacques Chirac having gone ahead and used the tracks without permission.

"We replied by fax, telling everybody we will not accept that they use our track. Now, if they break the law, I can say that our next president is a breaker of the law," explained Pedro Winter at the time. "I think that Jacques is 70 or something like that, so it would be like, 'Yeah, I'm 70, but I'm still in.'"

As for the adverts? For months, the furore that surrounded them in the holier-than-thou dance scene went on. They were accused of making money in cheap marketing exercises. It was suggested that they hadn't even appeared in the Gap ad, instead employing a couple of actors to wear the Daft Punk robot helmets. They were criticised for promoting a company like Gap, which had been accused of employing cheap sweatshop labour in third-world countries to maximise profits. And the Victoria's Secret ad was considered to be in bad taste.

"It was them in the ads wearing the crash helmets," exclaimed Pedro. "It was a crazy time for us. This story was really misunderstood; we had some bad, bad reviews about that. The fact is, in France, we were not as aware of Gap and the problems of them using third world labour. We were sad about that but if you start down that road, you can't use computers, you can't buy magazines. So that's why we decided to do it after all.

"In actual fact, we didn't get paid very much at all for the Gap ad," he continued. "They had the attitude that their ad was good publicity for the artist, so they gave us very little money for it. But it was so cool for us we had a crazy time in the studios at Universal, where nobody can usually go. We took those small carts and went around all the studios. We went to the house from Psycho and so on. For us, it was like party time.

"The Gap ad also helped us in the US. It didn't help break us but gave us a lot of attention. As did the Victoria's Secret ad to which we gave 'One More Time' to. To tell you the truth, that ad did bring us some money but we wanted to do it because it was a famous French photographer Dominique Esserman. She shot Giselle, who is a beautiful model for the ad. We did it because it was just sexy because it was Giselle dancing to 'One More Time' and who could resist that? For a band like Daft Punk to break the US you have to do ads because it is so big. Daft Punk want to reach as many people as they can. Not for the money, though. They have already sold two million records so they are already comfortable."

Winter revealed another reason why the band felt that the ads were a good idea. It was all about growing up.

"It was a time when Daft Punk wanted to turn a page and liberate themselves," he said. "Thomas and Guy-Man are both very shy. They did *Homework* and did very well with it but kept their underground living. But

Discovery represented the next stage which was more adult and so they were more prepared to take what life was offering them."

When *Discovery* was released in 2001, the sense that Daft Punk had matured was overriding. Gone was the need to emulate their heroes and be seen as an underground act. In their place was a far more commercial sound that drew on house culture, 80s electronic pop and even the power ballads of 80s rock. However, in accessing such obviously retro aspects, they forged a unique sound instantly recognisable as Daft Punk. Ironically it was a more modern-sounding record than *Homework*.

"Discovery has many influences," said Guy-Man. "But what we wanted to do was try and make music that captured that feeling of when you were a kid and you liked a record for what it was rather than if it was cool or not. We tried not to be influenced by underground or even mainstream. Just music as it is. So yes, we used disco, electro or glam rock. We wanted to try and get that naïve relationship kids have with music on *Discovery*. So we tried to include most of the things we liked as kids and bring that sense of fun to it. Which is why we included guitar solos on 'Aerodynamic'. Some people said it was bad taste, but we said it was honest."

Talking to DJ Times, Thomas further explained the attitude behind the album's making.

"It's been ambitious from the fact that we wanted to demonstrate that we could make music in a way that conveyed emotions, hooks and melodies. The production is what took the most time, as what we were doing would take a few days, rather than a few minutes like before. It's not difficult, it just takes time, and when it's ambitious, we started to feel that we could manage to understand how to make more than a simple club track. That's not to say that we don't like to do it anymore, but we wanted to be able to make music that was produced the right way, less random than the way we used to work. Before, things would just happen in a free way."

In the middle of recording the album, the duo's studio computers crashed and they lost some of their work. It was the ninth day of the ninth month in 1999. Naturally, the duo used the coincidence to create a new masked persona for their album.

"We became robots during the 1999 September trip, on 9/9/99," explained Bangalter in 2001. "We were just making music in the studio when suddenly there was a flash. It is not something that can easily be explained. It was not like an explosion, but there were lights and gold and silver powder was everywhere. When we finally woke up, the silver and gold powder became our robot faces. We do not know exactly what happened because when we woke up, we were just robots. What's funny is that we really like this look, so we're happy with it."

The band also launched the internet community Daft Club with the album to back this robotic image. Inside the sleeve was a membership card that enabled you to subscribe to the site. In return, fans got free downloads of new material and tracks by artists the duo were into. At this point, most musicians had only paid lip service to internet culture, but no one seemed to embrace it to the same extent as Daft Punk. They were quick to realise that they were able to access their fans, control the media, and support their own image development through this tool. The internet was a perfect invention for this shy duo. Playing with people's perception of what a musician should look like or even behave has long been at the heart of Daft Punk's media manipulation techniques and myth-making. However, musically too, they were determined to break the rules. *Discovery* was, if nothing else, a brave attempt to smash up everything that might have been referred to as the Daft Punk sound previously.

"This album was an attempt by us to break the rules again," said Guy-Man. "When we did our first album, house music was still quite new. But now it is everywhere established all around the world. At first, house music came to smash up the rules of rock, but now it is the establishment. So it has all these little rules like what beats you can use or what bpm a track should be, which was not what house music was about. So we were trying to make music that proved that house and electronic music can be made by breaking those rules. So we didn't make obvious references to Chicago or Detroit. We wanted to make dance music open and free-spirited again!"

"We wanted to do something different," added Bangalter. "We really wanted to work a little bit more on emotion and transmit not only the dance and powerful energetic beat but a bit more soul."

To attain this goal, they enlisted the vocal talents of Romanthony, whose vocals bookend the album on the single 'One More Time' and the Chicago meets Afrocentric digi-soul 'Too Long' and also Todd Edwards, who sings on the filtered house cut 'Face to Face'.

"We've always admired Romanthony and Todd Edwards. They also had a lot of influence on us because they have always been able to work and express themselves at a really high emotional level," explained Bangalter.

Despite Daft Punk's lofty ambitions with *Discovery*, the album initially failed to match the two million-plus sales attained by *Homework*. Indeed, as with the release of 'One More Time', the album was met with extreme views. On the one hand, people loved it, with at least one dance magazine declaring it to be the greatest dance album ever. On the other, some hated it. One-time Mixmag features editor Alexis Petridis declared his dislike for *Discovery* in his well-argued lead review in The Guardian.

He wrote: "Discovery comes studded with the sort of finger-twiddling, pseudo-classical solos that aspiring heavy-metal guitarists spent the 1980s trying to perfect. It also offers pomp-rock keyboard runs of which Rick Wakeman would be proud, and the return of the smooth mid-Atlantic funk ballad, beloved of both Phil Collins and commercial local radio 15 years ago.

The bad news is that this time, the salvage operation doesn't work. Forthcoming single 'Aerodynamic' illustrates its failings. There are pounding house beats, metal guitars, rococo synth flourishes and a Kraftwerk pastiche, but it all sounds disjointed and episodic. You can admire Daft Punk's desire to marry wildly differing musical cultures and their disregard for the stultifying conformity of dance music, but it doesn't make Aerodynamic any more fun to listen to.

But worryingly, most of *Discovery's* best tracks – hit single 'One More Time', vocal-house closer 'Too Long', the relentless 'Superheroes' – are those that stick closest to *Homework's* filtered disco blueprint."

The fact was that in the reverential tones of *Homework* they had created a genre called filtered disco – a stylistic straightjacket, in fact. Their claims that *Discovery* was all about being able to reintroduce house culture's original rule-breaking ideology could also be applied to their own output. *Discovery*, in other words, represented their attempt at escapology. And, despite the bad reviews, time proved that radical departure was the best thing the duo could have done. Indeed, *Discovery* is now regarded as one of the era's most influential albums. A point that is well-argued in Ben Cardew's book *Daft Punk's Discovery – The Future Unfurled*.

Ironically, given their stated desires with *Discovery*, the duo's continued output on Roule and Crydamoure were less confrontational. Guy-Man had worked hard at creating a label presence that found him searching out many of the producers who had influenced Daft Punk. As a result, the imprint played host to DJ Sneak (who is credited as being the true Godfather of the filtered disco sound) and Paul Johnson, among others. Le Knight Club also continued to release massive club singles and a CD compilation of the label's output appeared to critical acclaim.

On the other hand, Roule appeared to be more like a vanity label for Thomas. Among his releases was the 2002 soundtrack album, in the shape of the understated *Irreversible*. Also, that year, he teamed up with DJ Falcon for a second time to create the massive club smash 'I've Got So Much Love To Give', which featured a simple, twisting, hypnotic groove and a vocal hook looped to the point of insanity. It was house music created with the white heat hedonism of the dancefloor firmly in mind.

"We meant it to be very much a club track the way we want club tracks to sound," explained Bangalter. "All it is, is a strong and basic groove; which is what house music is all about, really."

The single represented a back to basics celebration that was a statement of intent that pointed an accusatory finger at those producers creating tunes with mainstream radio squarely in mind.

"Over the last two years, I do think that too many producers have been making music for radio rather than clubs. Which has had a negative effect," argued Falcon. "This record is for dancing to. If the radio doesn't play it, we don't mind."

"Club music should be direct and physical, with no immediate song structure or formula," continued Bangalter. "Daft Punk have experimented a lot with formats, mixing up different sounds and getting complex. But sometimes it's good just to get very simple."

The duo completed the track in July 2002, but rather than saturate Ibiza with it, they handed only one copy out. That was to long time friend Philippe Zdar of Motorbass, La Funk Mob and Cassius fame. Zdar played it out at Pacha in Ibiza. It went down a storm.

"It surprised me how quickly people knew about it," laughed Bangalter. "Because it is so basic and simple."

Every inch the measure of 'Together', the Bangalter/DJ Falcon collaboration from 2001, 'I've Got So Much Love To Give' celebrated the life-force of clubbing. Its narcotic simplicity echoes earlier times while also pointing to a bright and hopeful future.

"Usually, we get friends to hear stuff to get a reaction but this time, we just knew it was good," admitted Thomas. "We knew it was good because we were dancing in the studio all of the time we were making it."

"Dancing and smiling," added Falcon.

The period between *Discovery* and their 2021 'retirement' has been well documented through endless magazine and website articles, books and documentaries, so I won't outline the duo's next steps here. Suffice to say, they quickly moved into global pop aristocracy and became a dominating presence over popular culture through the first two decades of the twenty-first century. If Daft Punk are remembered for one thing, it will be the fact that they were the act most responsible for bringing the French Touch to the world's ears. They developed and delivered the blueprint for the sound, which would take others to the top of the charts around the world, and would rejuvenate the careers of Madonna, one-time indie kid Sophie Ellis Baxter and Kylie Minogue, among others.

However, it would probably be better to think of Daft Punk as the duo determined to tear up the rule books and take dance culture in a direction that no one expected. It was an attitude that tied them directly to the oppositional ideologies at work in the works of many of Paris' premier artists since World War II.

Love them, or hate them… That's all they asked of us.

THE MICRONAUTS – DOCUMENT AND EYE WITNESS

If Daft Punk were considered the French cousins of The Chemical Brothers thanks to the support shown by the UK duo in the early days, then a close relation would have to be The Micronauts. Not necessarily because of their music, but once again, they were championed by Ed and Tom Chemical.

The duo of Christopher Monier and Greek-born/Canadian-raised George Issakidis first met through the legendary *Eden* fanzine. George had approached Christophe intending to contribute. They struck up a friendship, and soon after, the Micronauts were born.

Christophe Monier had, of course, been a face on the Paris techno scene since day one. In 1989, the young Parisian attended the city's first rave, which was promoted by Manu Casana. Two years later, as previously mentioned, he would team up with Patrick Vidal to record as Discotique. Their 'Sexe' single was the first release on Casana's Rave Age Records. Monier would deliver singles under the names Eurostars (with Tom Bouthier), Nature and Impulsion.

Throughout this time, Monier had also been actively involved in the cultural side of the rave scene. He developed a strong understanding of the need to document the events taking place. With Eden, he created a fanzine that reported on all the underground happenings while also promoting other areas of the arts touched by the scene. In 1994 he also compiled an album that featured all the rising names in the scene. These included Daft Punk, Dimitri, Motorbass and Érik Rug. Unfortunately, he couldn't find a label to put the compilation out. Had he succeeded, though, the compilation would have defined the beginning of the French Touch years.

George Issakidis moved to Paris from Calgary in Canada in 1990. He'd gone to Paris to study History of Art at Le Sorbonne. However, his arrival coincided with the beginnings of the rave scene explosion. Soon his studies fell by the wayside as he chose to walk on the wired side of rave culture.

Christophe and George started making raw, acidic techno records together in 1994. Their first track, "Get Funky Get Down", was a dark, intense rollercoaster of minimal techno which drew as much on Underground Resistance as Derrick May. When Thomas Bangalter heard Monier playing the track at an Eden rave, he immediately offered his services for a Daft Punk remix. At this point, Daft Punk had only released 'The New Wave' on Soma.

'Get Funky Get Down' was first intended to be released on Brighton based imprint Loaded. However, due to numerous problems, things became delayed. So, in 1995 they issued 'The Jazz'/'The Jam' single through the label instead. They called the single trip house and scratched the legend "Warning: Loud stereo listening may cause full trip house effect' into the vinyl's run-out groove. Almost two years after it was first produced, 'Get Funky Get Down' was finally released on Phono Recordings. However, they requested an extra track and as a result, Christophe and George produced 'Back To The Bioship' in just one week.

It was around this time that they first met the Chemical Brothers at the studios of Radio Nova and gave them a copy of 'The Jazz' and a test pressing of 'Get Funky Get Down'. Tom and Ed were so impressed that they commissioned Christophe and George to remix their 'Block Rockin' Beats' single.

"They were doing an interview," explained Monier. "So we gave them promos of the records. Then they called and said that 'The Jazz' was in their set every night."

Also, in 1996 Monier teamed up with Tom Bouthier to record a single for Loaded under the Eurostars moniker. 'The Way' was a deep house cut that employed 80s electro-pop sequencers and heavily vocodered vocals that became a huge hit in the UK's house clubs. The renewed relationship with Loaded also resulted in Impulsion – a collaboration between Monier and renowned Parisian DJ Pascal R – and a commission to remix Pizzaman's happy house club smash 'Trippin' On Sunshine'. Pizzaman was actually a collaboration between Norman Cook and Loaded's owners, JC Ried and Tim Jeffries. It was a remix that was to again become a club hit in the UK. However, Monier's various collaborations still only received minimal attention in France.

This actually turned out to be a very positive thing. Without the pressure of commercialism being placed at the feet of The Micronauts, they were able to continue working their own style at their own slow pace. In 1998 they returned with a single that brought them major label interest. 'The Jag' appeared on a French-only white label. Still, the interest it caused among the big beat DJs of the UK, along with the increased interest received by French Touch acts in the wake of Stardust, resulted in a deal with Virgin subsidiary Science (also the home of Photek).

The single was released officially in 1999. The press and club reaction was phenomenal. Once again, they received huge support from The Chemical Brothers and their entourage. DJ James Holroyd could be heard spinning 'The Jag' every night before the Chemicals on their *Surrender* tour. As the year drew to an end, the track was placed in the *NME's* top 50 singles of the year. If that wasn't all, a remix of Underworld's 'Bruce Lee' delivered earlier that year was placed at #3 in the paper's remixes of the year list. Also released to huge response in 1999 was *Why Is It Fresh?*, The Micronauts' compilation of old electro cuts from Jean Karakos' renowned French electro label of the 1980s, Celluloid. By the early 21st century, Karakos owned the leading French dance label Distance, specialising in licensing international artists to create mixes and productions for the domestic French market. They subsequently had a huge presence on the global scene through these releases.

To add to the euphoria surrounding Monier that year, his Impulsion track 'The Trip', with a brilliant mix by DJ Pierre, became an instant club classic when it was released that summer.

With the amount of attention The Micronauts got throughout 1999, the scene looked set for them to go global in 2000. A mini-album, *Bleep to Bleep*, was released to acclaim but it proved too uncompromising for the general public's tastes. In a review for Amazon (when the platform employed music journalists to pen reviews), Louis Pattison summed up the problem:

"… a duo that pick up the experimental baton where LFO stumbled and fell. Those comparisons to The Chemical Brothers are fairly lazy; the

Micronauts offer nothing of their funky, rock-friendly mainstream nous. Rather, *Bleep To Bleep* ranks alongside the brutal innovation of Laurent Garnier's *Unreasonable Behaviour*, with the Micronauts dictating their brand of weird science like the last remaining acid pioneers."

The mainstream's loss was the underground's gain, however, as *Bleep to Bleep* proved to be a dark masterpiece of brittle electro beats, surging sub-bass and spluttering rhythm clusters.

And then, nothing. Just as the world was expecting their long-awaited full-length album, Christophe and George split up. The problem, it would seem, was productivity.

"Well, let's just say we had a different attitude towards the actual industrial side," explained Monier, sitting in his apartment with a view of the Parisian suburb he called home. "He was more relaxed about this than me. So we have gone our separate ways."

Monier retained the name The Micronauts and delivered a handful of mixes (Mirwais' 'Miss You', Scratch Massive's 'Keep On Workin'' and Bosco's 'Action' to name but a few). However, he moved his studio into his flat in a high-rise apartment block. Today his studio equipment dominates the living room and the mixing desk has a view of the city that is nothing short of spectacular.

It is one of the ironies of the French Touch explosion that the very man who was there from the beginning, documenting, promoting and DJing, never quite reached the heights that people expected. However, it could be that Monier's perversely underground attitude would provide him with enough kudos to carry on releasing eagerly awaited and much respected records for some time. Already he had shifted his focus towards the growing electro scene in Paris and it looked certain that he would re-emerge with classic after classic in future years. In reality, however, Monier's next release as The Micronauts would not arrive until 2018 when he dropped the *Acid Party* EP, followed by the electro-fuelled album, *Head Control Body Control*.

MUSIC SOUNDS BETTER WITH YOU –
THE FRENCH TOUCH DEFINED

Given the fact that so many styles of music went into the creation of the French Touch it is perhaps a shame that it became internationally recognised through the biggest hits of the era. Daft Punk may have been accused of introducing the filtered sound, but Stardust's 'Music Sounds Better With You' turned it into a pop phenomenon. Given the level of success that the track achieved, it was perhaps inevitable that others would emerge with a similar sound.

The main tracks that would be held up as the definitive sound of the movement came in the shape of the huge hits 'Lady' by Modjo and 'Starlight' by The Supermen Lovers. Although these tracks appeared to have been created with some level of integrity (they were, if nothing else, brilliant pop records), what followed was a rush for DJs and producers to get a piece of the filtered disco pie. However, the international success of the latter tracks brought with it a torrent of jealous abuse from some of the people within the scene. Where once the French Touch had appeared to be a disparate selection of DJs and producers, all unified by a collective love of music, the commercial success of a few production crews (two of which were considered to be outsiders) opened the cracks in the scene like a sledgehammer.

"To live here and see how the success of three tracks made people crazy was strange," recalled Guillaume Atlan, aka The Supermen Lovers. "People lost their minds. It was incredible. They wanted to be a part of it, but they were saying that Modjo and Supermen Lovers didn't want to share their success. What is crazy is that I had no problem sharing. In the beginning, I was positive about it. I was open to collaborating or doing some things together. Then they got aggressive. I don't know why. Suddenly I was hearing that the same people were against me."

The sudden cliquish response of the original French Touch crews toward these outsiders revealed a class and regional division that lay at the very heart of Parisian culture, where people become defined by the places they grew up. It is an attitude that relates directly to the feudalism of France's history and is today translated via a strong acceptance of hierarchy. The inner sanctum of the French Touch seemed to operate like the palace courts of Bastille's history.

For Supermen Lovers, one of the problems was that Atlan didn't come from a dance background but openly admitted that pop music was his main focus until he heard Daft Punk. Even then, he was never a clubber.

"I don't feel a part of the French Touch hype," Atlan said. "I'm not from the dancefloor, so I'm always on the outside. So I can see things from a different perspective. I think it's strange how people took Daft Punk's music and tried to make money out of it. Here in France, it became something unbelievable. Five years ago, they gave hope to people to make music, but everything today is on a down. The young producers now are disgusting because they're all taking the Daft Punk sound to make money. What is strange is that it's the people from electronic music that have taken the sound and exploited it. People like David Guetta, for example."

Another problem, he maintains, comes from a much more fundamental problem within Parisian society. Controversially, the fact he is Jewish was turned into an issue in the media.

"All the Versailles people were brought up and educated in a very Catholic way. And you know, a lot of the people from the magazines grew up there too," he said. "Me, I'm Jewish. All my friends when I was growing up were Jewish. I never thought there could be a link between that and the music I make, but then I started seeing articles in one magazine that showed me as a Jewish person. I was like, 'what the fuck?'. We did a live show at the Rex and the critic was like, 'yeah, good vibe, good sound but one problem; the only people were wearing gold and...', well they described Jewish people from North Africa. When I saw that I was furious. It really made me realise how cliquey people are. Paris is like this. I always thought that music was open to everyone, but they made me realise it wasn't.

"What is incredible is that 'Starlight' encouraged a lot of Jewish kids to make electronic music," he continued. "Nowadays, Jewish people are coming to me and saying that they're making music, and into this music

and that music. There's this Jewish scene now. I never thought that would be possible or necessary. I thought the music was important, so I can't understand how people were making the link."

Of course, the irony is that Atlan had no desire to become a figurehead for the Jewish youth in Paris. Indeed it's this very segregation that he is against. Indeed he likens the attitude to the rules of the playground.

"I think you have to go back to when we were 15 or 16, all the people from Versailles, or from Montmartre where Daft Punk are from, we would all meet sometimes at the same parties, I think the problem goes back to this time because people keep to their crews. We weren't in the same crew. And when you grow up, I think a lot of people base their relationships with people on the same ideals as the playground. For me, French Touch is a playground, no different to when we were 15 or 16. It's like people haven't grown up. And that's a big problem.

"But all I want is to make music. I don't want to be hanging out with Daft Punk," he emphasised. "But when I made 'Starlight' and it was popular. I expected people from the French Touch to be saying 'great record, well done'. But people were just indifferent. They acted like Supermen Lovers didn't exist. They just took everything too seriously. For a lot of people who just buy music and don't care about the hype, Supermen Lovers was as big as Daft Punk. But for the French Touch, they couldn't believe that someone who wasn't from their crew, who they used to see at these parties when we were kids, was getting success. It's just like they're still in the playground."

It is one of the great ironies of the French Touch phenomenon that, just as music from France was getting the global recognition it deserved, people started to react against the hype. It is a fair comment that any musician wants to be accepted according to their own merit and not part of some hype. However, as we have already seen, the better producers were able to rise above the whole phenomenon and become entities unto themselves anyway.

This reaction against the French Touch among artists and media like in France has resulted in the near death of the scene.

"In France now, to be a part of the French Touch is as bad as being a boy band," exclaims Supermen Lovers' Guillaim Atlan. If the scene had become the culturally divisive environment that Atlan outlined, the death of French Touch might not have been such a bad thing. Indeed, his comments shed fresh light on France's structural racism and subsequent responses in popular culture. It's fair to say that right-wing leaders like Marine Le Pen leaders could not have found popularity with structural divisions along the lines of race and religion.

SO... WHAT CREATED THE HYPE IN THE FIRST PLACE? AND WAS IT A GOOD THING?

"It's something I've been asked so many times and I always say the same thing – it's a combination of two things. First of all, the UK press was interested in a few early acts and it became maybe a trendy thing. That exposure made people, DJs, promoters, distributors, labels look at France. So people in France started to believe in their worth. They felt that they could start a label and take more risks."

Thomas Bangalter, 1997

Despite claims by Thomas Bangalter that only two forces were at work, there were actually several events that evolved over the years and then conspired to create a focused movement between 1995 and 1999. The first came with that change in attitude amongst the French dance scene. Because house and techno were mainly instrumental musical forms, the spoken language was no longer the barrier that it represented in the rock and pop era. Suddenly French artists (as with many other countries around the world) realised that they could be accepted in the global dance scene.

With this even playing field, many people set about creating the foundations and infrastructure for dance culture in France. Christophe Monier takes this up: "The foundations and connections of the French house/

techno scene have been strongly set by Manu Casana, *Eden* fanzine, *Coda* magazine, record label manager Éric Morand, DJs Laurent Garnier and Érik Rug, journalists like Didier Lestrade, musicians already releasing tracks on foreign labels, like Ludovic Navarre on Belgian labels, Érik Rug on Toronto Underground, Jerry Bouthier on Stress, me on Dark, Phono, Loaded and Azuli to name but a few."

These events colluded to effect a change in the attitudes of French youth.

"The French musicians were tired of being mocked (not without reason...) by the rest of the world," added Monier. "They decided to react and to use the new and more affordable home studio technology to become better than the rest of the world. It was, of course, an unconscious motivation, and I haven't said this goal has been reached, but at least the overall level increased."

This latter development may have created a growth in musicians creating electronic music in France. However, it didn't necessarily mean that the rest of the world would be interested. It is fair to say that the success of St. Germain's *Boulevard* album created enough interest outside of France for people in the wider media to start taking the country more seriously. What happened next, however, is where the hype began.

The UK dance media had recently grown from being a largely independent world, with small publishing companies issuing magazines like *Generator*, *Herb Garden*, *Jockey Slut*, *Mixmag* and its weekly sister title *Update*. Then suddenly, the major publishing companies recognised that there was money to be made from the dance scene. The first sign of the major publishers getting involved came with Emap's purchase of *Mixmag* in 1994. A year later, IPC (who published *NME* and *Melody Maker*) launched their spoiler title, *Muzik*, off the back of *Melody Maker's* Orbit dance section. With the large publishers on board came the demand for results. Editors were subsequently under pressure to be the first to the big story, create an assumed allegiance with the event, and then claim the phenomenon for the magazine.

Previously dance magazines had been all about reporting on the culture. Now they were trying to drive it. The end result was the loss of quality journalism and a gradual end to the importance of music over lifestyle. The genre that immediately benefited from this sudden change in media culture was drum & bass. Supported for a couple of years and then dropped like a dead weight. The same happened with trip hop, big beat and UK garage – even though all of these genres carried on developing and, in the case of drum & bass at least, enjoyed greater commercial success without the media spotlight.

At this time, the first wave of the French Touch was also met with the media's hunger for hype. And it was one press and promotions office that sold the hype to the editors – POP Promotions. They represented Motorbass, Dimitri from Paris (and the rest of Yellow Productions), Source Lab, Artefact, Pro-Zak Trax, and Versatile. Realising that most of their artists wouldn't get column inches alone, the PR company started to sell Paris rather than the artists. The media bit and suddenly, journalists were hopping the channel to check out this new scene. Interest was subsequently high enough for other artists to get caught up in the growing hype.

This coincided with a major change in the transport system that would have an enormous impact on the lives of English and French youth – the Eurostar.

"I'm sure that Eurostar is a big part of the French Touch story," confirms Pedro Winter. "The DJs started to go to London on Eurostar to buy records from Black Market and, in 1996, all of the record industry was chasing Daft Punk, meeting them in their offices. It meant that the industry was taking the Eurostar to talk about Frenchy music."

The next event was possibly the most important. Three excellent albums came out of Paris in two months: Motorbass' *Pansoul*, Dimitri from Paris' *Sacrebleu* and the *Source Lab 2* compilation. Amazingly, all three albums were given the Album of the Month spot in Muzik. First came Dimitri from Paris and Source Lab in the same month, and then Motorbass. As a triumvirate, the albums suggested France was a hotbed of undiscovered talent. Suddenly the entire UK music industry went looking around the studios of Paris for their own slice of the hype.

As these three were followed by similarly strong releases from *Super Discount* and producers like I:Cube, it then seemed impossible to avoid the French scene. As has been pointed out to me by numerous French producers, the UK press always referred to Paris as being France. With this hype came the major label interest, which brought a certain amount of power for the artists who were subsequently signed.

"Majors like Virgin France or Barclay (a Universal branch) decided to be predatory to the scene by investing massive amounts of marketing money on their protégés and occupying the media," confirmed Monier.

The subsequent release of Daft Punk's *Homework* set up a pattern for French artists signed to Virgin. In the UK, the media expected a major French artist album every January. First came Daft Punk, then Air, and finally Cassius. After this, the media had lost its excitement for the French scene, and it became difficult to launch new acts.

The final piece in the hype jigsaw was quite simply perfect timing. The French Touch boom time, as represented by the two million-plus sales of Daft Punk's *Homework*, coincided with the global dance market reaching critical mass. Dance culture had gained global popularity with acts like Underworld, The Prodigy, Orbital, Fatboy Slim, The Chemical Brothers and, of course, Daft Punk making inroads into the live music and album markets. At the same time, the top DJs were able to charge breathtaking fees to spin a few records.

The very same people would discover that the market started to downsize a few years later. The initially bad sales of albums like Daft Punk's *Discovery* came directly from this shrinking market. By the time of Modjo's 'Lady' and Supermen Lovers' 'Starlight', the French Touch had also reached saturation point with a dance media and public hooked on the latest hype. Quite simply, Paris no longer represented the underground. Even though it still boasted producers and DJs sitting at the cutting edge of dance music like the rest of France.

"In the UK, it has changed," suggested Pedro Winter. "I used to get many, many phone calls, but now people only call when they're after Daft Punk remixes. The UK is not open-minded or interested in what is going on anymore. I don't like the English attitude in the record industry, even at Virgin. Maybe two years ago they were all saying, please send us some

French music but now they only choose one from five projects.

"I think they should remember what French people gave them. But now they say, 'we told you techno music was fake, that it would only last ten years and that it was always drug music'. Even people in France have started to say this. I tell you, it's a bit quick to forget about the techno artists."

So, given the post-hype reaction, was French Touch a good thing?

"I think it was pretty positive," argued Gilb'R. "What I never understood was that after a while, people were dissing the scene. I understand that people got sick of the filtered sound, and there were a lot of people copying that sound, but there was a lot more to it than that. For me, it's just a question of quality. If it is good, it's good. If it's shit, it's shit. It's as simple as that. And I think this is the same with filtered house. There are still good tracks, but most are shit. It's up to the producer to take that idea and add something deeper."

Dimitri from Paris supported these feelings: "I think French Touch was a good way for the artists to get known by the rest of the world. After that, people didn't look at France in the same way. And the hype was deserved. There was really good music in the first place. Daft Punk had an innovative sound and I have a lot of respect for what they have done. I think most of the producers deserved the success they got. And I think that the rest of the records that people liked would have been popular without any French hype.

"There was this panic thing when everything French was supposed to be good, and a lot of people jumped on the bandwagon for money reasons as opposed to artistic reasons. But nobody remembers those people today. Everybody who is still around today deserves to be there because of the music that they did.

"Also, French Touch opened the doors for a newer generation to come in. People like Llorca and Alexkid are really interesting. I remember people asking me if I thought it was going to last and I kept saying well, so far so good. And I'm still playing a lot of French stuff now. People like DJ Gregory, who is one of the best producers in the world. You know, people should forget the French thing. As long as we are on the same level as the others, then that's the main thing."

This claim from Dimitri is perhaps one of the most positive effects of the French Touch. It gave people, young and not so young, the incentive to explore electronic music. In many cases, this didn't mean an attempt to appropriate those filtered disco stylings or even be part of the movement. However, the increased confidence in electronic music at this time also meant that people were able to get signed far easier.

This in itself was a bad thing in some cases. For example, Supermen Lovers was signed to a major from Atlan's own Lafesse Records on the strength of 'Starlight'. However, as the album that followed showed, he hadn't yet been able to find his true sound.

"Today, I don't really know where Supermen Lovers are. I'm just learning how to make dancefloor tracks," Atlan admitted. "I've only been making this kind of music for three years, but it's more normal for me to write a song and not a dancefloor track. Four years ago, I started my studio. It was then I discovered I could make the music I wanted without the complexities of a band of musicians. So I started making this electronic music but as if I was a band and then I started to listen to dance music. But it wasn't because I went to clubs, but because I was working with samplers and got interested in the dance sounds and started to listen to how they used the machines.

"Then something strange happened to me," he continued. "I met this guy at a party. I was talking with him and he told me he was very rich. His family owns the riverboats. A month later, he phoned me and asked if I wanted money for the label. I said yes, please. Two weeks after, I had the money to buy the machines I wanted. Then one month later, I wrote 'Starlight'. I brought it out and straight away, it was massive. Now I think I made a lot of mistakes on Supermen Lovers. I didn't understand the music business. I didn't understand the hype. I just wrote a track and thought that was it. So I had to learn very quickly how to make an album, how to run a label and so on."

It is little surprise then that Atlan could not match 'Starlight' as a single. However, the album's other tracks were hints as to the sound might have been moving towards. Music that embraced his love of 80s electro-pop alongside funk acts like Cameo and Prince.

The Dax Riders was another outfit that benefited from the hype but were determined to tread their own path. Again, they were criticised by the French Touch underground, but their sound was a unique take on the ever-present Cameo effect with heavy P-funk stylings.

"We call it the Fresh Touch. That's what we're a part of, the Fresh Touch," laughed Olivier Roule, aka Daxman, who has gained a reputation for appearing naked when the band plays live. "We were always separate from the scene anyway. We came from a very different culture."

"And we're not rich people from Versailles who want to control the French Touch," added Cedric Azencoth as that ever-present class and wealth division in French society again reared its head. "We haven't been raised in rich households where it is expected that we will succeed in everything we do. We're just doing this for the music. So we're a part of a wider culture than French Touch."

"Originally, I was from Marseilles in the south of France," said Olivier on the band's origins. "I was making demos and sent them to Cedric, who actually ran one of the first electro labels in France, Omnisonus, which started in 1993. When I came to Paris when we met, we discovered that we both had a love for riding Dax motorbikes."

That was 1994, and a month-long stay in Paris for Olivier resulted in him moving to the city to create a dance outfit with Cedric. They called themselves the Dax Riders, after those motorbikes, a number of which are lined up in the band's offices. They then released several dancefloor tracks through their own Subscience label and a track on the 1997 compilation *The Future Sound of Paris*. Following this, they released a compilation of their singles through Warners in 1998.

While the Dax Riders were still recording their first tracks, Olivier had also formed a funk band. The singer was one-time model Nicolas Berger-Vachon. In 1999 the Dax Riders duo were asked to tour in support of their Warners album and they decided to enrol the services of a singer. Nicolas was the perfect choice. And Dax Riders were now a trio.

Their sets were mainly jams. However, when they listened back to some of the tracks, they realised that a new sound was starting to emerge.

So they decamped to Marseilles to record an album in Olivier's partner's garage. Within weeks of finishing the record, they had signed to Universal.

"We had met these two people and didn't know that they wanted to sign us at first," laughed Olivier. "We had become friends while we were playing live and when we had finished the album they asked to listen to it. A few days later, we signed with them."

2001's resulting album *Back In Town* found the trio pushing their 1980s electro-funk influences to the fore. Indeed where so many French artists claimed an influence from Cameo, it was in Dax Riders that the full effect of the group who created electro-funk classic 'Word Up' can be heard. Also evident is a deep love of the music of Michael Jackson.

"We also love Giorgio Moroder and all of that 80s disco electro sound," added Nicolas. "And Prince, of course."

"It's the music we grew up with," continues Olivier. "Our generation had all of this music on the radio, which the previous generation didn't."

That the older generation hadn't grown up with electro music on the radio hadn't stopped some of them from being just as influenced by the dance revolution and the French Touch. Just as 80s French pop crooner Jakkno dropped his traditional pop chanson style favouring full-blown electro-pop in 1981, so too outfits like Grand Tourism explored electronic music in 2000 in a way that belied their background in rock 'n' roll. The standout track 'Les Courants d'Air', a smooth electronic soul lament featuring the vocals of Chicago folk legend Terry Callier. And through their label Fakir, they delivered the downtempo-funk fuelled *Funkorama* in 2002.

"We were definitely influenced by French Touch to believe in the fact that we could do things for ourselves," explained band producer Jim Clarke. "Also, for everyone involved, electronic music meant that anyone could do it. The machines freed people, so age is no longer an issue. This represented a new way of creating music and all true musicians naturally look for new ways of expression."

If the French Touch had had a positive effect on some people, it was perhaps predictable that techno DJ and producer Manu le Malin wasn't enthused about it.

"When French Touch came out, France was suddenly considered a house country, but this wasn't really true," he argued. "People thought we were all into filtered disco, but that was fucking rubbish. Laurent Garnier never did a filtered house track; he never played it. Ever. Fifteen years after he started and he's still packing the Rex Club and he only plays serious music. No, the problem with that French Touch thing is that everyone outside of France thought that we were a house country. It took about a year and a half to get rid of the hype.

"Also, because of the French Touch, some people were forced to go to Germany," he added. "People like The Hacker, or Vitalic who would blow you away, man. He did a remix of one of my tracks because he wanted to do a hard track rather than a house track. And he made a fantastic tune for my label. Because there are the techno artists getting attention, all of a sudden, French Touch just disappeared. Now it's just French artists. But they were forced to go to Germany to get noticed because no label would touch them here."

Ironically Manu's last point may actually turn out to be one of the more positive aspects of the French Touch. It created a reaction among the more underground artists to forge a new sound. This would create the next wave of French electronic music.

There was one other positive aspect of the French Touch, however. With the spotlight on Paris came a wider interest in France. As a result, labels throughout the country gained increased exposure and support. One label, which had been present throughout the hype, was Pro-Zak Trax from Bagnolet. An eclectic label that had some success with albums by 7even Dub and Aleem in 1997, but it wasn't until the worldwide success of Kojak that they were noticed beyond the rarefied circles of DJs and the dance media.

Kojak were the combo of DJ Gregoire and DJ Vas, augmented by the vocals of Jayhem. Their first single as a trio was the 'Funk House for Your Funkt Head'; it sold 4,000 copies and brought Pro-Zak Trax to their doorsteps. As legend has it, the label was as excited by their live act as they were by the music. In 1998 Kojak were one of only two live acts programmed for the inaugural Paris Techno Parade. This followed a year of constant recording and gigging and by 1999, they had completed their debut album *Crime in the City*, which was released via Barclay/Universal Records.

The album found the trio fusing their combined influences of soul, hip hop, funk and classic house. In many ways, it followed all of the same blueprints as the French Touch frontline, but their sound was a lot warmer. The funk edge flowed with a much smoother glow while the house grooves dominated throughout. Sadly the extended filtered effects that seeped into the album's mix detracted from the trio of talents at work behind *Crime in the City*.

Soundsystem, the mix set that followed a year later, laid their influences bare. From hip hop's P-funkers Digital Underground to Juan Atkins' seminal Detroit techno guise Model 500, DJ Vadim's dark cut-ups to Ian Pooley's muscular funky techno, the astonishing mix set was cut up with a hip hop passion but delivered with the dancefloor aesthetic of house.

The combination of *Crime in the City* and *Soundsystem* suggested that Kojak may have been among the artists who would transcend the post-French Touch fallout. They had enough of their own charismatic sound to walk a solitary path and when they were at their best, they could burn dancefloors in even the coolest and most aloof cities on the planet.

In Lyon, two labels stood tall throughout the late 90s and into the new millennium. The first was Rotax, the second Superhuit. Rotax was founded by Pascal Rioux and Teddy G in 1997. Their aim was to make quality deep house music with a soul and jazz edge. The biggest success for the label came with the licensing of Pascal and Mr Day's *High Flying* album to Glasgow Underground in October 2000. This followed the huge underground success of their cover of 'It's a Disco Night', which was included on Dimitri from Paris' *A Night at the Playboy Mansion* mix set.

2001 sew the first proper album from Pascal & Mr Day, *The Lure of Melody*, again through Glasgow Underground. On the album, the duo extended the disco ambience of the early material to take in classic funk, old soul and R&B with the standout the slow soul funky wah-wah guitar grooves of 'Gotta Get Home' while Mr Day's vocals offered a Marvin Gaye-esque richness to the sonic brew. Also noteworthy were the vintage Motown meets smooth house classic 'On My Mind' and the garage inspired 'Shelter'.

Soon after *The Lure of Melody* came the duo's debut single for US imprint Guidance, 'The Bee Tree'. It proved to be Pascal and Mr Day's finest hour, thanks to its addictive, funky house style. However, their version of funky house was a million miles removed from that of the Parisian scene. There were no filters, no synths set on full phase and certainly no loose beats. 'The Bee Tree' was modelled on the classic Chicago house sound and fused with old school garage and underlined by an 80s bassline and gorgeous Fender Rhodes keyboard licks. The final ingredient, of course, was Mr. Day's sensual vocals. Like all of Pascal & Mr Day's material to that point, 'The Bee Tree' was an intensely spiritual record that touched on a very emotional level. It was hailed as a classic throughout the dance media.

Rotax (by 2002 run solely by Pascal) continued to grow through the release of material by newer artists, Vartan and Inner Visions. The label's singular vision allowed it the space to develop its own identity, which was far removed from the French Touch. Indeed in that part of Lyon, it was as if the Parisian hype never happened!

Superhuit, on the other hand, combined their walk down a lone path with an oppositional attitude. Their relationship with the French Touch was very much an antagonistic and inherently political one. Spearheaded by Olivier Pillet, aka Teo Moritz, the label has concentrated on deep and jazzy house, as exemplified through the stunning albums *Avenue* from 2001 and *Boogeyman presents… Walk So Lonely* from a couple of years later. If the existence of Rotax and Superhuit give the impression that Lyon is a hotbed of clubbing culture, then Superhuits' Teo Moritz would be forced to argue.

"Is there a good scene in Lyon? Absolutely not; there is just two of the best underground house label in France [Rotax and Superhuit], and that's all, the rest is a big fucking fashion and clubbing town with Bob Sinclar every week, but not a scene."

Other artists who came through in the period immediately after the French Touch included Montpellier's <<Rinoçerose>>, who featured the duo of academics Jean Philippe and Patou (Patrice Carrie). They took their name from a painting by a mental patient. Hence the strange spelling and the accents etc. Almost unique in the French scene, they created their house-scapes from guitars and only then added the electronic elements created by Johnny Palumbo. The first fruits of their musical union were initially released on a small Italian independent and were then picked up by PIAS, who released the 'Le Mobilier EP' in 1998. Throughout this time, the band's live shows (where they swelled to an 8-piece) picked up acclaim in France, making the band a regular at many of the country's festivals.

In 1999 the group signed to V2 following a support slot with Underworld in Paris. What followed was the album *Installation Sonore*. A breathtaking release that fused a wall of sound guitars and snaking house beats to hypnotic effect became a huge favourite with DJs everywhere. The second album, *Music Kills Me*, arrived in 2002 and showed <<Rinoçerose>> to have moved on somewhat. Their guitar styling was still in place, but the structures now included a wider range of dance influences. Sadly, it didn't have the same monumental impact as the first album but did include moments of sheer quality.

In the first two years of the new millennium, the French Touch became a curse to many artists. The hype had killed enthusiasm and suddenly, many of the leading producers faced an uncertain future. However, already things had started to mutate and by 2001, a new hype had emerged in the shape of electroclash. Among the biggest artists included in the so-called scene were a clutch of French musicians. Terence Fixmer, Miss Kitten, The Hacker, Oxia and Tampopo, to name but a few. None of them hailed from Paris. All considered themselves to be a part of the greater techno scene.

Suddenly France, the house nation, was returned to the techno roots of the early days of raving.

7. POST-FRENCH TOUCH: THE NEXT STEP OF THE NEW WAVE

"I think what we have happening right now is a new underground. You have your big-name artists and also there is a big underground scene which is not really techno but more hard. I think it totally reflects the minds of people right now. All the people like the Hacker and all those artists from the south of France, these people are influenced by German music. The club scene in France used to be really disco with the Respect parties and Dimitri in Paris but now all the big nights in Paris are big-name techno people like DJ Hell or Miss Kittens. Maybe the next big French hype will be a big chaotic techno sound."

Pedro Winter, December 2002

Just as the world's eyes were focussed on the ins and outs of the French Touch, so the techno scene continued to work away on the underground. Gradually a fresh sound developed that drew on an obsession with electro and added the favours of 80s electro-pop. However, modern programming techniques gave these comparatively light sounds a sense of darkness. It's a sound that basically reached back to the pre-acid house era of electronic music. The very period that inspired Detroit's seminal techno producers.

It was described as electroclash, although no one included in the scene called it that. That name sounded too much like hype. Sure leading light, Grenoble's Miss Kittin had once performed a track with Chicks on Speed called 'Electroclash Girl', but it was an ironic statement. No one in France called it electroclash. Nu Wave, perhaps. For argument's sake, it might be called nu-electro. Indeed twenty years later, it has undergone numerous mutations such as cold wave and electro-pop. But it was never called electroclash. Not by the scene, at least.

The next chapter of French dance music was this already unfolding before the French Touch had even started to collapse. However, there was a huge difference between this new sound and the hype surrounding the Paris scene. The new breed of artists came from all over France but predominantly from the south. More importantly, they were determined to keep things underground.

Not that this new development was the sound of serious young men and women locking heads in intense discussions about culture and ideology. No, these artists, producers and DJs had a sense of fun that made many of the purveyors of the French Touch seem like humourless bank managers. However, the resistance of France's nu-electro movement was very much against the original aesthetics of rave's ecstasy culture. Even though many of the producers and DJs had evolved through and were still very much a part of the free party movement, the fundamental ethos of the new movement was anti-rave.

Essentially this generation had abandoned the egalitarian concept of shedding ego and becoming one with a crowd. They rejected the concept of the seamlessly mixed set of anonymous records that were essentially DJ tools created to promote the hypnosis of the club experience. In their place, the nu-electro crowds adopted the 'everyone (we know) is a star' ideologies of the 80s new romantics. Personalities in the scene were larger than life. DJs spun records and sang over them; vocalists were exaggerated comic book characters with a stage presence that combined kung fu chic with Madonna's vogue presence. Running throughout was a trash aesthetic that would define the popular culture of the early noughties and inform pop stars like Britney Spears about style.

Above all, it was a scene that drew on the clique-ish ideologies of pre-rave clubbing. The ideologies of the 80s Parisian clubs where the velvet rope separated the 'beautiful people' and the proletariat. Indeed Miss Kitten & The Hacker's 'Frank Sinatra' celebrated the superiority complex of the rich and famous as represented by the velvet rope.

It was too easy to accuse the nu-electro movement of simple retromania. This was a scene that had grown through rave culture. It evolved as an undercurrent in the stream of techno development. Nu-electro could not have existed without the previous fifteen years of rave and club culture. Whether the producers created in a state of reaction to the dominant dance styles or as a homage to the musicians they grew up with, the simple fact was that the new generation could not unlearn what they had experienced. So what they did with their music was adopt and subvert the clichés of 80s electro-pop and filter them via rave's history.

Perhaps the most important thing that distinguished them from the French Touch was honesty about both retromania and class division. French Touch attempted to deny its obsession with old clichés and claimed to be recreating old sounds and new styles. French Touch claimed to be part of a classless rave society where everyone was accepted for their love of music alone. But history quickly shows the scene rife with inherently divisive attitudes based on class, income, region, ethnicity and religion. On the other hand, nu-electro celebrated that they were gorging on old music to create new. They embellished ideas around exclusivity and fractured society through their strict door policies. But their divisions weren't around traditional ideas but based on subcultural capital. To be included, you had to be in the know. The trashy people were the beautiful people now. It was every inch a rerun of the Blitz Club of the 1979 – 1981 London club culture.

Another huge difference between French Touch and nu-electro could be viewed through attitudes to sexuality and gender. While the Parisian French Touch scene was dominated by men who celebrated hyper-masculinity and straight sexuality, nu-electro was a far more sexually liberal setting with all sexualities encouraged while women were allowed far more space to create. This was certainly not a boys club.

Electroclash itself may have been celebrated through its collective name in the UK, Germany and the US, but nu-electro was still in its infancy in France. Furthermore, it was less located in the faux glamour of the New York, Berlin and London electroclash clubs. Its roots were tangled within the French free party movement. Even if its ultimate aims were very different.

One of the biggest names in the movement is Caroline Herve, aka Miss Kittin. Originally from Grenoble, she first started DJing in 1993 at parties around her hometown. Her first gig early in 1994 was in an old army fort in the mountains around Grenoble at a party organised by a group of art students from Grenoble Fine Art School, where she also studied. However, her first official gig was at a party in Annecy, 100km from Grenoble, with Erik Rug and other French DJs in April 94. Amazingly she had no turntables to practice on and only played records that she'd listened to and bought in a record shop in the days before the rave.

Over the years that followed, Miss Kitten became a high profile techno DJ on France and Europe's underground party scenes. She subsequently became renowned for the musical breadth within her sets that would move between full-on techno, ambient, rave classics and the odd Prince tune. All without ever losing the crowd. It was a skill perfectly captured on her excellent mix album *Radio Caroline*.

One of the most alluring aspects of Miss Kittin's DJ sets was her willingness to talk and sing over the tracks. This talent resulted in her delivering vocals on collaborations with fellow Gronoble artist The Hacker. Miss Kitten and The Hacker signed to DJ Hell's Munich label International Deejay Gigolos and went on to release a series of genre-defining records. Among them was the track that could arguably be called the global electroclash anthem, 'Frank Sinatra', with its risqué chorus of "suck my dick, lick my ass". The duo's live show became renowned throughout Europe and the US for her onstage persona's aloof, sneering irony.

As well as her material with The Hacker, Miss Kitten has provided vocals for Felix da Housecat, Detroit Grand Pubahs and Sven Vath. The latter produced an electro version of Gainsbourg and Birkin's 'Je T'Aime,

314

Moi Non Plus' for which Miss Kitten provided moaning that seemingly sneered at the original's submissive ambience.

The Hacker, aka Michel Amato, first started creating electronic music with a late 80s industrial group. He discovered techno early in the 90s and started producing techno and hardcore records under the alias XMF. In 1998 Amato founded Good Life Records along with Alex Reynard and Olivier Raymond (aka Oxia), through which both The Hacker and Oxia's album were released. Olivier Raymond had also run the Ozone imprint with techno artist Kiko since 1995. Based in Rhine-Alpes, Ozone released tracks by Oxia and Kiko, and Jack de Marseille. The Hacker also recorded for the label. Indeed both Ozone and Good life would seem to share artists.

The Toulouse area of France had witnessed the rise of two nu-electro outfits that threatened to achieve global success; The Eternals and Tampopo. The former signed to Benjamin Diamond's Diamond Traxx imprint. Their debut for that label, 'Walk For Me', contained all of the hallmarks of classic nu-electro through its combination of 80s synths rolling out electro hook lines over a techno-noir ambience and an electronic pop sheen. The trio's original soundtrack to the imaginary movie *Astropioneers* collected together a multi-hued selection of electro epics.

Tampopo, on the other hand, quickly became a part of the International Deejay Gigolos elite thanks to his electro-funk excursions that echoed the dissonance of Drexciya as much as it drew on Cybotron. In effect, his music epitomised the links that nu-electro had with the pre-techno electronic era while also underlining the Detroit references.

Terence Fixmer, from Bondues in the north of France, had also released his dark and lush electro tones on International Deejay Gigolo Records. His storming 'Electrostatic' was a big dancefloor hit, which led to an album deal with the Munich label. Fixmer also ran the Planet Rouge Records label, releasing his own material and tracks by Gemini 9. Teamtendo were a duo from Bordeaux who played live with Game Boy consoles dressed like giant teddy bears "like the ones you can see at Euro Disney, but far more perverse!" explained Tampopo. Musically they drew heavily on the brittle beats and bleeps of early electro.

Paris, too had been active in the creation of this scene. Numerous artists came through the 'naked' parties at The Pulp club. Among them was Scratch Massive, who represented the more melodic, theatrical edge of the electro movement. Feadz was a DJ and producer of some repute from Paris who joined the B Pitch Control crew while female DJ Jennifer was an exceptional talent. Originally from Nice, she was part of the Pussy Killers with Sex Toy. Sadly Sex Toy died in 2001; however, she was an important ingredient in the development of the underground electro movement.

Also notable was the Scandium Records imprint from Nimes, whose artists like Ultracolour and Southsonic took the 80s style but forged it with melodic techno. While the abrasive but playful techno of Paris' Active Suspension records was consistent in its high quality. Indeed O.Lamm's 'Snow Party' on the label updated Aphex Twin by drawing on the rhythm clusters of The Neptunes, the Casio soul of nu-electro and the strafed ambience of Arpanet – but without any of the easy to listen to qualities of these influences.

Also of interest were Hypo, whose 'Karaoke A Capella' combined snatched frequencies with references from electro culture. For example, the aptly named 'Newoldorder' combined the melodic rock solo basslines of New Order with uneasy dissonance. At the same time, 'Iancurtismayfield (Half a Duet)' lifted the hi-hat sixteens and Rotopad drums of Joy Division with reversed beats and noises to create a slice of analogue pop-noir.

Meanwhile, back in Paris, that man Pedro Winter started promoting a new band on his own Ed Banger Records that many heralded as the 'new Daft Punk'. Their name was Justice and their sound brought the French Touch in line with electroclash to decidedly inconsistent effect. Their debut album *Cross* (2007) had no real sense of breaking new ground so much as continuing a legacy. As an album, it was unchallenging with a comforting predictability at its core. Perhaps unsurprisingly it was critically acclaimed. Indeed it was embraced by electronic musicians and producers with many from disparate styles including The Prodigy's Liam Howlett heralding its brilliance. In reality, Justice held none of the urgency and creativity of either the French Touch or electroclash scenes that preceded it.

With the continued emergence of artists from a constantly evolving underground still inspired by the Parisian turn of the late 1990s, France will continue as a force on the international dance music scene. However, what the story, from discotheque to *Discovery*, or musique concrete to nu electro, revealed was that France's history is rich with innovative electronic music talent. Indeed, electronic music is sewn to the tapestries of French culture and a deeply hued part of its traditions – even if most people are unaware of these largely hidden histories that have occasionally bubbled up to the surface of popular culture.

The continued growth of these alternative electronic pathways depends on artists' ability to transcend the limitations imposed by hierarchies of aristocracy, which existed as much within electronic music as in everyday life. This attitude goes into the actual perception of the music created domestically, which relies on a stringently defined sense of belonging. When Daft Punk attempted to remove the sense of cool from their *Discovery* album, they were actually attacking the hierarchical culture. They were railing against the dictates of style while also attempting to shed their Frenchness by adopting non-nationalistic robot personas. In 2001 Daft Punk took on an international identity.

And dance music at its finest has always been an international force.

SPECIAL THANKS TO THOSE WHO PRE-ORDERED TO BOOK

Anton Ardakov, Simon Baggley, Richard Barrett, Arlando Battle, Guillaume Bucholz, Todd Burns, Shane Cashin, Yvonne Duffield, Paul Greenwood, Eric Ferrer Guiteras, Tim Forrester, Thomas Hnatiw, Mark Holmes, Simone Hutchinson, Paul Jobson, Simon Kemp, Neil Lumsden, Mufeed Mahmood, Steve McLay, Anthony Morrow, Tom Ralph, Jaime Rosso, Jes Sewerin, Ryan Simoneau, Pablo Smet, Gregory Smith, Leigh Strydom, Michele Tessadri, Richard Weeks, Mark Wood.